LIFE ON THE HOME FRONT

Life on the Home Front

Montreal 1939-1945

PATRICIA BURNS

Véhicule Press

Published with the assistance of the Canada Council for the Arts, the Canada Book Fund of the Department of Canadian Heritage, and the Société de développement des entreprises culturelles
du Québec (SODEC).

Cover design: J.W. Stewart
Cover photograph: Condrad Poirier. Children gather rubber for salvage, Rosemont, Montreal, 29 April 1942
Fond Conrad Poirier P48,S1,P7495
Bibliothèque et archives nationales du Québec

Typeset in Minion by Simon Garamond
Printed by Marquis Printing Inc.

First printing, November 2012;
second printing December 2012.

LIBRARY AND ARCHIVES CANADA CATALOGUING IN PUBLICATION
Burns, Patricia, 1939-

Life on the home front : Montréal 1939-1945 / Patricia Burns.
Includes bibliographical references and index.

ISBN 978-1-55065-341-0

1. World War, 1939-1945--Québec (Province)--Montréal.
2. Montréal (Québec)--History--20th century. 3. Montréal (Québec)--Social life and customs--20th century. 4. Montréal (Québec)--Social conditions--20th century. I. Title.

FC2947.4.B87 2012 940.53'71428 C2012-903086-4

Published by Véhicule Press, Montréal, Québec, Canada
www.vehiculepress.com

Distribution in Canada by LitDistCo
www.litdistco.ca

Distributed in the U.S. by Independent Publishers Group
www.ipgbook.com

Printed in Canada on recycled paper

To the memory of my sister Connie
1959-2009

Contents

A book like this could not have been attempted without the help of so many people who allowed themselves to be interviewed and others who shared their knowledge of the war years. Good friends and family members offered me encouragement and support in a project that was delayed quite often by life's happy and sad intrusions. I would especially like to thank my daughter Erin Olizar Fowler and my son-in-law Major Rory Fowler for their unstinting support, and my sister Mickey Naisby, who read the manuscript and offered pithy and extremely helpful advice. Mickey was also a wonderful source of encouragement during the down times—and there were many—in the writing of this book. I could not have done it without her.

Alan Hustak and Pierre Vennat, both brilliant historians and authors were always there to answer my many questions. The late Andy Melville offered support, lent books, gave advice and generally was one of my most enthusiastic cheerleaders whenever I "felt a book coming on." I shall miss you, my good friend.

The "Friday Afternoon Gang" at the N.D.G. Legion (Branch 24/106) which is composed of both WW II and Korean veterans were unbelievably helpful in getting me in touch with a time about which I had no memory. Stu Vallières, Dave McCrindle, Frank Stanway and Jim McCann were the ones I bugged the most with my countless questions. Although these gentlemen were away fighting for most of the war years, they certainly remembered the restaurants, bars, theatres, train stations and the general mores of the times. I owe an undying debt of gratitude to them. To the others who helped bring the war years to life: Allen, Pat, Mickey, Gerry, Iris, Bob, thank you, thank you very much. It was so much fun remembering with you.

Vaughn Maiolla gave me moral support and untold hours

of practical computer help throughout the project. Catherine Richards offered much helpful advice on a troublesome chapter and Joanne Schoeler Fitzpatrick and Marie Andrée Robinson helped immensely with French translation.

Jane Naisbitt, Head of the Military Research Centre of the Canadian War Museum in Ottawa gave me much detailed help in locating information. The staff at the Concordia University Library was also extremely helpful in my research as were Ian Fleming, the archivist of the Toronto YMCA, Don Pidgeon of the Knights of Columbus and Michel Tassé of the Salvation Army. Especially helpful, also, were the Honourable Marlene Jennings, Executive Director of the YM-YWHA/ Montreal Jewish Community Centres and Shannon Hodge, archivist of the Jewish Public Library.

A big thank you to my friend, Sheila Kindellan Sheehan, noted author of crime novels, who provided practical advice and moral support. Special thanks go to those who allowed me to interview them. You shared your time, memories and photos with me. Without you, this book could not have happened.

The following friends and acquaintances helped me in myriad ways. Whether you introduced me to people I eventually interviewed, lent an ear or provided interesting and relevant information, your help was precious to me: Ann Ascoli, Giovanni Barillaro, the Bieler family, Josée Bois, André Bricault, Ron Charland, Norma Chyka, Vicki Cole, Betty Coughlin, Patricia Crichton, Dr. Serge Durflinger, Rosemary Elson, Bernie Farrell, Mrs. Guffler of St. Boniface Catholic Parish, Dr. Maureen E. Kiely, Vic and Sue Kuwabara, Patricia Mathers, Frank Moritsugu, Carmela Panetta Papandrea, Tamara Shacter and John Tweddell. I ask forgiveness of those I may have forgotten to mention. Please know that your contributions were also very much appreciated.

Heartfelt thanks go to the wonderful publishing team at Véhicule Press for allowing me, once again, to record a bygone time. Simon, Nancy, Vicki, Maya, you have been wonderful and so easy to work with.

A Note on Terminology

There have been so many changes in Montreal and Quebec since the 1960s that a note on usage is necessary. I have used the names and terms that were common at the time such as "French Canadians" which has now been replaced by "Québécois." Street names, cities, landmarks and areas were then Rosemount, Three Rivers, Mountain Street, St. Lawrence, St. Mark, St. Matthew, and St. James Market. St. James Basilica would later become Mary, Queen of the World Cathedral (Marie-Reine-du-Monde). Names with French spellings, like Barré and Jeanne Mance were invariably pronounced by English speakers as "Barry Street" and "Jeen Manse". Dorchester has since become Boulevard René Lévesque except for a short stretch from Clarke Avenue to Atwater at the eastern edge of Westmount. Fletcher's Field is now Parc Jeanne-Mance. The Catholic cemetery now known as Notre-Dame-des-Neiges was always referred to simply as Côte-des-Neiges Cemetery. The city at that time included, or was adjacent to, many separate municipalities like Verdun, Outremont, Montreal West, and Westmount etc., which provided their own services and, in some cases, ran their own school boards. For simplicity I have used "French" and "English" to define the linguistic divide and the inhabitants of the city.

Introduction

NOT BEING OF SCHOOL AGE when the war ended, I don't have a memory of a jubilant teacher announcing the end of hostilities and sending me home to rejoice with my family. Living on a leafy street in the Montreal district of Notre Dame de Grâce (N.D.G.) also meant that I was spared any knowledge of a housing shortage during and after the war. The war intruded on our family in a cruel way when my Aunt Eileen's son and only child, Gerald Hartman (17th Duke of York Hussars), was killed in France in the Battle of Caen in 1944 but, this too, passed unnoticed by me. My father worked in Civil Defence and, I imagine, patrolled the streets looking for Nazi spies and unheeding citizens flaunting the blackout laws. While he did this, I was probably asleep clutching a teddy bear. Our family all enjoyed our mother's Sugarless Butterscotch Cookies that were made with Crisco vegetable shortening instead of butter—obviously a wartime recipe. We had a garden on a plot down the street but it was just a garden, never called a Victory garden. The oblivious nature of childhood meant that I was totally unaware of the sacrifices being made all around me during the war years.

My memory comes alive only after the war had ended. Instead of hearing the inspiring and measured tones of Winston Churchill as he promised to vanquish the "Nawzees", my first radio memories are of hearing strange names like "Shinekieshek" and "Mahatma-gandee" who obviously had taken up centre stage in the world's dramas. Playing outside on the street—as we all did in those days—children would show me leftover blue ration coupons but rationing of food was a concept I couldn't begin to understand. There was a poor demented fellow who walked the neighbourhood whom the children called Crazy Johnny. Some said he suffered from shell shock and I was told that this was because he had been in the First World War. If so, he would soon be joined by thousands of others as they returned home with new demons. As a teenager later on, I always felt so sorry for the alcoholics I would meet on St. Catherine Street and wondered how sad it was that they probably started life as beautiful and loved babies dressed in blue only to end up in their present state. Many, if not most, of these were probably veterans suffering from what we now call Post Traumatic Stress Disorder.

In the fifties my sister Mickey and I would go down to the basement to practice our tap dancing and Mickey remembers seeing a helmet on the wall. Was it what our father wore as a member of Canada's Civil Defence team? In elementary school, my friend Sheila Meehan and I could not restrain ourselves from writing KILROY WAS HERE on the blackboard when the teacher's back was turned. I had no idea who Kilroy was and why he was here but it seemed an important statement to make. Another time my friend, Jocelyn, told me how amusing it was when her parents returned from the St. Patrick's Ball with a group of friends and all the men lustily sang, "Praise the Lord and Pass the Ammunition". Of course, these veterans probably knew a lot about ammunition and how to pass, aim, conserve, respect and, most importantly—duck it.

In reading about the Royal Visit of 1939 and of the manner Queen Elizabeth charmed her way across Canada, I was reminded of my own contact with her extraordinary presence. In 1987, while on an official tour to mark the 125th anniversary of her regiment, the Black Watch, she attended a morning service at the Church of St. Andrew and St. Paul on Sherbrooke Street. I had always been impressed with her down-to-earth friendliness, her devotion to duty and support of the British people during the dark days of the war. I also admired her for her reputed overspending ways, her ability to down a gin and tonic before noon and her love of *risqué* jokes and Scottish country dancing. So, on Sunday, June 7, I went with my daughter, Erin, and her friend to stand on Sherbrooke Street across from the church to try to get a glimpse of perhaps the most beloved royal of all, the "Queen Mum". A tiny figure, she emerged into the blinding sunlight to the applause and cheers of the assembled crowd. Then she stopped, looked directly across the street to where we were standing, tipped her head to seemingly get a better look as if to say, "There you are. I was hoping you could make it." It was an incredible moment never to be forgotten. I now understood her power over people.

While writing this book, I was reminded many times over of the unifying effect of music and song. Both French- and English-speakers had a wide repertoire of songs that could be sung at parties, in work camps, on rail cars during the Depression or heading off to war, in army camps, in hospital wards overseas, in Europe wherever Canadians gathered or on buses when girls went to entertain the troops in Montreal. In English some of these standards were "The Maple Leaf Forever", "Danny Boy", "When Johnny Comes Marching Home", "I Love a Lassie", "Roamin' in the Gloamin'", "All Through the Night", "Auld Lang Syne", "Billy Boy", "Land of Hope and Glory", "Waltzing Matilda", "Cockles and Mussels", "For Me and My Gal", "The Rose of Tralee"....the list of these old favourites is endless and everyone also knew war songs, hymns and Christmas carols. How sad that we have lost this musical legacy.

Having a father who was too old to enlist was the singular most important factor in my being protected from what so many families were experiencing. I did not lose precious years with him and our large family is not separated by a war-related age gap. My father was spared physical and mental problems suffered by so many veterans. I also did not have to say good-bye to a favourite older brother who might never return and my mother did not age (as so many mothers did) worrying about three or four children serving for up to six years in places they hardly knew existed before the war. I will forever be grateful that, except for the loss of our cousin, my family was mercifully spared. My gratitude to those who sacrificed their lives or spent long years away from home, sometimes losing physical ability or mental stability and emotional peace, knows no bounds. May we never forget the sacrifices of their generation and cherish their memory forever.

The veterans who returned did not usually like to talk about their experiences and Canadian textbooks are remarkably silent on Canada's contribution to victory. As former soldiers and the family members who supported them age and pass away, I hope this book, in some small way, will commemorate those years of sacrifice, fear and hope on the home front.

[CHAPTER ONE]

September 1939

No Peace in Our Time

ON MONDAY, SEPTEMBER 4, 1939, Montrealers prepared for the coming week. Horse-drawn delivery wagons clopped and wobbled through the morning-misted streets guided by men delivering milk and bread to all the households on their routes. Breakfasts, which might include cereal, eggs, toast, prunes, tea and coffee, were hastily eaten. Those who forgot to turn their bread over in the toaster had to spend a few minutes over the kitchen sink scraping burnt bits off their toast to get the desired golden colour. Large families lined up to use the only bathroom and mothers got ready to do the weekly laundry. Those with jobs took the streetcar or walked to their places of employment. Students were enjoying their last taste of freedom before heading back to school in the next two days. The Robert Simpson Company was selling girls' tunics for $4.98 and blazers for $2.98. A crisp white blouse to complete the outfit would set parents back another 98 cents. Boys could be outfitted with a four-piece suit—two breeches (usually called breeks), jacket and vest—for $11.50. Not everyone, however, had the money to do much shopping. The unemployed in poorer areas of the city prepared for another monotonous day. They might spend many hours sitting in front of their timeworn flats on chairs brought outside for the purpose, or hanging out of their upper windows leaning on pillows and smoking Sweet Caporals or Turrets (20 for 25 cents) while watching the passing parade of humanity.

War had been a hovering menace for many weeks. The invasion of Poland on September 1 brought England into the conflict and Canadians knew that it was only a matter of time before they would also become embroiled in a war that would have unforeseen consequences. On this particular Monday, Montreal suffered its first war casualties. The headline of the *Gazette* of that day blared: 1,400 PASSENGERS IN ATHENIA REPORTED SAFE AS GERMAN SUB SINKS MONTREAL-BOUND LINER. The *Gazette* provided more information: SEVERAL KILLED BY TORPEDO BUT ALL OTHERS ARE RESCUED 200 MILES OFF SCOTS COAST. Only hours after Britain declared war on Germany on September 3, the *Athenia*, a liner owned by the Donaldson Atlantic Line Ltd. and built for the Glasgow/Liverpool- Quebec/Montreal passenger trade, was mistakenly torpedoed by the German submarine U-30. Most of the passengers were Canadian but there were also 300 Americans on board. The final toll was ninety-three passengers and nineteen crew members killed. Hannah Baird of Verdun, a member of the Canadian Merchant Marines who was serving as a stewardess on the ship, perished and is acknowledged as Canada's first death of the war. Three-year-old Gladys MacFarlane and her mother, also from Verdun, were among the dead. One notable Montrealer who was killed was Fred Blair, a prominent musician and the organist of the Church of St. Andrew and St. Paul. The child whose funeral was the most publicized, however, was that of ten-year-old Margaret Hayworth from Hamilton. A thousand people met the train that transported her body home and her public funeral was attended by all the political luminaries of Ontario, from the mayor of Hamilton to the provincial premier and his entire cabinet. Now, it was hoped, Canadians would realize the true nature of the enemy.

Young Elspeth "Penny" Pentland Gélineau of Verdun could have been another Montreal casualty but for her parents' premonition: "I was nine years old when I sailed alone to Scotland on board the *Duchess of Bedford* in June 1939. After spending three months visiting relatives, my passage was booked to return to Montreal on board the *Athenia*. My parents, realizing war was imminent, changed my passage to the *Duchess of York*. There was a threat—a very real threat it was found out—that there might be German submarines in the Gulf of St. Lawrence. My first sight as I arrived home was seeing my father standing on the pier to welcome me home waving his closed umbrella in the air with his hat on top of it. I then found out that the *Athenia* had been sunk. My mother was very quiet and, I'm sure, very thankful that I was safe."

The evening of that same day, as many movie goers headed out to see *Goodbye, Mr. Chips* starring Robert Donat and Greer Garson at the Loew's Theatre downtown on St. Catherine Street, another attraction drew a huge crowd. Paul Gouin, the leader of the L'Action Libérale Nationale (National Liberal Action) party, held an anti-war rally at Maisonneuve Market that was carefully monitored by more than thirty policemen. A long list of speakers declared that French Canada was not prepared to be cannon fodder for Britain's war. They were willing to help by sending aid to England on a C.O.D. basis but demanded a referendum be held on Canada's involvement in the war. Amid cries of: *"Vive la Revolution!" "Nous n'irons pas à la guerre." "Laissez les Anglais y aller." "C'est la faute des juifs." "A bas les Anglais."* Gouin stated that it was not just a race thing and that many English Canadians were also against conscription. Montreal would have to get used to many such rallies in the coming years that many hoped would not be as vitriolic as the conscription crisis of the First World War, which saw bloody riots in Quebec City. The mood in French Canada then was that they did not want their sons ripped from the bosoms of their families to die for the British Empire. Now, a mere twenty-two years after the World War I conscription crisis, Prime Minister Mackenzie King knew he had some very difficult choices to make.

Military authorities in Montreal began preparations for war in late August. Montreal, as a port city and the country's largest metropolis, had to be protected from saboteurs and fifth columnists. Soldiers began to guard bridges, train yards and other points that might be targeted. Armed teenage members of the Victoria Rifles Reserves were sent out to guard the Lachine Canal and the railway bridge to the Mohawk village Caughnawaga (now Kahnawake) to prevent agents of the Reich from disrupting the Dominion. By September 1 the Defence Department had created the Canadian

Active Service Force which meant that volunteers would be sent overseas if needed. One thousand men a day swamped Montreal recruiting centres, which obliged the military to take over the old Grand Union Hotel and parts of the United Theological College to handle the crowds. On September 6 the Atwater Market was requisitioned by the military as a food-supply depot and as a centre for recruitment and training. By the middle of September fifteen medical centres were examining 700 men a day. New recruits were also given medical exams at the newly reopened Place Viger Hotel. At the same time, 3,500 Montreal women offered their services as volunteers—making coffee and taking courses in first aid and nursing. This was all they could do since the military had no place for them at the time. The Régiment de Maisonneuve was the first in Canada to fill its ranks with volunteers for overseas service. This fulfilled the dream of Lieutenant-Colonel Robert Bourassa, the commanding officer of the regiment and a successful lawyer and World War I veteran. Lt.Col. Paul Grenier of Les Fusiliers Mont Royal (FMR), having received a call to begin enlisting men, took over the Motordome—a former garage near the corner of Sherbrooke and St. Denis streets—on September 2. After a cleaning crew removed the oil stains and painted the cement floor, it quickly became an arsenal. Hundreds of young volunteers to Les Fusiliers, after passing a medical exam, began marching in Lafontaine Park and up and down all the streets near their armoury on Henri Julien. This was not only to introduce them to military discipline but also to put their patriotism on display and encourage recruitment. As uniforms had not yet been issued, they were still a motley lot. It seemed that French Canada did not speak with one voice.

Around the same time, The Royal Montreal Regiment situated at 4625 St. Catherine Street in Westmount was advertising for recruits. They had to be physically-fit British subjects between the ages of eighteen and forty-five with a minimum height of 5 feet 4 inches. Priority would be given to high school graduates and those with special skills or training. Many answered the call to the colours. Sixteen-year-old boys with squeaky voices had to be tactfully turned away as did one fifty-nine-year-old who gave his age as thirty-eight. When Captain Whiteman asked incredulously, "*How old*?" the would-be recruit admitted his real age and said that he was fit as a fiddle and had served through the last show and could do it again. Many other older men with newly-dyed black hair were also turned away from recruiting centres in Montreal. This scenario was repeated all across Canada.

In spite of the alacrity with which many young men signed up, the mood in Montreal was subdued. If Canada had to go to war, it was seen as an onerous duty imposed on a population still recovering from the losses of World War I. It was naively hoped that the far-away dictators who bestrode the world of the late thirties could be dealt with by someone else. This war, however, could not be wished away. When England declared war on Germany it was only a matter of time before Canada followed suit. In 1931 the British Parliament passed the Statute of Westminster which gave Canada control over its foreign policy. The Canadian Parliament, after a debate lasting three days, agreed to go to war and Prime Minister Mackenzie King sent a message to King George VI on September 10 announcing that a state of war now existed between Canada and the German Reich. During the debate, Quebec MP Maxime Raymond, while not opposing the war, offered a cautionary warning: "The French Canadian of Quebec is attached to the soil he tills and recognizes only the obligation to defend its own soil." Ernest Lapointe, the minister of justice, saw the necessity of war to "protect Canada from the tyrannical doctrines of Nazism and communism." Lapointe, in newspaper headlines, proclaimed the loyalty of Quebec but his approval was contingent on the government's promise never to impose conscription as it did in 1917.

Madeleine Cloutier Méthot and her two sisters grew up in comfortable and sheltered circumstances on Berri Street. Her uncle, Lieut. André Vennat, FMR; two cousins, Capt. Aimé Lefebvre, FMR, Alexandre Brisebois, RCAF; and her boyfriend and future husband Guy Méthot all volunteered for service. She recalls her feelings at the outbreak of war: "September 1939. A new uneasiness spread across Montreal. Canada was at war. We thought of all the young sons and married men who would soon be called upon to serve their country. To my mind, it was like a curtain coming down in the theatre. Suddenly we were in darkness and everyone stayed home. Life continued, however, and we had to think of the families who needed help."

Carol Lodge was a young teenager from working class Point St. Charles enjoying the end of her summer holiday in Plattsburgh, New York over Labour Day weekend: " I was about to begin grade nine at Montreal High School when we heard on the radio that the war had begun. My father was greatly upset but, to a kid of thirteen with no experience of war except from the movies, it seemed exciting. Incidentally, my two friends and I went up in an airplane that same afternoon. Half-hour flights in a small plane were quite the thing at holiday and beach resorts in the 1930s. Much to my parents' disgust, the short plane expedition was of greater interest to us three teens than the world-shaking events soon to commence."

Dave McCrindle heard about the war while driving back from Ottawa: "I was seventeen years old and in the rumble seat of my brother-in-law's car. I heard it on CFCF radio. Christopher Ellis, a long-time broadcaster announced it. I figured pretty soon I would volunteer and I did."

In the late thirties, Montreal was just recovering from the Depression which had struck a cruel blow to Canada's metropolis. In 1932 a third of the city's poor were on relief payments from the city that barely kept body and soul alive. In the mid-thirties, a family of five in Montreal received $5.05 a week during the winter for food, $1.35 for heating, 75 cents for clothing and monthly rent allowance of $10.50, as well as 90 cents for electricity. While many received some help from charitable organizations that were run along religious lines, the poor often helped themselves by exchanging services, bartering and accepting aid from family and neighbours. A minority of the unemployed were involved in demonstrations, rallies and strikes at public works sites. Many turned to God and pilgrimages to St. Joseph's Oratory, and the Tuesday devotions to Our Lady of Perpetual Help at St. Ann's Church in Griffintown were extremely popular. At one point, it was estimated that 1,200 people were being fed daily at a local soup kitchen. Young children were kept busy scurrying down to the corner store to buy a small bag of coal to provide heat in the crowded flats. Warmth could also be had by sharing a bed with three or four siblings. Ragged hand-me-down clothing, worn shoes stuffed with cardboard to extend the life of the soles and children drooling as they passed pastry shops and could smell, but not buy, the wonders inside, were the order of the day. Supper quite often meant a thin soup made with a bone begged from the butcher "for the dog". Children were known to faint from hunger in class while others couldn't go to school if it wasn't their day to wear the only coat or pair of boots the siblings shared. The one-child-a year policy of the Catholic Church worked well in an agrarian setting but meant extremely cramped quarters in the city. Lt. Filiatreault, a Montreal policeman was the father of twenty living children. His first wife gave birth to twelve, of whom two died and his second wife bore him eleven, of whom one died.

The poor sometimes resorted to burning doors in their rental flats to provide heat. May 1st was the traditional moving day and, for the poor, moving was cheaper than paying rent. As possessions were piled on rickety carts or horse-drawn wagons for the move, landlords noticed that the empty dwellings sometimes had more rooms than doors. Evicted tenants sitting on the sidewalk surrounded by their worn possessions were a common sight. The Montreal Unemployment Relief Commission and charitable organizations like the St.Vincent de Paul Society could sometimes assist in finding new accommodation. Despair led many to commit suicide and even murder family members. New immigrants were particularly vulnerable because they had fewer resources and were subjected to harsher treatment by the police when they couldn't pay their rent and faced eviction. Many jobless immigrants were forcibly returned to their home countries. According to Arthur Fraser (a francophone despite his English-sounding name) who lived on Sanguinet Street: "People didn't work. You used to see them in their windows all day. If you were on relief and someone didn't like you, they would go outside and phone the city and tell them that you were working—washing clothes or something—under the table. Then your name would be crossed off the list. Once a year the priest used to pass to collect the church money and the janitor threw him out. He went to get help from the priest and never got nothing." Not all of the clergy were cold-hearted. Many of the young men from other provinces who rode the rails ended up in Montreal looking for work. At one time over three hundred men were sleeping outside around St. Lawrence Boulevard. They were fed, morning and night, by nuns from a nearby convent. The poor also had a friend in Frank R. Scott, the McGill lawyer, poet, civil libertarian and socialist who was deeply affected by the Depression and sought to alleviate the problems of inequality by helping to found the Cooperative Commonwealth Federation (CCF), which later became the New Democratic Party (NDP).

Those who had jobs often worked under Dickensian conditions. A woman operating a sewing machine would earn $3 a week. If she took too many bathroom breaks or asked for a deserved bonus, she did so at her peril. With so many willing to take any job at all, the bosses knew that they had it made. In that dog-eat-dog world many became wealthy. Fortunes were also made in real estate if someone had the cash to buy up the cheap properties that were available. For the rich, life went on and even improved. Food was extremely cheap and, in 1933, the going rate for a live-in housemaid ranged between $15 and $30 a month. A chef earned $40 a month. A male bank clerk was paid $7 or $8 a week which included working a half-day on Saturday. Prices were low; a pound of round steak sold for 19 cents. You paid $1 for five gallons of Joy gasoline if you were lucky enough to own a car. Many of the poor sold their possessions before subjecting themselves to the shame of accepting relief. For many young men who realized they were just one more mouth to feed in a large family, there was always the option of putting a harmonica in a back pocket and heading out to see Canada in search of a job by "riding the rods".

The middle class who had jobs were better off. Sometimes they had their salaries reduced but, since prices were low, most managed to live reasonably well. The fear of much of the wealthy business class was that any attempt to provide social assistance to the masses would lead to indolence and socialism. The Montreal *Gazette*, which was the mouthpiece of St. James Street, in an editorial stated, "…..it is sheer madness to tell idle and shiftless men and women that the state will step in and save them from the penalties of their violation of fixed social laws." Sir Edward Beattie, president of the CPR and a bachelor who certainly did not have to worry about hungry mouths around his table, lived in a four-storey greystone on Pine Avenue that boasted a racquet court. Although not opposed to unemployment insurance or relief in principle, he worried about "the effects of its application upon the individual." Surely, the well-to-do thought: Anyone who *really* wants to work can find a job. Left-wing politicians, social workers and unions tried unsuccessfully to bring in unemployment insurance benefits but this was only put in place in 1940 after a constitutional amendment agreed to by the provinces.

The challenges of the Depression and the looming war were to be managed by a Canadian prime minister whom many considered to be unprepossessing in the extreme.

Liberal Prime Minister William Lyon Mackenzie King was to lead Canada through the war and oversee the transition to peace. A dour-faced man of immense talent and academic accomplishments—a total of five university degrees, the last one from Harvard—he was sadly outclassed in the charisma department by the titans of the day like Roosevelt and Churchill. King left a detailed diary that provides us with a good understanding of his personality. He was egotistical, a hypochondriac with a martyr complex, a sexually-repressed lifelong bachelor, wealthy but parsimonious, mother-fixated, a racist and anti-Semite (not uncommon at the time), a man with a highly developed interest in the world of séances and fortune telling but a devout Presbyterian nevertheless. While aloof and rather prim in public, his friends said he could be charming and sociable and enjoyed good food and fine wines in moderation. What is clear is the utter loneliness of the man. He often commented that he had no one with whom he could share his political victories, and, for friendship he relied on his neighbours near Kingsmere, his country house in the Gatineau Hills. One in particular, Mrs. Joan Godfroy Patteson, a close platonic friend and confidante shared his interest in the occult. King owned a total of four Irish Terrier dogs and, in a touching interview in 1944, he described the seventeen-year relationship and loss of the last one, "his little friend Pat".

In spite of his eccentricities King was Canada's tenth and longest-serving prime minister (December 1921-June 1926, September 1926-August 1930, October 1935-November 1948). He brought many skills to the job: hard-working and intelligent, he had an unerring feel for the needs of the Canadian people. Widely travelled, his work in social settlement in England gave him an understanding of the conditions of the workingman. He worked tirelessly to bring

Prime Minister William Lyon Mackenzie King

Premier Maurice Duplessis

harmony to potentially divisive situations and groups in a newly-industrialized country. An astute politician, in the lead up to the war he assured pro-British Canadians that if Britain were drawn into a major conflict Canada would not stand by and do nothing. Meanwhile, his Quebec lieutenant, Ernest Lapointe (who believed that neutrality was morally wrong) told French Canadians that Canada's interests were to be the only consideration in such a decision. Thus, King was able to create a consensus between the two linguistic groups and assure that Parliament would agree to a declaration of war.

King was not, however, a good judge of character. After meeting Hitler in 1937, he described him as "a simple peasant" and, in a memo to Governor General Lord Tweedsmuir, he stated, "I am perfectly certain that the Germans are not contemplating war, either with France or Britain." He also put on his rose-coloured glasses when taking the measure of Mussolini. This grandson of the rebel, William Lyon Mackenzie, did not see any irony in his admiration for a dictator who imposed order, discipline and respect for authority on a recalcitrant and fractious country.

Mackenzie King's counterpart in Quebec was anything but unprepossessing.

It was always a standing joke. Driving through the Quebec countryside in the 1940s and '50s motorists would always be shocked by the sudden change in the quality of the roads until someone said, "Oh, this town voted (or didn't) for Duplessis." The man whose legacy still divides Quebecers, Premier Maurice LeNoblet Duplessis, was born in 1890 near Three Rivers. The son of a successful local politician, he was known as a popular, successful and well-behaved student with oratorical skills, who loved to read but wasn't too keen on sports. He studied at Collège Notre Dame in Montreal and, after obtaining a law degree from Laval's Montreal branch (now the University of Montreal), he opened a law practice in Three Rivers where he made many contacts that would serve him well in the future. As an eligible local bachelor, he cut a dashing figure and was charismatic, sociable, amusing and the proud owner of a large Winton car. His eyes, intelligent and sparkling, were his most notable physical feature. His family tree included judges, senators and councillors. His maternal grandmother was Scottish/Irish and he was never anti-English. He fell in love with Augustine Delisle but deferred to his family's wishes and gave her up because her father was a coal merchant. No daughter of a man "in trade" would be acceptable to the Duplessis family. He, like Mackenzie King, would remain a lifelong bachelor and suffer bouts of loneliness. Although there were rumours about the private life of Mackenzie King, there was always the odour of sanctity about him. With Duplessis there was a whiff of debauchery as he tried to cope with his love of alcohol and women. When drunk, he could be nasty and unpredictable. In 1943 at the age of fifty-three and with health problems, he finally gave up drinking. In his later years his affairs were limited to "safe" (married or separated) women who were respectable but unavailable for marriage.

Beginning in 1923 Duplessis was involved in provincial politics as a Conservative. In the election of 1936 he became premier with his newly-created Union Nationale Party, which swept away thirty-nine years of corrupt Liberal government. However, "*plus ça change*", his eighteen-year tenure in office was known as "*La Grande Noirceur*" (The Great Darkness). He had a saying: *Le ciel est bleu; l'enfer est rouge.* (Heaven is blue-UN; Hell is red-Liberal). For those on the "*bleu*" side who remember him fondly he was hard-working, gave Quebec stability, protected the primacy of the Catholic Church and French Canadian culture, resisted godless communism, provided electrical service in rural areas, built roads, hospitals and universities even during the Depression, and managed to balance the budget for fifteen straight years. The list goes on: he was a devout Catholic who worked with the Church to promote its view of society, fought for provincial rights, was against conscription, brought American investment to Quebec, gave Quebec its *fleur-de-lys* flag. For his enemies he was an authoritarian tyrant not unlike those we were about to fight across the sea. Their list was just as long: persecution of dissidents, union busting, graft, patronage, rigged elections (truckloads of goodies—whiskey, food, nylon stockings, shoes etc.—brought into a town just before an election could guarantee votes), denial of liquor permits to supporters of the Liberal Party, restriction of free speech and assembly with the notorious Padlock Law which was in effect from 1937 to 1957, allowing American companies to buy Quebec's natural resources and pay their workers extremely low wages, and a refusal to adopt basic social services because of a fear of creeping socialism.

One of the most reprehensible chapters in Duplessis' reign was the story of the Duplessis Orphans. Since funding from the federal government was higher for mental institutions, beginning in the 1940s the premier, with the cooperation of the Catholic Church, arranged to have thousands of illegitimate children institutionalized in asylums or orphanages that had been reclassified as hospitals and operated by the clergy. Medical experimentation sometimes resulting in death, harsh treatment and sexual abuse were the lot of many. Understandably, when released as adults they were totally unprepared for life outside the walls. Their saga, which continued into the 1960s, was only nominally dealt with in 2001, and remains a terrible blot on Quebec's history.

Duplessis spent the years between 1939 and 1944 as leader of the opposition. On September 23, 1939 he lost the snap election he had called on the basis of the conscription question. The Liberals promised the electorate that no French Canadian would be sent to fight in Europe and Adélard Godbout became premier of Quebec. With the war nearing an end in 1944, *le Chef* was returned to power where he remained until his death in 1959.

A politician who would be sidelined for most of the war was the always-interesting mayor of Montreal.

HOUDE FREED. ON ROUTE HERE. screamed the *Gazette* headline of Thursday, August 17, 1944. "Mr. Montreal", Camillien Houde, had finally been released from internment. The advance notice allowed Montrealers to prepare for the grand reception that awaited the former mayor of Montreal that evening after four years away from the city he personified. After spending the night in Sherbrooke with his wife, Georgette, and three daughters, he emerged from the train in Central Station, looking much slimmer and wearing a green suit with the ribbon of a Chevalier of the Legion of Honour in his lapel. A reported ten thousand supporters met him at the station and exploded with joy upon seeing their hero. Weeping women threw flowers and car owners honked their horns incessantly. Some even stood on top of their cars to see better. The crowd chanted "*Il a gagné ses epaulettes*" (He's earned his stripes.). Blinding flashbulbs popped while jostling citizens shouted their frenzied cries of welcome. Fifteen minutes later when the applause of the crowd finally subsided, Houde gave a speech in French and English. Then he and his family drove slowly in a convertible as part of a welcoming convoy, threading their way through the cheering masses to his home on St. Hubert Street where he again thrilled the huge and enthusiastic crowd, speaking three more times from his balcony before calling it a night. So ended the story which began on August 2, 1940 when, as mayor of Montreal, Houde went on record as saying the National Registration Act was the first step towards conscription which King had promised not to impose on Canadians. He advised the men of Quebec to refuse registration and, three days later, he was arrested by officers of the Royal Canadian Mounted Police (RCMP) and the provincial police as he left City Hall. Charged under the Defence of Canada Regulations and stripped of his office, he was immediately taken to Camp Petawawa, Ontario where he donned the regulation internment garb and became Prisoner Number 694. He spent his time at Petawawa chopping wood for the camp stoves. Transferred to Minto, New Brunswick in 1941, many hours were passed playing Chinese checkers and ice skating. Not surprisingly, he was the most popular man in both camps. His impression from those years was that the Communist prisoners were more interesting than the Fascists. He might have been released earlier but he refused to agree to conditions of keeping the peace and not interfering with the war effort by giving speeches—the last condition a virtual impossibility for the consummate politician. His anti-conscription stand, considered seditious behaviour, did not sit well with English Montrealers (or with the rest of Canada) but they eventually forgave him. To meet him was to like him and few could resist his love for people and his genuine conviviality.

Born in the working class area of St. Henri in Montreal in 1889, Camillien Houde was the only one of ten children to survive beyond the age of two. His father's death meant that he had to go to work at a young age to help support his mother. After trying careers from baking to banking, he found his true calling in politics. He first tested the waters by being elected a Conservative member of the Quebec Legislative Assembly for St. Mary (Ste. Marie) in 1923 where he served off and on for ten years. Federal politics also interested him (he could hardly resist an election of any sort!) but he made his name as mayor of Montreal when he was first elected in 1928. He was elected four times between 1928 and 1944. Physically he resembled a clown more than a statesman. His homely looks—bulging eyes, potato nose and rotund figure —did not prevent him from becoming an iconic Montreal figure. He had a flair for the theatrical, a smile that could light up a village, a wicked sense of humour and the common touch which made him a darling of the masses, both English and French. He could also be impulsive, pugnacious and outrageous. He tackled the problems of the Depression head on by instituting a municipal sales tax even though it cost him re-election in 1936. He walked a fine line as the city grappled with its dire financial situation. Montreal was hugely in debt but Houde always put the welfare of the people first and was prepared to sacrifice municipal solvency to see that the poor were taken care of. He even helped to distribute funds donated by the Saint Jean Baptiste Society to poor areas of the city. His personal generosity was also noted and his home was always open to the needy. His make-work projects left a huge legacy to the city as well as providing needed jobs. These included the Atwater, Jean Talon and St. James farmers' markets, the Botanical Gardens, chalets on Mount

King George VI and Queen Elizabeth on the balcony of the Windsor Hotel, May 18, 1939, just months before the outbreak of war.
Université de Montréal, Services des archives.
Fonds William Henry Atherton.

Royal and in Lafontaine Park, viaducts, public baths and, of course, the public toilets which were called *camilliennes* in his honour.

He was not, however, a man given to rhetorical restraint. Just a few months before King George and Queen Elizabeth were to visit Canada in 1939, in a speech to the YMCA on the subject of war in Europe, he stated, among other things: "If war comes, and if Italy is on one side and England on the other, the sympathy of the French Canadians in Quebec will be on the side of Italy." As expected, this provocative statement angered English Canada. In Quebec, it even shocked those who were opposed to Canada's involvement in the coming war such as Paul Gouin, Adrian Arcand and the newspapers *Le Devoir* and *L'Action Catholique.*

There were seeming contradictions in his views. Loyal to the British Crown (he had been made a Commander of the Order of the British Empire in 1935), during the royal visit he absolutely charmed the King and Queen with his complete self-confidence and effervescent personality. After the royal visitors signed the Golden Book at City Hall and went out on the balcony to greet the huge crowds that awaited them, Houde famously stated: "You know, Your Majesty, some of those cheers are for you also."

After his release from prison the *p'tit gars de Ste. Marie* was returned to office in the civic election of 1944 by a 15,000 vote majority. He remained mayor until 1954 and died in 1958 at the age of sixty-nine. The man who never became personally wealthy was remembered fondly by the many people who survived the Depression because of his generosity and foresight. Many just liked the colourful man who had been a part of their lives for so long. Thousands lined the streets to watch one of the largest funerals ever seen in Montreal. After lying in state at City Hall, a firemen's band lead the procession to Notre Dame Basilica where his funeral Mass was celebrated. Thirty cars were needed to carry the flowers and the mourners included Premier Maurice Duplessis and many members of his cabinet, Montreal city councillors and two Montreal Canadiens hockey players, Maurice Richard and Butch Bouchard. He rests in Côte des Neiges Cemetery in an Italian marble replica crypt of Napoleon's tomb.

All three leaders, King, Duplessis and Houde had perfectly-honed political instincts. Only Mackenzie King was to see the war through in office. While Houde chopped wood for his internment camp stove, Duplessis worked in opposition to regain his former job as premier. These three men would be involved in another very important event of 1939—the month-long royal visit of King George VI and Queen Elizabeth to Canada in May and June—the first ever for a reigning monarch, just months before the outbreak of war.

The royal visit was meant to garner support for Britain in the coming war. Queen Elizabeth, the Queen Consort, was a woman of effortless and unflappable charm. Lovely and always chic, she was called "The Smiling Duchess" and won the hearts of everyone who met her. King George was a sympathetic figure; slight and shy, with the weight of the British Empire on his shoulders. While Canada waited with bated breath for the event, Quebec was the big question mark. Would French Canadians spoil the welcome and embarrass the government? The sticky question of protocol was another matter and would be debated *ad nauseum* at Rideau Hall and Laurier House. Who would be the first to welcome the King and Queen to Canada? Traditionally, that honour would have gone to Governor General Lord Tweedsmuir, the King's representative in Canada, but as the elected leader of the senior Dominion, Mackenzie King insisted on being the first to greet the royal couple when they arrived in Quebec City. Not missing a chance to personify Canada's new political power and with his hypochondria shelved for the duration, he stayed glued to the side of the royal couple during the gruelling visit and even accompanied them on the New York and Washington leg of the journey, making copious notes for his diary along the way. Lord Tweedsmuir was given a holiday to enjoy the warm weather and was only responsible for the Ottawa part of the visit and for the final send-off in Halifax. When the royal couple stepped off the *Empress of Australia* on May 17 in Quebec City, they were welcomed by Prime Minister Mackenzie King and

Premier Ernest Lapointe, both suitably plumed and uniformed, and other dignitaries. The soldiers of the Royal 22nd Regiment (Van Doos), dressed in scarlet tunics and bearskin busbies, provided a smart backdrop to the welcoming ceremony. Guns boomed out a royal salute, the bands played and the crowds went crazy, cheering and waving from the first moment the King and Queen appeared until they left the city. Journalists went into reverential rhapsodies describing every detail. What was not generally known was that two Royal Navy cruisers which accompanied the *Empress of Australia* carried the British crown jewels and 3,550 gold bars from the Bank of England to safekeeping in the Sun Life Insurance Building in downtown Montreal. The next and more challenging test was Montreal which, as it turned out, was an even bigger success.

Houses and businesses in all areas of the city were festooned with pictures of the King and Queen, Union Jack flags, banners and bunting. Crowds in their Sunday-best filled the streets and squeezed onto small balconies, staircases and lawns along the route to catch a glimpse of history in the making. Just in case the east end of Montreal was reluctant to get out and cheer, Cardinal Rodrigue Villeneuve wrote a pastoral letter which was read in all Catholic churches in the province. In the letter the Prince of the Church ordered the population to receive the King and Queen with respect and dignity. The populace was ready and the politicians held their breath. The royal couple arrived at Park Avenue Station at around two p.m. on May 18 and, after being greeted effusively by Mayor Houde, started their tour of the city in a maroon convertible, part of a motorcade that included the prime minister and the mayor. They were escorted by the handsome mounted soldiers of the 17th Duke of York's Royal Canadian Hussars in their black and gold uniforms and busbies. The cars drove through Outremont, down Park Avenue and past Fletcher's Field. They then headed east and visited Delormier Stadium where thousands of French- and English-speaking Catholic children cheered themselves hoarse. Then it was over the Jacques Cartier Bridge to the fort on St. Helen's Island (St. Helen's Island would become POW camp Number 47 during the war housing mostly Germans and Italians) and back again to City Hall where they signed the Golden Book. Then, up the hill they went to McGill University's Percival Molson Stadium where thousands of Protestant schoolchildren would be next to shout their appreciation for the royal couple. Then the motorcade made its way to the chalet atop Mount Royal where the King and Queen were served tea by socially suitable young ladies. Phyllis Eperson was waiting patiently with other Girl Guides on the mountain and remembers: "The Guides and Scouts (I was a Ranger by then, a senior guide) all waited on Remembrance Road (formerly Shakespeare Road) to greet the King and Queen. It was a beautiful day and the flowers were all out. We waved like mad and were so pleased to see them." The procession continued along Sherbrooke Street in the Golden Square Mile and headed to the Windsor Hotel where a thousand of Montreal's elite would attend an evening banquet. At the end of the long, exhausting day, organizers and the police breathed a huge sigh of relief. The Hussars' horses did not

Phyllis Eperson (third from left) with a group of Rangers.
"The Guides and Scouts (I was a Ranger by then) all waited ...
to greet the King and Queen"
Courtesy of Phillis Esperson.

panic; the welcome was spontaneous and genuine. The few medical emergencies were manageable and lost children were soon recovered. Unfortunately, one man suffered a heart attack and died but there were no unpleasant scenes from embittered communists, anti-conscription demonstrators or other malcontents and the welcome in French-speaking areas exceeded all expectations. The only sour note was caused by the petulant bickering of the politicians involved. Duplessis boycotted a luncheon given by the Canadian government in Quebec City because his seat was not close enough to the royal couple. He turned up in good spirits that evening for a dinner when he made sure that Mackenzie King would be given an inferior seat. In Montreal Mayor Houde and Mackenzie King had a dispute over who would sit in the second and third cars in the motorcade. Houde won, displacing King.

Quebec City had been a brilliant success and thousands of people had lined the streets of Montreal to welcome the British King and Queen. Yes, it could be said, Quebec was on side and would probably support the coming war.

[CHAPTER TWO]

Montreal — *Montréal*

Daily Life And Political Strife

MONTREAL IN THE EARLY 1940S was unique in Canada, not only because of its dual linguistic nature but also because the majority of people rented their homes. The duplex or triplex style of housing—often with outdoor staircases—which had two or three flats one atop another, made for crowded neighbourhoods and a lively street life. There were also single-family homes in many areas of the city such as Westmount, Notre Dame de Grâce (N.D.G.), Outremont and Point St. Charles. The well-to-do and many of the middle class had central heating and hot water on demand. This meant that they could bathe often, even once a day. For those who had a coal furnace in the basement, the coalman regularly delivered a supply that was fed through a chute into a coal bin beneath a window. Feeding the furnace and tending it was a job that generally fell to the man of the house or a stalwart son or two. Others heated their homes with one or more small coal stoves that were strategically located throughout the house. A network of large ceiling pipes delivered the heat to all the rooms and these pipes had to be cleaned on a regular basis. A water heater would be fired up for baths, which happened traditionally on Saturday night. In many poor districts of the city bathroom facilities were primitive with only a cold-water faucet in the kitchen sink and an enclosed toilet in the corner. While small children could be scrubbed clean in a metal basin, adults had a harder time keeping presentable, especially the men who laboured in hot and dirty factories and foundries. They could wash themselves over a sink or take advantage of the public baths sprinkled throughout the city. Families could also pay a visit to a luckier relative with a tub. Many women washed their hair only once every two or three weeks. Although the deodorized society was still a long way in the future, fastidious ladies could buy Mum or Odo-Ro-No deodorant. Lifebuoy soap, with its famous red colour, kept B.O. (body odour) at bay and was widely advertised with slogans such as "From head to toe, it stops B.O.". Lux and Palmolive soap were also popular with women. Sunlight soap was used by almost everybody for almost anything while Listerine mouthwash kept both sexes kissable.

In English homes, those who could afford magazines read *Maclean's, Chatelaine, Time, Collier's, Ladies' Home Journal, Newsweek* that sold for between five and fifteen cents. On coffee tables in French homes, one could find copies of popular magazines like *La Revue populaire, La Revue moderne* (for women) and the intellectual *La Relève.* Canadian pulp magazines dealing in romance, crime, western, mystery and science-fiction sagas could be found in both English and French for those who needed a little more spice in their life. (The War Exchange Conservation Act which was passed in 1940 restricted the importation of American pulp magazines and comics thus giving a shot in the arm to Canadian writers and publishers.) Telephone exchanges had colourful names like: WIlbank, HArbour, FRontenac, MArquette, DExter, WEllington and CHerrier which were followed by only four numbers. Many households shared "party lines" which allowed for interesting eavesdropping sessions.

Housewives, who rarely worked outside the home unless they were widowed or struggling immigrants, had their hands full with taking care of children who came home from school for lunch. Monday was wash day, Tuesday ironing day and so on until Sunday arrived and allowed a bit of a break for going to church or visiting relatives. There were no miracle fabrics and tea towels, bed sheets, tablecloths (used every day) and napkins (usually used less often), blouses, dresses and men's and boys' shirts all had to be bleached and starched, if necessary, before being ironed. Clothes could be hung outside to dry in good weather but rainy or winter weather meant that lines of laundry were hung in the house or basement. There were also many laundries in the city that were happy to save you the trouble if you could afford their services. Most homes had a treadle sewing machine and mothers were kept busy making clothes for themselves and their families. Smocking dresses, embroidering, crocheting, knitting, canning and preserving in season made for a busy life. Babies' cloth diapers had to be washed and holes in sweaters, socks and stockings had to be darned.

Families rarely went to restaurants. A dinner out was something parents did on their wedding anniversary or other special occasions. Then there was the cooking and baking. Not everyone could afford the cakes, tarts and crumpets delivered by the bread man every day. Not only were home freezers unheard of, a majority of homes had only an icebox. A sign in the window let the ice man know that ice was needed and, in he came, dripping a huge block which would last a couple of days. On very hot days, children loved to get a sliver of ice (stolen or donated by the iceman) to suck on and cool off. Refrigerators had, of course, been invented but only became a common household appliance after the war. If a family wanted to have ice cream for dessert, one of the older children would be dispatched to the ubiquitous local corner store to buy a brick of Neapolitan, chocolate, vanilla or strawberry ice cream, which, when sliced, was a rare treat. After dinner, a kettle of water was heated, some Oxydol, Rinso or other soap powder (used both for dishes and laundry) was added to the dishpan. In large families where older children were expected to help out, the fight was then on for whose turn it was to wash or dry the pile of dirty dishes. Better-off families could afford to hire help, and gardeners, chauffeurs, charwomen, nannies, seamstresses, cooks and housekeepers made life easier and allowed more time, especially for the women, to have a social life playing bridge or volunteering in churches, schools and hospitals. Couples could also take advantage of Montreal's exciting and vibrant entertainment and restaurant scene.

For the average family as well, there was still a lot of fun to be had. Picnics, visits to relatives, dropping in on friends, outings to

Lafontaine Park or Mount Royal to feed the ducks at Beaver Lake, day trips to local beaches like Plage Laval, Cap St. Jacques and St. Joseph du Lac, or even to Plattsburgh Beach, all helped to make life interesting. Old Orchard Beach in Maine was a popular holiday destination as were the many vacation spots in the Laurentians for those who could afford to go for a week or two. For the many who couldn't afford to leave the city, Balconville would have to do. There were many race tracks to be supported (although the one in Dorval closed to make way for the airport which opened in 1941) and countless all-male taverns where hard-working men could go, order a Black Horse or Dow beer, discuss work, sports, politics and the perfidy of bosses.

Radio was in its heyday and there were shows to please everybody. Among them were Amos & Andy, Fibber McGee and Molly, Baby Snooks and the scary The Shadow ("Who knows what evil lurks in the hearts of men? The Shadow knows!"). The variety show The Happy Gang was another favourite: ("Knock, knock. Who's there? It's the Happy Gang! Well, come on in!"). The Aldrich Family had perhaps one of the most well-known signature sounds in radio, "Henreeeeee! Henree Al-drich" followed by a squeaky adolescent voice, "Coming, Mother" as it followed the adventures of a bumbling but loveable teenager through the social minefield of youthful misadventures. For fans of Bing Crosby, his dulcet tones would introduce the theme song of the Kraft Music Hall program: ("Where the Blue of the Night Meets the Gold of the Day.") French audiences often listened to music programs from the United States but talented writers like Robert Choquette and others wrote captivating shows like *La Pension Velder*, *Métropole*, *Un homme et son Péché* and *Vie de Famille*. Boxing matches and hockey games were popular with both French and English, of course. Wartime restrictions meant that time on the radio had to be provided for political speeches and other relevant programming. Lorne Greene (nicknamed "The Voice of Doom") delivered the latest war news to a worried and attentive English audience. Those who had short-wave radios could tune in to news from all parts of the world.

Many did and were sometimes kept up half the night following the Allied progress.

Families shopped for food at large markets, small independent grocers, butchers, bakeries and fruit stores or did business with chains like Dominion, A&P, Thrift Stop and Shop or Steinberg's, most of which offered home delivery. Dionne's on St. Catherine Street catered to the carriage trade and offered five deliveries a day. Anyone wanting a bottle or two of alcohol had to visit one of the Quebec liquor commission outlets (Commission des Liqueurs de Québec). It was a daunting process. Walking in the front door of the store (which looked like a Soviet government office), one checked the price of the desired bottle which was displayed on the wall, lined up at one of the caged windows at a long counter and gave the order to one of the employees who would then retrieve it from the supply that was hidden in the back.

Churches were an important element of life in those days. As well as offering spiritual succour, they held fairs, bazaars, concerts, plays, recitals and other events that brought people together. Catholic parishes all over the city regularly held processions. One of the most popular was the feast of Corpus Christi—*La Fête-Dieu*—in June. The streets were a sea of black and white as lines of priests and altar boys accompanied the consecrated Host the priest carried in a golden monstrance. Fraternal groups and parish societies, some carrying banners, would accompany the parade and flower petals would be scattered by the young girls of the parish. The large crowds of the devout—all dressed in their Sunday best and waiting reverentially—would fall to their knees as the Host passed. In English areas not as thickly populated and with a large Protestant element, there was less of an audience but no less pageantry. These processions ended back at the church with a service of Benediction of the Blessed Sacrament. In English parishes, strong voices would fill the church and shake the rafters with "Tantum Ergo" and "Holy God, We Praise Thy Name". The Divine Praises would be recited: Blessed be God. Blessed be His Holy Name… and so on until: Blessed be God in His Angels and in His Saints. Then it was over for another year and everyone would walk home, grateful for the longer hours of daylight that signalled the coming of summer.

Children in most areas of the city had a rich play life in the streets that were, for the most part, free of cars and thus safe. For the boys, there were always friends or brothers available for a game of baseball, kick the can, hide-and-seek or a bicycle adventure. Some cigarette packages came with cards that had pictures of planes on them. Boys gathered and threw them one at a time against the street curb. The lucky fellow whose card was closest would pick up all the cards. "*Drapeau*" was a warlike game played with a broomstick and a rag representing a flag on top of it. Making model airplanes and ships from kits was also fun and, sadly, foreshadowed the role many boys would soon play in the real things. French boys in the east end of the city played "*le moineau*" (tip it), a game involving a broomstick and a smaller piece of wood and, being hockey crazy, started practicing on the street in the fall until they could get on the ice when the city rinks were set up in the winter. Then there was general mischief. "Clinkers" (partially-burned lumps of coal) were collected from train tracks and brought home to contribute to the coal supply. Tittering over the women's underwear ads in the Eaton's catalogue or playing "doctor," if one could find amenable girls, were two other popular hobbies. Stealing tomatoes and carrots from a neighbour's garden was fairly innocent but often the mischief escalated from aiming at birds with a slingshot or BB gun and breaking windows to more daring deeds like ringing in a false fire alarm, pulling streetcar trolley poles off the lines or stealing flares from the CNR at the Turcot Yards to put on city poles and set afire. Small metal pieces, also stolen from the CNR, could be used as "track bombs" and placed on streetcar tracks. This terrified the poor unsuspecting conductor whose fate it was to ride over one of them. Not getting caught was the big excitement but, if the bad boys were caught, it often meant a trip to Juvenile Court on St. Denis Street where Judge Nicholson could mete out a couple of days in custody.

Mischief for girls was a bit tamer. With one or more friends assembled for the fun, one girl would telephone a store and ask, "Are you on St. Catherine Street?" The answer was yes and then the brave girl would say, "You'd better hurry and get off. A streetcar is coming." A quick hang up and then the stifled laughter could be unleashed to a full roar until the next phone call with a variation on the theme. Ringing doorbells and running away was a common thing to do when coming home in the dark from a Girl Guide meeting. Both boys and girls played marbles which were carried in pockets or mesh bags. If their parents could afford the Crown Royal brand of whiskey which Seagram's had created in honour of the royal visit of 1939, then collections of marbles could be trotted around, especially by girls, in the regal purple and gold bag that came with its purchase. As well as many of the same games that boys played, skipping rope and bouncing lacrosse balls were games that girls enjoyed and there was a rich repertoire of chants that went with each one. Choosing sides for any game meant that all the children stood in a circle and put their fists (the potatoes) in front of them. One child banged on the fists while reciting: One potato, two potato, three potato, four, five potato, six potato, seven potato, more. On "more", one hand was eliminated and placed behind one's back until only one fist was left. All these games were played until it was time to go home for a meal or, if played after supper, until "the street lights come on" when all had to scurry home.

Mary Prendergast Ebel, who grew up on Melrose Avenue in N.D.G. remembers: "We spent a lot of time skipping and playing hopscotch, tag and run-sheep-run, which was a two-team game like hide-and-seek. We also had never-ending baseball and kickball games which the boys let us join—probably when there was a shortage of team members! We played with tennis balls that would sometimes go down the open sewer grate. We would get a rake and fish them out if the "gunk" was high enough. If it wasn't, we had to wait until the city guys came to clean the sewers. Then they'd fish out two or three balls that we would wash off and make ready for another game. It was "finders keepers" in these circumstances. We also spent hours practicing the art of walking on the metal-railing fences which were in front of many houses." Mary's father was a CPR policeman who worked at the Angus Shops. On his days off, Mary, her parents and three sisters and one brother would go on picnics to a beach in Lachine or to parks in Westmount or Montreal West. These destinations were reached by foot or streetcar. On these outings, cans of Klik, Kam, Spam or tuna would be brought and opened to make sandwiches. In the fall, there was apple picking in Cote St. Luc—with fewer than 800 residents, it was the countryside at the time.

Another fun thing to do was to walk to the corner store that had a seemingly endless selection of penny candy in bins. This took money, of course. A generous allowance at the time was five cents a week. If you had already spent it, your mother might let you return

A World War II era photograph of happy children playing on Melrose Avenue in N.D.G. Mary Prendergast is second from left, first row. *Courtesy Mary Prendergast Ebel*

bottles to the store for a refund, thus replenishing your capital. Children who received no allowance and were desperate for money could always steal bottles from a neighbour's garage or shed. When the bell over the candy store door announced the arrival of one or more children, the bored owner would stop whatever he was doing and patiently wait for the big transaction to come. For kids, it seemed they had died and gone to heaven. There were coconut balls, chocolate-covered "honeymoons", candy kisses, red and black liquorice, liquorice pipes, sponge candy, small packages of candy cigarettes, tiny cones filled with candy, wax false teeth that could be chewed and were filled with a sweet liquid. A nickel would buy you an Oh Henry!, Sweet Marie or Neilson's Jersey Milk chocolate bar, an ice cream cone or a Popsicle which could be shared with a friend. B-B Bats, a toffee treat on a stick were another option. When rationing was introduced in 1942, it became harder for children to satisfy their sweet tooth, not to mention the huge impact on the family's food supply. The candy stores were not as opulent as they once were and much of what was available had an unusual taste. Artificial flavours and ingredients used to make candy and chocolate bars did not fool the children who complained of the "different" taste of their favourite treats. Chocolate bars were in short supply with many being sent to the troops overseas. Ice cream, Coca-Cola, chewing gum, Life Savers all became almost treasured memories. By 1944 production of candy and soft drinks was down 50 per cent from the pre-war years.

If there was no one around to play with, children had cut-out and colouring books, jigsaw puzzles, books, bolo bats, scrapbooks and yo-yos to fill the time. It was the Golden Age of Superheroes but the adventures of Superman, Wonder Woman and Captain Marvel could not be enjoyed in Canada because of the ban on American comics. But, *nil desperandum*, talented Canadian artists and writers came to the rescue and produced heroes like Nelvana of the Northern Lights, Captain Wonder, Thunderfist, Whiz Wallace, Commander Steel, Johnny Canuck and others who were quite prepared to fight the bad guys and the Axis tyrants. These comics had coloured covers but were printed in black and white. The war years came to be known as the Golden Age of Canadian comics with more than twenty original titles being produced. This would end when American comics again flooded into Canada after 1945. Howard Dearlove was not at all impressed with the local selection: "Good comic books were hard to get. The ones they had here were lousy. You had to go to the States. My grandmother had a cottage up near Cornwall in Summerstown and we used to get in boats and row up the Salmon River to Fort Covington in New York and get the good Walt Disney, Superman and Batman comics. We also used to go for the Fleer's bubble gum which we couldn't get here."

In Church-run Quebec, French kids were often limited to reading comic strips with Catholic and nationalist themes. Stories about the Bible, saints, Church prelates, missionaries and martyrs were plentiful. The monthly *Hérauts* was one example. Newspapers like *Le Petit Journal* and *L'Action catholique* carried strips like *La Fille du brouillard, Sergent Belle-Rose* and *La Toison d'or*. The bi-weekly newspaper *François* featured humorous cartoons like *Les Loups-garous de Beauchàtel* and adventure stories like *Yves l'Aventurier* and *Robino.* When boredom set in, as it often did, it was sometimes alleviated by sitting on the front step just thinking about life or daydreaming. Ambitious kids could make the rounds of neighbours and, depending on the season, offer to shovel snow or cut the grass, providing money for more candy or comics.

For those who loved swimming but had no access to a lake, there was a public beach on St. Helen's Island and the Natatorium in Verdun was open for business. There were also numerous indoor pools sprinkled around the city. Tennis was another option for those who had the equipment and lived near a court. In the winter there were hockey games, skating, sledding, tobogganing, fort making and snowball fights. Children also got a lot of exercise walking back and forth to school four times a day in often below freezing temperatures. Sometimes you could hitch a ride on a bread or milk wagon if the driver liked you or happened to be your friend's father or uncle. Horses were everywhere; milk, bread, coal, fruits and vegetables were all delivered by wagons. Ragmen would clip-clop down back lanes and offer to buy "RAGS, BOTTLES, OLD CLOTHES". The arrival of the "chip" wagon was an occasion for buying a greasy treat for five cents. The number of horses meant rather untidy streets and, in the summer, the city used a water truck to spray the roads. Some small children were terrified as these huge aquatic monsters rolled down the street loudly spewing torrents of water.

As children became teens, the world opened up a bit more. Arthur Fraser had great times: "The six of us in my gang used to go to the movies on St. Lawrence Boulevard. There was a vaudeville show and two movies for twelve cents. At the French theatre, they had three movies for the same price. Chocolate bars and ice cream cones cost five cents. Orange Crush used to have pieces of orange in it at that time. Kik cola was sold in big bottles for six cents and there was another soft drink called Denis. They used to sell cigarettes by the penny or you could buy packages of five, ten, twenty or twenty-five. They also sold fifty cigarettes in a metal box but they were usually sold around the holidays."

Trips to Belmont Park were always fun for families and young people looking to meet interesting people of the opposite sex. Situated on the banks of Rivière des Prairies (the Back River), Montrealers got there by boarding the No. 17 streetcar to Cartierville at the Garland Terminus. Arriving at the front gate, visitors were notified that the entrance fee for adults was 20 cents and for children, 10 cents. Another sign of the times said: "No zoot suits." Once inside, it was a sensory overload of noisy rides, music, screaming children, banging noises from games, the crack of rifles from the shooting gallery, the smell of snack food, cotton candy and toffee apples. A papier-mâche figure of a fat, shaking, laughing lady with very red lipstick called "*la grosse femme*" or "Laughing Sal" graced the park midway. Her incessant laughter was due to a recorded soundtrack. One of the most popular rides was the Cyclone, a huge wooden roller coaster which went clicking over the tracks slowly until the turns and descents that were taken at stomach-churning speeds. There were also exciting rides like the Roll-O-Plane, Caterpillar, Octopus, the Whip, Tumble Bug, bumper cars and more sedate rides like the Carousel and Ferris Wheel. There were sideshows of "freaks" like the bearded lady and other unfortunates. Picnic grounds, boat rides, a dance hall and a roller skating rink as well as a section for kiddie rides rounded out the attractions. It was a perfect place to forget your troubles and have a good time.

Visitors to Montreal could see the sights by taking a ride on an observation streetcar. These were magnificent open cars with tiered seats and intricate railings painted gold. Ensconced in rococo splendour, one passed such sights as the Oratory, the University of Montreal, Fletcher's Field, the Motherhouse of the Congregation of Nôtre Dame and Westmount Park with its floral clock. And all for twenty-five cents! Another tourist attraction was the Midgets Palace (le Palais des Nains) at 961 Rachel Street East. This home was decorated with Lilliputian furnishings by Philippe Nicol for his wife Rose and son Philippe and was open to the public. The Wax Museum was another popular destination. Scenes of martyred Roman Christians and heroes of New France like Jeanne Mance and Jacques Cartier were guaranteed to stoke religious and patriotic feelings.

Those families with money naturally had a more varied life with holidays, visits to cottages, tennis and ski lessons but for the ordinary child, the street was where the action happened unless there was a park nearby. Community-minded groups sometimes organized outings to Mount Royal and some children were lucky enough to be sent to summer camp to escape the city heat. Until the discovery of the Salk vaccine in the 1950s, regular epidemics of polio, also called poliomyelitis or infantile paralysis, were a terrifying reality for families and definitely put a pall on children's activities. It was highly contagious and often left its victims with paralysis. Eating fuit or going to a public swimming pool were done with much trepidation until the danger passed.

* * *

The most salient fact about Montreal was that it was linguistically divided. St. Lawrence Boulevard (called the Main) separated the English west end from the French east end. Some working-class neighbourhoods in the west end, like St. Henri and Point St. Charles, had both French and English living side by side. This closeness led to great friendships and sometimes marriages. If the children would sometimes kick over the traces and recreate the Battle of the Plains of Abraham on the way to their separate schools, the positive thing was that most children in these areas quickly became bilingual. Insults were one way to start your bilingual career. "*Mange la merde*!", "*Maudit anglais*" "*Bloke*" "*Tête carrée*", screamed the French kids while the English ones bellowed, "Go home, Frenchy", "Frog", "Pepsi!", "French pea soup". Another area with both English and French was Maisonneuve in the east end. Dave McCrindle remembers: "I grew up on Leclaire Street in the Maisonneuve area. A good proportion of our neighbours were British who all worked at Vickers. Our French neighbours were nice people and there was no strife at all. As young boys we would sometimes fight with the French kids but, if we didn't have French kids to fight with, we'd fight with the English kids. As a matter of fact, some of my French chums were among the first to join up in 1939 with the Régiment de Maisonneuve." If many of the English felt that the French were "priest-ridden" and undereducated, the French had the satisfaction of knowing that they had more fun than those uptight English, who could barely manage a smile, ate boring food and had no "*joie de vivre.*"

French-Canadian men were often bilingual—even becoming an elevator operator in downtown Montreal required English. The predominance of English in a city with a French-speaking majority would have serious repercussions in the coming decades. Conversations between unilingual English and French housewives in poorer areas were often managed in sign language as these women hovered over rickety back balconies hanging out laundry. Help, when needed, was generously given by both groups. In mostly English areas of the city, such as N.D.G. and Westmount, the only

French people many saw were delivery men and city workers.

Montreal, being the business hub of Canada and a major seaport, attracted many immigrants who hoped to better their lives. The Jewish population of Quebec was estimated to be 63,697 in 1941. The wealthier ones lived in Outremont or Westmount while the newcomers struggled to make a living in factories or as shop owners whose stores lined St. Lawrence Boulevard and who tended to live in the same area. Sam Steinberg's mother opened a grocery store that soon became a respected and innovative supermarket chain that gave the more established ones a run for their money. The black community was mostly centered in the St. Antoine-St. Henri area, although many also lived in other districts like Park Extension, Ville Emard, N.D.G. and Verdun. The small Chinese community lived in the La Gauchetière Street area and many Chinese men worked as cooks and launderers before setting up their own businesses. Italians, Ukrainians, Poles, Germans, and other ethnic groups also crowded into the city and set up communities mostly in the downtown area. The churches and social centres that they built helped them assimilate to a new country while retaining ties to the old. While many learned French, the welcome mat was not put out for them in the French school system, so the children of immigrants usually went to English schools and quite often ended up trilingual. Public schools were set up along religious lines so Catholic children in English schools benefitted by having a parochial education. English Protestant schools were quite similar to those in Ontario with the singing of "God Save the King" and framed pictures of the monarch on the wall. With less emphasis on religion, these schools accommodated Jewish students who had to celebrate the Christmas and Easter school traditions even if the school had a majority Jewish student enrolment such as Baron Byng high school on St. Urbain Street. While the children of immigrants might aspire to higher education and better job opportunities, St. James Street, the financial centre of Montreal, was run by the English or more precisely, the Anglo-Scots. It was a closed society of prominent families such as the

Molsons and the Refords, many of whom lived in Westmount and in downtown Montreal's Golden Square Mile. They frequented the same clubs such as the Mount Royal, were educated at exclusive schools including Trafalgar and Lower Canada College, holidayed at Métis Beach, Tadoussac or Cacouna, sailed, played golf, polo and tennis and usually intermarried. The wealthy French, many of whom lived in Outremont, were equally patrician and included the Beaubiens and Gérin-Lajoies. They also had their clubs, like the St. Denis, and enjoyed lives of quiet opulence. Their children attended private schools like the Jesuit-run Collège Jean-de-Brébeuf for the boys and Villa Maria for the girls. The large Irish community had fanned out across the city, but many still lived in the working-class areas of Griffintown, Verdun and Point St. Charles. A city map of Montreal clearly indicates the dichotomy between the two groups sharing the same language. Strathcona, Sydenham, Braeside, Aberdeen, Argyle, Churchill and Trafalgar are all streets in Westmount while Griffintown and "The Point" have street signs that read: Dublin, St. Patrick, Hibernia, Brennan and Sullivan. Those Griffintowners, however, who wished to have a toney address could always choose to live on Prince, Duke, King or Queen streets.

St. Catherine Street was the most important shopping street in the city. Ogilvy's, Simpson's, Eaton's, Morgan's (now The Bay) were large department stores in central downtown while Dupuis Frères was east of St. Lawrence and served a mostly French clientele. Department stores offered home deliveries and C.O.D. payments and their trucks were busy delivering packages large and small all over the city. Woolworth's and Kresge's were also popular destinations for smaller items and a quick lunch. In those days the apostrophe reigned supreme west of the Main. Dinty Moore's Restaurant, Bryson's Drug Store, Lindsay's Record Store, Murray's Restaurant, Layton's... the list was a long one until the passage of Bill 101 in 1977. The French Language Charter, which restricted the use of English in commercial signs, was an attempt to assert the city's French character. To Montrealers in the 1940s, the idea that the English language would not dominate the business world forever was unthinkable. Generations of unilingual English workers had made a good living working in banks, stores, and insurance companies and for large employers like the Bell Telephone Company, Montreal Light, Heat and Power, Dominion Textiles and Northern Electric. It was also very common for French Canadians to speak English to one another when doing business. It was an accepted fact that the sun rose in the east and set in the west and business was conducted in English.

Visitors to Montreal could not help but notice the endless landscape of Roman Catholic churches, seminaries, convents, parish schools, church-run hospitals, orphanages and homes for the insane. Many of these institutions were sombre-grey in colour and rather intimidating to the outsider. Stern-faced priests, religious brothers and nuns in religious habit were a common sight and the peal of church bells a regular reminder. The Catholicism in Quebec was ultramontanist, an ideology in which the Church was accepted as as a divine institution headed by a Pope who was infallible in matters of faith. The state and the Church worked as one and, between them, every aspect of life in French Quebec was governed. Schools, universities, trade unions, social action groups, parish organizations, women's groups and Church-sanctioned newspapers all combined to stifle dissent, something that worked in a society where outside influences like radio were still fairly new. Belonging to the "one, true Church" carried a heavy responsibility. The faithful were told how to think and act and were expected to behave or face social and religious ostracism. There were the seven deadly sins that were to be avoided; the Ten Commandments to be followed and the rules of the Church regarding holy days, fasting and abstinence to be obeyed. Occasions of sin were also to be shunned. Even *thinking* about sinning was a sin. Dances and movies, especially those from Hollywood were to be avoided but documentaries on nature, agriculture, crafts or the perennial favourite, *Maria Chapdelaine,* were acceptable.

Although men were expected to lead pious lives, women carried the full weight of the endless exhortations to perfection. Birth control (except for the rhythm method) was a mortal sin and they were expected to bear many children, keep a spotless house, defer to their husbands, dress modestly, see to the religious observation of their family while keeping a pleasant demeanour at all times. Schoolchildren learned arithmetic by finding the answer to such problems as: If Anne says five "*Notre Pères*" a day, how many does she say in one week? Prayers were said upon arriving at school, before and after each recess and lunch break and before going home for the day. Religious authorities regulated the registration of births, marriages and deaths. Divorce was available only by applying to the federal government in Ottawa. This authoritarian Catholicism very often led to a xenophobic view of society. There was distrust of "foreigners"—English-Canadian or American businessmen who were seen as exploiting a people whose religion and language they did not respect. Socialists, liberals, Jews and communists (often considered one and the same) were, to many, beyond the pale. In Louis Hémon's, *Maria Chapdelaine*, one of the most influential novels in French-Canadian history, the English are described thus: "Around us the strangers have come whom we like to call barbarians. They have taken all the power and have acquired almost all the money."

English-speaking Catholics followed the same Church rules but with a lesser degree of insularity. While intermarriage with Protestants was not approved, in most cases English Catholics and Protestants lived side by side quite successfully.

While these negative feelings about outsiders can be understood in a population suffering from the psychic scars of the Conquest, they were by no means particular to Quebec. Canada had not covered itself with glory in this regard. Racism was not an aberration but a way of life for many. Strict immigration laws at the beginning of the twentieth century were put in place to ensure that Canada remained a White Anglo-Saxon nation. Northern Europeans were welcome. Unwelcome were immigrants from Eastern Europe and the Baltic countries (although exceptions were made for agricultural workers). Those in the "Special Permit" class were Italians, Greeks, Syrians, Turks, blacks, Orientals and all Jews except those with British citizenship. From 1933 to 1939, Canada had the worst record of any western country for accepting Jewish immigrants fleeing persecution. While the United States admitted 140,000 and Brazil admitted 20,000, Canada accepted only 4,000. In June of 1939 the transatlantic liner *St. Louis* with 907 Jews aboard seeking asylum, was off the coast of Nova Scotia. They had already been denied entry to Havana although they had valid visas. Canadian authorities turned them away and the passengers then sailed back to Europe to face an uncertain fate. All across Canada immigrants were subjected to racism and exploitation. McGill University had a restricted enrolment policy regarding Jewish students and many English in Montreal were quite prepared to go along with the bilingual message seen in St. Agathe in the thirties: *AVIS Les juifs ne sont pas désirés ici. Ste-Agathe est un village canadian français et nous le garderons ainsi.* (NOTICE Jews are not wanted here in Ste. Agathe, so scram while the going is good.) Golf clubs had signs reading, "Restricted Membership" and ads for resorts in the

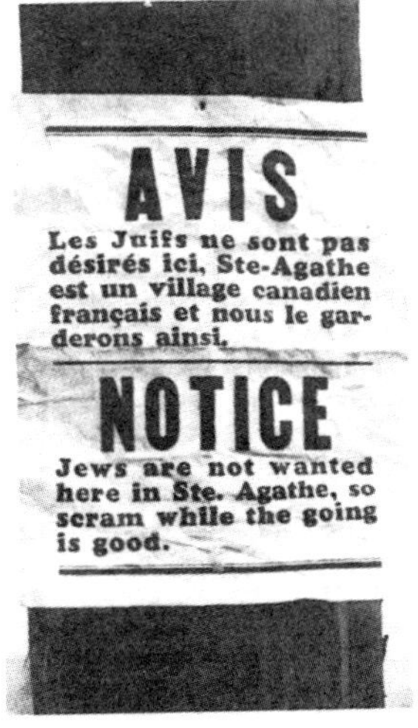

Laurentians often specified, "Restricted Clientele". Blacks and Chinese in Montreal faced relentless job and housing discrimination. Eastern European immigrants with names that were difficult to pronounce were all classified as "Polacks" or, in the case of Italians, *les spaghettis,* wops or dagos.

The political philosophy which defined Quebec in the 1930s and '40s was corporatism, a definition of society approved by the Pope which was a compromise between liberalism and communism and was intended to right the problems of the Depression. The countries that exemplified it the best were Italy, Spain and Portugal. France's Marshal Pétain, the Vichy government's *Chef d'Etat* and collaborator with the Nazis, was also much admired. In a corporate state all sectors of society worked together to ensure order and social peace. Dissent was replaced by collaboration. This, of course, worked better in a state that was homogenous and in Quebec that meant Catholic and French Canadian. Private property and free enterprise were encouraged but "godless communism" was totally rejected. Left-wing and liberal thinking also had to be curtailed for the common good. The man who best embodied these views was Abbé Lionel Groulx. A priest, professor, author and public speaker, he had taught Canadian history at the University of Montreal since 1915 and had imbued his students with his own view of the past, which was that nothing good had come out of Confederation. He wanted the provincial government to work within Confederation to improve the economic status of French Canadians and give them back pride in their heritage. He is considered the spiritual father of Quebec nationalism and is an icon to many Quebec intellectuals. A racist and an anti-Semite (although he occasionally remembered his priestly mission when he stated that racism was unchristian), his message resonated with many who wanted a strong Catholic and French-speaking society on the shores of the St. Lawrence.

Communism and fascism were the two major competing ideologies of the time and it was against this backdrop that the country had to adjust to a new direction. The world knew what communism had done to Russia but fascism was relatively new and, in the case of Spain and Italy, seemed rather benign. The Canadian government was totally opposed to communism which, during the Depression, represented a threat to social order. Prime Minister Bennett blamed foreigners for the many converts to communism and their successes in the labour movement and deported thousands back to Europe. Those who couldn't be deported were hounded by the RCMP and often jailed. The Communists blamed Bennett and the Depression for the need for a new social order. Montrealer Fred Rose was a Communist politician and union worker who was jailed in the 1930s for organizing the unemployed. He placed second as a Communist Party of Canada candidate in the 1935 federal election in the mostly Jewish working-class riding of Cartier. Banned early in the war, the Communist Party was renamed the Labour Progressive Party. Rose was elected to the House of Commons under its banner in a 1943 by-election in a four-way race, even beating out David Lewis of the CCF. Many of his Jewish constituents thought communism was the only answer to fight Hitler's Fascism. After the war and with Cold War hysteria heating up, Rose again became a target. Accused of spying and with no way to defend himself against such non-specific charges as conspiracy, he was expelled from Parliament in 1947 and jailed for four and a half years. After his release, the RCMP made sure that he couldn't find work in Montreal and he returned to Poland to get needed medical help and try to restart his life. His Canadian citizenship was revoked in 1957 which meant that he had no opportunity to return to Canada to clear his name. He died in1983.

Canada was slow, however, to see the looming threat of right-wing extremism in Europe. The Spanish Civil War, which started in 1936, was the shot across the bow for what lay ahead for the world. When General Francisco Franco (leader of the Nationalists), aided by Nazi Germany and Fascist Italy, wanted to oust the Communist-supported Popular Front government, the Mackenzie-Papineau Battalion, or Mac-Paps was formed in Canada to fight on the Republican side as part of the XV International Brigade. They were a varied group of individuals—communists, intellectuals, leftists and idealists—and all were champing at the bit to fight Franco and preserve democracy. Many were working class people whose experiences during the Depression had turned them against capitalism. Their commander was Edward Cecil-Smith, a Montreal journalist and union organizer. Dr. Norman Bethune, a doctor at the Royal Victoria Hospital, also left for Spain to set up a Canadian Medical Unit. Bethune, a member of a prominent family from Gravenhurst, Ontario, was won over to the communist cause when, as a doctor in Montreal during the Depression, he was appalled by the lack of medical services for the poor, which he often provided free of charge. Canada did everything possible to prevent these recruits from volunteering by making it illegal to serve in Spain. Anyone suspected of going was denied a passport and the RCMP spied on all leftist organizations. Speakers coming to Montreal to explain the Republican side of the war in Spain were greeted with hostility and shouts of "*A bas les communistes*". Very often and predictably "*A bas les juifs*" was added to the refrain. Of the 1,546 Canadians who volunteered, 721 were killed. When the veterans returned, they were often hounded and harassed by the Mounties and denied employment. It is ironic in the extreme to realize that these soldiers who were in the vanguard in the fight against fascism were pariahs in their own country which would soon be involved in an all-out war against the Axis. Many did, however, volunteer to serve in World War II but many others were turned down as they were considered unreliable. A few were simply past caring and had no interest in crossing the Atlantic again to fight.

One man who strutted across the political stage with impunity at this time was Adrien Arcand, Canada's self-proclaimed *führer*. A thin, intense man, he was born in Montreal and, after studying journalism at McGill University, edited several anti-Semitic newspapers in the 1930s, among them *Le Fasciste Canadien, Le Miroir* and *Le Goglu*. A federalist and an anglophile, he received money to fund his newspapers from no less a supporter than R.B. Bennett, the prime minister of Canada from 1930 to 1935. Bennett also hired Arcand as his chief Quebec electoral organizer in the federal election of 1935. He had friends in high places in England as well. Secret funds were sent from Lord Sydenham, a prominent Fascist sympathizer in the British Conservative Party, and he corresponded regularly with the chief of the Imperial Fascist League. He had a signed photo of Hitler on his office wall and was in close touch with German Nazis. In 1938 Arcand was chosen leader of the Parti de l'Unité nationale, which was comprised of elements of his own Parti National Social Chrétien which he had founded in 1934, the Prairies-based Canadian Nationalist Party and Ontario's Nationalist Party. He was anti-communist as well as being an anti-Semite. He believed in the supremacy of the white race and advocated shipping all Jews to Hudson Bay after stripping them of their civil rights. His dream was to fashion a strong fascist government in Canada within the Commonwealth and to rule Canada when the Germans had successfully defeated the Allies. Although he tried very hard to recreate Nuremberg in Canada with swastika flags, blue-shirted followers practicing their Nazi salute and goons with swastika armbands standing guard at every meeting, he was never a serious threat as his party membership only numbered 1,800 across Canada. Msgr. Gauthier, the archbishop of Montreal, condemned Arcand's group in 1938 and little space was given to him in the press. As a friend of Duplessis, however, he was allowed free rein in Quebec and was well protected by the police wherever he went outside of Quebec, unlike the treatment shown to suspected communists. A cagey politician, in meetings in Toronto, he played up his loyalty to the British Empire, and in Quebec he ranted against the evils of communism and appealed to anti-war sentiment. His strong federalism, however, made him unpopular with many nationalists. At the outbreak of war, he toned down his rhetoric to avoid becoming a fifth- columnist target. His dreams came crashing down in May 1940 when his party was banned and Arcand and ten of his followers were arrested for "plotting to overthrow the state". Interned for the duration of the war, he regaled other prisoners with stories of how he would govern Canada when

Hitler won the war. The internment experience did not change his ideas and he remained politically active and an unrepentant Nazi until his death in 1967. The French-language newspapers of the day such as Montreal's *Le Devoir* and Quebec City's *L'Action Catholique* defended the social teachings of the Church and were anti-Semitic, anti-conscription and racist in content. (By 1943 *Le Devoir* was reporting on German atrocities against the Jews but in a limited way). However, the Montreal newspapers *La Presse* and *Le Canada* (the Liberal Party paper) and Quebec City's *Le Soleil,* with much wider circulations, never indulged in racist rants. Starting in the mid-1930s, these papers attacked the Nazis, were pro-democracy and called for tolerance of the Jews. Jean-Charles Harvey, a left-wing lecturer, radio commentator and author incurred the wrath of the Church by denouncing its power and, as editor of his own weekly newspaper, *Le Jour,* from 1937 to 1946, opposed anti-Semitism and encouraged an all-out fight to defeat Germany.

Another maverick who disagreed with Abbé Groulx's vision of society was Télésphore Damien Bouchard, an anti-clerical Liberal who was active in municipal and provincial politics. A member of the Canadian Senate, his outspoken ways led to his downfall. In his maiden speech to the Senate he criticized the power of the Church in government affairs. Reviled on all sides, he lost his position as president of Hydro-Québec and because he was a political liability he was forced to resign from Premier Godbout's Cabinet. Being an independent thinker had its price.

Those fighting conscription for overseas service were a force to be reckoned with. Henri Bourassa, the esteemed and highly-educated founder of *Le Devoir,* was an important leader in the debate. He had been a successful politician in his youth, becoming mayor of the small town of Montebello in 1890 when he was only twenty-two years old. Active in both federal and provincial politics, he helped to create the Nationalist League (*Ligue nationaliste*) to promote his vision of Canadian autonomy and equality for English and French Canadians within the British Empire. As an independent Liberal for Labelle, he resigned his seat in the House of Commons in 1899 to protest against the sending of Canadian troops to the Boer War. His stance did not change and he was opposed to conscription in both world wars although he was not against Canadians volunteering to serve.

André Laurendeau, a Sorbonne-educated journalist, politician and broadcaster was born in Montreal in 1912. His thirty-year career in public life saw him evolve from a racist, anti-Semitic separatist who, with a few friends, founded a movement called Jeune Canada which preached the need for a homeland for French Canadians called "Laurentie," to a man who, later in life, worked for Canadian unity. As a Christian humanist, he was concerned with the plight of the common man and the need for Canada to respect Quebec's unique culture. From 1963 until his early death in 1968, he served as co-chair with Davidson Dunton on the Royal Commission on Bilingualism and Biculturalism which worked to bridge the gap between the two linguistic groups. Five years before his death he denounced the radical early period of his life as youthful folly. In 1942, however, as a member of the *Ligue pour la défense du Canada*, a group formed to protest conscription, he was in the forefront of those opposed to conscription along with Paul Gouin, Jean Drapeau, a young lawyer and future mayor of Montreal and Michel Chartrand, the firebrand nationalist and former monk born to an affluent Outremont family who devoted his life to easing the plight of the working man and trying the patience of the establishment.

In June 1940 Canada adopted a soft form of conscription in the National Resources Mobilization Act (NRMA). Between 1940 and 1946, all persons over sixteen years of age had to register to allow for the best use of human resources in the war effort. There was to be no conscription for overseas service but men were required to train for various periods of time for home defence only. With the entry of the United States into the war in 1941, many breathed a sigh of relief that a powerful and wealthy ally was now on side. Canada was alone among the Allies in having soldiers who were divided into "overseas service" and "home defence" categories. Under pressure from the

Conservatives, Mackenzie King's government planned a national plebiscite on April 27, 1942 to ask the Canadian population to release them from their promise never to draft men for overseas service. Several of King's Quebec Liberal MPs quit at this time and many joined the *Bloc populaire canadien* when it was formed to campaign against the government. Mackenzie King was loath to divide the country with this issue but it became necessary because recruitment had fallen off and many more men would soon be needed as reinforcements. To paint the situation in very broad strokes: English Canadians were in favour of all-out war because of their close ties to England. French Canadians were not in favour of fighting for the British Empire, while immigrant groups were mostly indifferent but compliant.

With the very unity of the country at stake, Mackenzie King was between a rock and a hard place trying to please English and French Canada. The ambiguous phrase "not necessarily conscription, but conscription if necessary" did not fool the *Ligue pour la défence du Canada*. They organized a demonstration for the No side on February 11. Most realized that although Quebec would probably vote no, the vast majority of Canadians would vote yes, thus nullifying Quebec's decision. Jean Drapeau, one of the leaders of the demonstration, was keen to join more seasoned protesters like Abbé Groulx and André Laurendeau. Leaflets were distributed weeks before the event, which was to take place in the St. James Market Hall on the corner of Amherst and Ontario streets in the east end. Henri Bourassa, the venerable war horse of French-Canadian rights was to be one of the speakers. At 7 p.m. the rally began with a full hall and a crowd of more than a thousand shivering and stamping their feet in the cold outside while listening to the speeches on loudspeakers. Many were young men who would be most affected by a yes vote. The first speaker was Drapeau and he vented his rage against the domination of his people by all manner of foreigner. Many speakers followed with the same impassioned rhetoric but the rally was not pro-German in any way. Many sang "O Canada" and a British flag was burned. When Bourassa finally got to speak, he gave a reasoned, calm and balanced talk in which he said violence was not the answer. He further stated that many Canadians were also against conscription and were "no less Canadian" than his audience. The applause for Bourassa was lukewarm but outside the crowd was heating up and then they ran amok. Streetcars had their windows smashed and a small group of young soldiers, with more bravado than common sense, taunted the rioters and were attacked. The usual refrains: "*A bas la conscription*" and, in a variation on a theme, "*A bas Steinberg*" could be heard. The police could not break up the crowd and eight, including two captains, suffered injuries trying. Rocks and pieces of ice flew through the air and small groups then roamed through neighbouring streets breaking store windows and trashing taverns. Even a "house of ill repute" on Ontario Street was invaded and suffered about $350 in damages. Eighteen hotheads were arrested and spent the night in cells. The result of the plebiscite was predictable. While English districts of Montreal voted yes, the east end voted solidly no. The outcome was that Quebec voted 72 per cent against conscription while, across Canada, 64 per cent were in favour. Armed with this support in English Canada, King, the shrewd politician, did nothing for the moment that would antagonize Quebec.

Not everyone was in favour of *La ligue* and its aims. Radio-Canada, the French-language arm of the CBC, denied them airtime as they were directed to by the federal government. Although many Catholic clergymen were supporters of Pétain, Cardinal Villeneuve thought the war was "a struggle for Christian civilization" and supported an all-out effort for Allied victory which included buying war bonds, praying and periodic fasting. He also issued a pastoral letter in favour of conscription which probably influenced some young men to enlist. Others, even certain devout Catholics, considered him a sell-out and irreverently referred to him as "Newtown, O.H.M.S." (On His Majesty's Service) or "Kid Villeneuve".

The men conscripted under the terms of the NRMA and known derisively as Zombies were fed, outfitted, trained and paid the regular soldiers' pay for staying in Canada and guarding its shores. Badly treated and often badly behaved, these bitter, restless home-defence troops were sent to British Columbia to await a Japanese invasion that never happened. In August 1943, they joined an American force sent to expel the Japanese from Kiska in the Aleutian Islands. They were prepared for a difficult battle as the Americans had suffered a high casualty rate in their attack on Attu Island in May. As it turned out, the Japanese had already abandoned the island but four Zombies were killed by booby traps. By all accounts these conscripts acquitted themselves well as they spent a few months on barren and foggy Kiska before returning to the mainland. One misconception that still remains in the national consciousness, is that the Zombies were all from Quebec. In fact Quebecers were only a third of the total; many were of German or Ukrainian background while others were the disgruntled sons of neglected First World War veterans, idealistic pacifists or bitter Depression boys. Canada had given them an option and they had taken it. Still, desertions were high and morale low as these young men waited out the war.

There were many who felt that French-Canadian men who did not want to serve overseas had valid reasons for this decision. Canada had been their home since the early French settlements were established in the early 1600s and they saw no reason to enmesh themselves in yet another European war. Many who might have served in the navy or air force were discouraged from doing so. The lack of French-Canadian regiments meant that recruits might be integrated into English units that were not prepared to welcome them. The pervasive racist attitude of many English-speaking officers and men, the lack of a Catholic chaplain and many conscripts' inability to speak English all figured in their decision. Even French-speaking enlisted men were often given a hard time and told to "speak White". For the thousands of recruits of all ethnic groups who had rushed to volunteer for overseas service and the dangers it entailed, these arguments did not wash. They were fighting to restore sanity to a beleaguered world and were prepared to lay down their lives in that cause. Many harboured bitter thoughts about the "cowards and malingerers" who did not understand the global scope of the terrible threat to liberty the free world was facing. The public, many of them bitter and angry parents of three or more sons and daughters in uniform, had little patience for Mackenzie King's fence sitting and wanted the enemy defeated as quickly as possible with all the resources of Canada put to use. The final chapter in the conscription crisis would only be written in 1944.

Anti-conscription protestors assembled at Champ-de-Mars on March 23, 1939, five months before war was declared.
Canada Wide Feature Service Ltd. Collection
Bibliothèque nationale du Québec

[CHAPTER THREE]

Let's Go Canada!
Allons-y-Canadiens!

CANADA HAD ONLY BEEN at war for fifteen days when the word came down from Ottawa that recruiting centres in Ottawa, Toronto and Montreal could not accept any more volunteers. There were many reasons for the surge in patriotism. The boys who used to stand in line at soup kitchens were lining up again. This time, they were no longer society's pariahs but its future heroes. They needed a job and Canada needed them. They would be clothed, housed, fed and trained and, what was more important, the generous sum of $1.30 a day (seven days a week) would be their pay. If three square meals a day and a new pair of boots were not enough, they were also promised medical and dental care—dentures or eyeglasses, if needed, included. Servicemen overseas had to remit half their pay (usually around $20) to dependents at home. The monthly Soldiers' Dependents' Allowance paid to the wife of an army private in 1942 was $35 with $12 each for the first two children, $10 for the third with $8 each for fourth, fifth and sixth children. A wife with two children received about $79 a month which did not quite cover expenses while soldiers overseas were also chronically short of money and reduced to bartering free cigarettes for goods.

Others, the sons of privilege, did not need the perks but their sense of duty meant that they also had to answer the call. Many men who had jobs were willing to give them up for the duration. Montreal's long military tradition, both French and English, meant that those whose fathers and grandfathers had served were willing to take their turn. Public and peer pressure was also a strong motivator and many signed up with their brothers and buddies.

In a country full of uniforms, those not wearing one had some explaining to do. Walking around town and impressing everyone with your snazzy new uniform that indicated your patriotism was also an intoxicating thought. What more did a young man need! Underage boys, keen to join the big show, would do anything to enlist, including lying about their age and threatening their parents that they would run away or do some other drastic deed like joining the merchant marines if they did not accept their decision. Adventure was also a prime motivator. The thought of travelling to foreign countries was exciting to many young boys, some of whom had never ventured more than a few miles from home. Yes, of course, one might get killed but the feeling of invincibility granted to youth meant that most thought these bad things only happened to others.

The words of Horace's ode which can be found on many church memorials: *Dulce et Decorum est Pro Patria mori* (It is sweet and fitting to die for one's country) had been disabused by the First World War anti-war poetry of Wilfred Owen and Siegfried Sassoon but, in spite of this, a new generation was ready to fight again to defeat tyranny. Those of British background had no problem rushing to the aid of England. Many had grandparents, aunts and uncles who still lived in Britain and whom they would sometimes visit when on leave. Many French Canadians had been devastated with the fall of France and were willing to help liberate their *mère patrie.* Jewish recruits had a more compelling reason as they knew exactly what Hitler was capable of. Members of all ethnic groups in Montreal rushed to enlist to serve Canada and prove their loyalty.

For some older married men with families it was an excuse to escape babies and bills while recapturing lost youth. For under-employed family men, it was a way to pay those bills and provide for their families. It was also an easy out from an unhappy relationship. While men in the black community were more than willing to serve, they would face discrimination as they had in World War I. Although fully qualified to do many jobs, they usually were shunted to service roles and ended up washing dishes or cooking.

In 1941, the community, led by Reverend Charles Este, formally protested against racism in the forces and, as the war progressed, things improved.

Having made the decision to enlist, young men from all backgrounds headed to recruitment centres that were set up throughout Montreal. They had to be British subjects (as Canadians were at the time), of good character and between the ages of eighteen and forty-five. They were not accepted for duty if they were needed on farms or were involved in other essential war or civil work. Single men were called up first. Examining doctors were guided by the pamphlet, *Physical Standards and Instructions for Recruits 1938* and placed recruits in different categories, from "A" (fit for general service) to "E" (unfit for service).

Depression boys did not all fulfill the conditions to be in the "perfectly fit" category. Any young man not accepted for medical reasons was given an "Application for Service" lapel badge that he could wear and thus avoid being called a Zombie or "yellow". As soon as recruitment began, standards of sight, hearing, height and weight were quickly lowered in order to meet requirements.

By December, 1939 aliens (not including enemy aliens) who were resident in Canada on September 1, 1939, were accepted. Another change came about in October, 1940 when Americans could enlist without swearing allegiance to the Crown. In December 1942, married men between nineteen and twenty-five had to register for compulsory service. By the spring of 1943, seventeen-year-old boys could sign up with their parents' permission and those previously rejected because of remediable health problems were encouraged to try again.

There was a complete menu of choices for those who were accepted. The air force and navy were the most popular and had a surfeit of volunteers but the army was also waiting to process them. Those who wanted to join a particular regiment had a wide choice: Montreal was home to the Black Watch (Royal Highland Regiment of Canada), the Fusiliers Mont-Royal, the Royal Montreal Regiment, the Canadian Grenadier Guards, the 17th Duke of York's

Royal Canadian Hussars and the Régiment de Maisonneuve, among others. The Sherbrooke Fusiliers had set up a recruitment centre in the Viger Hotel. Many Montrealers eventually served in regiments drawn from all across Canada from the British Columbia Dragoons to the Fort Garry Horse, and French-speaking men were found in English-speaking regiments and vice versa. Recruits could opt to serve in different branches or corps such as: artillery, engineers, signals, ordnance, provost, service, medical, dental, and others. The educational range of recruits was immense. There were university graduates, both French and English, to fill officer ranks but, since there was no compulsory, free education in Quebec until the Liberal Premier Adélard Godbout introduced it in 1943 (against much opposition from the Church), there were many applicants who had not spent a day in school and were functionally illiterate. Others had three or four years of schooling and a recruit with two years of high school was considered to have had a decent education.

By 1944, Britain was suffering a shortage of junior officers in its ranks so Canada sent 673 French-and English-speaking lieutenants and captains to England to serve with British regiments. This "Canloan" program was voluntary and these officers served with distinction and won awards for bravery but suffered a high casualty rate. First World War veterans were also called back to the colours to join units of the Veterans' Guard. Their main responsibility was to guard POW camps in Canada but they also performed other duties.

For young English-speaking boys, it was a foregone conclusion that they would support the war. Philip Aspler was one of them. In 1939 he was living with his widowed mother and twin brother, Gerald in downtown Montreal. "When the war started, I was only fifteen years old and, like every young boy, I wanted to see Hitler get his. It was only when you saw your friends starting to die that you knew it wasn't all peaches and cream." Both brothers enlisted but, due to a foot injury sustained in an assault course, Philip was assigned to Military District 4 Headquarters, which occupied six floors in the Sun Life Building on Dominion Square.

The RCAF had great appeal for many young men. Flying a plane with your goggles shining in the sun and a white silk scarf flying in the wind was the dream, but the sad reality was that the air force had one of the highest mortality rates of any of the services. That didn't deter Stuart Vallières who came from a bilingual background and explains how he enlisted: "Like everybody else my age, we felt it was the thing to do. My dad had been in the Royal Canadian Flying Corps in World War I so I thought the RCAF was the place for me. All my friends in N.D.G. had joined up and I wanted to be with them. We moved from N.D.G. to Nitro near Valleyfield because my father, my sister and I were working at the C.I.L. (Canadian Industries Limited) explosives factory and, since it was considered essential war service, I was a long time getting called up. It was only when I threatened to join the merchant marines that the personnel department said I could leave to join the air force and I ended up at 427 Lion Squadron when it was formed. I left for England in 1942."

Dave McCrindle's first choice was the air force: "When I turned eighteen in 1940 I went to the Air Force Recruiting Office on Bishop Street. I didn't have the educational qualifications so they sent me to McGill University to take a special test. I passed the test, went back and said, 'When do I start?' Then they told me that I wasn't heavy enough. I was 5'7" and weighed 120 pounds. They told me to come back when I weighed 130 pounds. Two weeks later, I went back weighing 133 pounds. The reason for my weight gain was that every day I drank two quarts of Jersey milk (which was like cream). Then I was told I was too young. I said, 'You mean to say that you put me through all this crap and now you're telling me I'm too young. You know what you can do with your air force!' So then I joined the Non Permanent Active Militia (NPAM). We were in the army but we still kept our day jobs and trained evenings and weekends and spent three weeks training at Farnham. I was waiting for the 3rd Medium Battery to mobilize which never happened. In January, 1941, I enlisted as a reinforcement for the 7th Field Battery and was switched to the 35th Light Anti Aircraft Battery in England."

Lorne Hamilton was born in Kenora, Ontario in 1910 and

came to Montreal in 1932. Working his way through McGill University, he graduated with an M.A. in Education. "In 1940 I was recommended by the School Board to take leave from my teaching job at Montreal High and become the educational organizer for the Canadian Legion Educational Services. I worked for them for two years until I joined the navy. The purpose of this organization was to upgrade the educational standards of those in the armed services. There were recruits who could not read—in Joliette there were about 150 men in a special camp learning to read and write and to speak English. After they reached a certain standard, they were moved out into the regular stream of recruits. I had an office with a library and a secretary in the School Board on McTavish. I remember visiting almost every English military camp in Quebec. (A French-speaking organization visited the French camps.) We organized classes by hiring part-time teachers to teach in the evenings. These teachers were always glad to get the extra work and, indeed, the extra pay.

"I joined the navy on October 26, 1942. I was thirty years old, married, and a university graduate. They were looking for people to do instruction duties and so on and they were willing to give me a commission right away. There was also the social pressure. As soon as the bands start playing and the uniforms appear you can be sure that people are influenced greatly by that. The third reason was that I could see that I would have to enlist if the conscription got down to my age level and then I wouldn't get a commission. It was also a rather clean job, unlike the army and air force. You travelled and were able to get home on occasion. In the army one might be away for years. I was sent to Halifax for about four months for training and then was at HMCS Donnacona on Drummond Street until 1946. I was a lieutenant and my job was part administrative and part teaching. I had to instruct the ratings mainly in such things as elementary school mathematics and English for those who needed it. Many had minimal educational standards which had to be raised. These recruits, both French and English, were at Donnacona temporarily for basic training and then were shipped out to other places for further training. The Wrens (Women's Royal Canadian Naval Service) lived in the Presbyterian College at McGill University and did many jobs at Donnacona like clerical work and operating the switchboards. If one wasn't married, there were a lot of opportunities!"

The Gray family of N.D.G. had four sons in uniform: Frank, RCAF, shot down and killed over Germany; Hubert "Dodd", RCAF, survived two tours of operations, Wilfred, RCAF and Ernest who served in the navy. Another brother was waiting in the wings as an air cadet while the youngest brother was too young to be involved. At the age of ninety (2010), Hubert Gray recalls: "Can you imagine a mother with four sons overseas! When I left, my mother's hair was black and when I came back five years later, it had turned completely white. I think mothers are the ones who should get the medals. My dad didn't say too much and kept it all to himself."

While some parents bade farewell to a treasured only child, other Montreal families made sacrifices similar to that of Dodd Gray's mother and father. The six Murphy brothers, John, Thomas, Joseph, Herbert, William and James all went on active service in the navy. The Goldwater family had three sons in uniform, Jack, David and Nathan. The Bennett's had five sons and one daughter serving their country. Four Lahaie brothers, Gaétan, Marcelin, Deguise and Rostrand all served with distinction in the army. The three Elkin brothers of Verdun, George (navy), Charles (army) and Frank (air force) and their sister, Olive (Women's Volunteer Reserve Corps), all donned uniforms. Incredibly, on D-Day, the three brothers, without knowing that it would be a family endeavour, took part in the invasion of Normandy. George, the oldest was in a corvette, Charles landed on Juno Beach and Frank was flying overhead in a Halifax bomber.

The resistance to the war in many French circles in Montreal and Quebec was well known. What was less well known is that there was a long tradition of military service in the province and many young men were already attached to militia units—many of these little more than social clubs—and regiments in 1939. The common thinking was that the Quebec-France connection had been broken centuries before but there still existed the blood bond and many carried names that could be traced back to Normandy. At a time when many English were calling themselves British, Quebecers were calling themselves *les Canadiens* and many were willing, like Gen. Jacques Dextraze (one of Canada's most decorated heroes) to join up and fight "for Canada".

The fact is that Canada's unpreparedness for war extended to the ability to absorb many French-speaking recruits. After the First World War, there was only one permanent French unit, the Royal 22nd Regiment. The Canadian Army in 1939 had so few French-speaking officers that they did not have the manpower necessary to train men in French. The navy had a hard enough time getting its force together and the idea of French-speaking ships was untenable. The best the navy could do was to give Quebecers a twelve-week course in English at a special base, HMCS Prévost in London, Ontario. The RCAF had a French-speaking bomber command squadron, the 425 "Alouette" Squadron that began operations in October 1942. Flying Wellington bombers, the crew of "425" had more than 100 airmen out of a total of 131 who were French Canadian. As they were attached to the RAF, some aircrew were British and the ground crew was mixed so the language of command had to be English. This accommodation given to the crew of 425, was much appreciated by the men leading to high morale. Although it was impossible to fight a completely bilingual war, in 1941 the government did make an attempt by translating hundreds of manuals and pamphlets into French and opening bilingual staff schools and officer training programs. French-speaking public-relations men were sent out to encourage recruitment and suitable candidates were invited to apply for officer school. Eventually, by 1944, 80 per cent of instructors in Quebec could speak French. Many bilingual recruits served in English regiments such as the Black Watch and a few were transferred from French to English regiments to act as translators in France. While some Quebec regiments served only in Canada, there were four French infantry battalions, one artillery regiment, one engineer battalion as well as other units serving overseas.

Arthur Fraser got caught up in the war by youthful bravado. "I lived on Sanguinet Street in the red-light district. It was tough and you had to be in a gang because all the other districts had gangs. We were six in our gang and one of our fellows, Roland Bilodeau, was in the peacetime army. When the war started he said that he was going to sign up and go active. So the five of us followed him to the Fusiliers Mont-Royal Armoury on Pine Avenue and enlisted. I asked the fellow who received us if we would all stay together in the war. Sure, he told us, no problem. I cheated about my age because you had to be eighteen and I was only seventeen. That's the reason. Our friend was joining active and we had nothing in our minds beyond that. We didn't know the army and we didn't know the future. I also didn't have a job because the man who owned the store where I worked told me that he would have to let me go because he said that the government would call me up sooner or later. My mother was really disappointed. She didn't say too much but I knew she was very sorry that I joined up. I think she knew that I would have to join sooner or later. I know she was sad."

Of the six friends who enlisted: one served as a messenger; three were killed at Dieppe on August 19, 1942 (including Sgt. Roland Bilodeau) and Arthur and another friend were taken prisoner in the same battle. The next three years were a nightmare menu of prison camp life; being shackled for fourteen months and, finally, the long forced march away from the advancing Russian Army in the last months of the war. Arthur Fraser returned to Canada in May 1945 weighing ninety pounds and looking at least two decades older than his twenty-three years.

René Héroux was one of five brothers in uniform. "We lived on Brébeuf Street right near Laurier Park. My mother, Marguerite Mallette, spoke English because her mother came from Ireland. My father, Lucien, didn't speak English but, anyway, they got along and had twelve children. There were eight of us living when the war started. My father worked for forty-eight years as a milkman for J.J. Joubert milk company. He worked seven days a week and

It's hard to believe that these photographs are the same person. On the left, the 17-year old Arthur Fraser, a fresh-faced recruit of the Fusiliers Mont-Royal. On the right, the ninety-pound 23-year-old veteran after incarceration as a POW.
Courtesy of Arthur Fraser.

never missed a day.

"We were a small family compared to others on Brébeuf Street. *Les Poiriers* had eighteen, *les Monettes* had twenty- two and *les Viaus* had eighteen or nineteen. Most of the guys didn't sign up and probably some were deserters. There was a lot of talk like, 'We don't want to go to war to defend the English.' I was young at the time but my answer was, 'I'm going there to defend the French. The French need us.' I was also a boxer and not afraid of anybody so I could talk like this.

"My oldest brother, Léo was married so they didn't take him. My youngest brother, Raymond, was seven years younger than me and too young to go. All of us, except Raymond, were working for J.J.Joubert and making good money when we were called up and had to go. André, Maurice, Roland and Edouard signed up. André was wounded on D-Day on Juno Beach when he disembarked with Le Régiment de la Chaudière. (We used to call them the "Buckets") He returned to Canada in October or November of 1944 and the newspaper *Le Canada* took a picture of his arrival. In the photo are my parents and all five brothers in uniform.

"Of the five of us, I went the furthest. I started as an instructor in St. Jerome when I was nineteen and could have stayed there for the rest of the war but I wanted to go overseas. I wanted revenge for my brother, André. I saw action in Holland and Germany with Les Fusiliers Mont-Royal and after the war I volunteered to go to Japan."

The men who served Canada in the Merchant Marine wore no uniforms, did not come under military discipline and while not forced to sail, the majority did. Without them, however, it is debatable whether the war could have been won. They protected the lifeline between Canada and Europe by making more than 25,000 voyages during the war, carrying desperately needed personnel and goods. Most of them served during the Battle of the Atlantic which was patrolled by "wolf packs" of German submarines. Merchant mariners also had to contend with the brutal weather conditions of the North Atlantic and could not expect rescue if torpedoed. Early in the war, the RCAF could only offer air support part of the way across the Atlantic. Flight decks added to merchant ships later on helped to solve this problem. The navy organized the merchant ships into convoys that had armed escorts but, in spite of these precautions, they suffered a very high casualty rate. They have been called the unsung heroes of the war and, for a long time, were not given the recognition due their sacrifice. Women also joined the merchant marines but not in large numbers and at least five died while serving as stewardesses, cooks and wireless operators. The female radio officers, after being trained in Canada, had to go to New York to sign on with the exiled Norwegian merchant navy which, unlike Commonwealth ships, allowed women to serve.

The roles of both men and women had great bearing on the success of the war effort. The Corps of (Civilian) Canadian Firefighters accepted over four hundred volunteers, of whom only half were professionally trained. Sent to England, they helped British firefighters put out blazes caused by bombing. Both male and female pilots were needed to fly Canadian-built aircraft to England. They were assigned to one of three groups that managed to successfully get 10,000 planes overseas: RAF Transport Command, RAF Ferry Command or the Atlantic Ferrying Organization.

Many organizations recognized the need to bring comfort to service personnel serving away from home. Nearly 600 volunteers from the Knights of Columbus, the Salvation Army, the YMCA and the Canadian Legion War Services Incorporated served overseas. Their duties included everything from showing movies to operating canteens. The Red Cross and the St. John Ambulance Brigade assisted nurses and ambulance drivers. Many of the female Red Cross volunteers came from privileged backgrounds and adapted to difficult battlefield conditions. The Newfoundland Overseas Forestry Unit sent 3,500 men to help harvest trees in northern Scotland or serve alongside the British Home Guard.

There were personal, political and religious reasons for not enlisting. Young men who were Mennonites, Doukhobors or the smaller number of conscientious objectors (who had to prove their beliefs) were sent to work camps instead of military camps. They had to serve for three or four months and were paid 50 cents a day. This category did not affect many men in Quebec. For those who didn't want to enlist, both English and French, marriage was a quick option at the beginning of the war. Two hundred and ten Jocistes, (Jeunesse ouvrières catholique) who were members of the Catholic Workers' movement, married in a mass ceremony in the Delormier Baseball Stadium before a crowd of more than 20,000 on July 23, 1939. These couples had prepared for and were committed to embarking on a marriage with Christian values but, with war a distinct probability, they also pre-empted enlistment requirements by which single men would be called up first. For purposes of military service registration, single men were those who were single on July 15, 1940. On the weekend just before the deadline, there were 800 marriages in Quebec. It was said that one woman in Quebec received four marriage proposals in one day and jewellers quickly ran out of wedding rings. Quebec was not alone in the rush to the altar. Vancouver reported that in one three-hour period one hundred marriage licences were issued. Those living in Ontario and Saskatchewan were out of luck because there was a waiting period which meant that the deadline could not be met.

There were young men who just didn't have a taste for war and were determined to avoid it. Some preferred to profit from the booming economy while staying safe. University students could hide themselves in the halls of academe on a deferment. Military deserters, absentees and draft delinquents in hiding were chased down by either the RCMP or the Military Police who would even ring the doorbells of neighbours to try to get information. Reluctance to serve meant that two Montreal regiments, the Régiment de Maisonneuve and the Fusiliers Mont-Royal as well as other Quebec regiments suffered from the lack of reinforcements. By September 1944, the Régiment de Maisonneuve was short 276 men and the Fusiliers were 333 under strength. The desperate situation was helped once conscription began later that year but many thought it was "too little, too late".

The reaction to the reluctance of French Canadians to enlist was predictable in English circles but always tempered with respect for the ones who did.

Phyllis Eperson: "We felt resentment towards the attitude of many French Canadians at the time. and sometimes thought of them as cowards. In a way, we could understand that there had been a big break between France and Quebec. There were French regiments, of course, and one of our French-Canadian friends, Guy, joined the air force and got shot down within six months."

"Frank" (not his real name): "There was always antagonism against French Canadians. Many didn't enlist but those who did were very good soldiers. A few of my friends (in uniform) were beaten up when they went to a night club in the east end. The Provosts had to go in the bush to get resisters and I know for a fact that they were threatened if they went into certain small towns. They threatened to blow up the hotel where the Provosts stayed. One of my Provost friends shot and killed a man but in the court martial he said that the man fell over a twig. He was after this guy who kept running and he shot him."

Mike Caron's father, Rolland, left the Montreal Police Force at the beginning of the war and joined the Army Provost Corps. "My father called himself a French Canadian and was perfectly bilingual. I don't have much detail about the time he served but I do remember him saying that he would have much preferred serving overseas than having to chase healthy and strong lumberjacks into the woods."

Madeleine Cloutier Méthot was very involved in the war effort and had family members on active service. "There were always people who were against the war but they didn't bother us. In our parish, St-Louis-de-France, everyone seemed to be united about the war. I was young and didn't go out at night so I never saw any anti-conscription riots. Our next-door neighbour signed up and, for many men who had no work, it was a good opportunity for them to earn money and prepare for the future."

Canada was slow to follow the lead of Britain, which had recruited women starting in 1938. Canadian women wishing to serve their country were forced to start their own auxiliary volunteer corps, which they did all over the country. The Women's Volunteer Reserve Corps (WVRC) was one of them. Active in Quebec, Ontario and the Maritimes, it was organized along military lines and stayed operational until the end of the war although some members of the group joined the Canadian forces when that option became available.

Nearly two years after the start of war, it finally became obvious to the government that due to the shortage of manpower they would have to accommodate women in the armed forces. Just in case wanton "camp followers" got the idea that they would be accepted, the warning was issued: "Only Respectable Women Need Apply".

Women at the time usually lived at home until they got married. Now, they were expected to serve alongside single and married men which did not sit well with many soldiers and their wives. False rumours of the sort of women recruited and their behaviour did not help the situation. This was highly insulting to the many educated, talented, adventurous and refined women who were not happy with the traditional supportive roles they were expected to fill on the home front and wanted to serve in a more active way. Their desire to serve also challenged prevailing ideas of authority and division of labour. Charlotte Whitton, who before becoming mayor of Ottawa was the president of the Canadian Welfare Council, did her best to counteract these rumours, which were more prevalent about women serving in the army and air force. Her intervention helped because, from waitresses to debutantes they enlisted and, like the men, they had different reasons and motivations. Many came from military families. Some had brothers and boyfriends overseas and felt they could better help the war effort by going active. Others felt that their talents were needed and they could contribute in a more meaningful way by being in uniform. They were willing to put up with Spartan conditions in training while learning skills from office work to welding. The air force was the first to open its doors to women in July, 1941 with the slogan "They serve that men may fly". The young women initially recruited were carefully chosen from good families with social connections. By 1945, more than 17,000 women had served in the RCAF Women's Division (WDs). Their senior officer was Kathleen Walker from Montreal, the widow of an RCAF group captain.

The army very shortly followed suit and, by the end of the war, more than 22,000 women had served in the Canadian Women's Army Corps (CWACs). Margaret Eaton, of the famous Toronto family, rose to become director-general of the CWACs so the "respectability" standard had been more than met by the army! For those wishing to apply—even those without foxhunting ability—they had to be "in excellent health, at least 5 feet tall and 105 (or within 10 pounds above or below the standard of weight laid down in medical tables for different heights), with no dependents, a minimum of grade eight education, aged eighteen to forty-five and a British subject". About 3,000 CWACs served overseas and four were injured in a V-2 missile attack in Antwerp while those serving in Britain faced the same dangers as the English public.

The Women's Royal Canadian Naval Service (WRCNS or Wrens) accepted nearly 7,000 women. The navy, the "senior service" (and the snobbiest), was the last one to accept women (July 1942) and their standards were very high. Many potential recruits got the impression that the navy was looking to recruit only beautiful, intelligent debutants with shiny hair and manicured fingers. The Canadian director of the Wrens was Adelaide Sinclair, an economics professor at the University of Toronto.

One group that did not have to do any trailblazing were nurses (known as nursing sisters) as they had already been part of the military tradition since serving in the North West Rebellion in 1885. In World War 1 nearly 3.000 Canadian nurses had served and forty-seven had been killed. In World War II more than 4,000 Canadian nursing sisters served in the three branches of the service with most of them serving in the army. For those serving near the front lines, not only were they in physical danger but they were the first to see and tend the horrific injuries war produces. They were often unprepared for the heartrending condition of the young men they treated and were touched by their deep gratitude. The only two Canadian servicewomen taken prisoner were nursing sisters Kay Christie and May Waters who went with "C" Force to Hong Kong in 1941 and were POWs until 1943 when they were repatriated in a prisoner exchange. More than 1,000 nurses served in Canada at the sixty military hospitals that were then in operation.

Once in the service, women contributed in countless ways, thus releasing men for overseas service. From the dishwasher and cook to the wireless operators, parachute riggers and mechanics, they all contributed in ways that made these trailblazers proud. Their courage and competence also broke down prejudices and won the respect of their male officers who would later say they didn't know what they would have done without them. They were paid two-thirds of a man's salary, which was later raised to four-fifths. This was justified by some because women in the forces were doing mostly "women's work" and not fighting. More than 50,000 eventually served in the three branches of the armed forces. Their contribution and competence was acknowledged by all and left a lasting legacy for future generations of women. They transformed the armed services as they transformed Canada.

Norma Duckworth Dillon grew up on Delormier near Beaubien. Having a father who was the secretary-treasurer of *The Standard* meant that the family was steeped in war news and Norma couldn't wait to sign up. Her choice of service was decided when she met an attractive young man at a local tennis court who was planning to enlist in the navy. Having told herself that John Dillon was the man she was going to marry, she announced to all her friends that she was also going to join the navy when she turned eighteen.

"On my eighteenth birthday, March 31, 1943, I was at work at Canadian Westinghouse in the Dominion Square Building. I phoned my father and told him that I was going down at lunchtime to join the navy. Dad, who had been in the First World War, said, 'Wait and I'll come with you'. He came with me to HMCS Montreal on Mountain Street and waited downstairs while I went up to join. Then he took me out for lunch at Murray's. I was the oldest of eight but my brothers were too young to join so my father and my grandparents were pleased. At first my mother was upset and then she came around. As the oldest child, I was her right hand. I babysat and helped her by working in the house.

"I was sent to HMCS York in Toronto. We were given our first uniform but, after that, we had to pay if we needed to replace anything. Since I was a stenographer, I became a captain's writer and took dictation from the captain. I also took all the notes if someone did something wrong on a ship and there was a trial. When I read the navy rules and regulations I was annoyed when I discovered that male writers and female writers didn't get the same pay. A male would get paid for so many words a minute but I just got my

Norma Duckworth Dillon, March 1944.
"I wouldn't have missed this experience for the world."
Courtesy Norma Duckworth Dillon.

$40 a month pay so sometimes, when they buzzed for me. I just wouldn't go. *I wouldn't go!*

"I felt very proud wearing the uniform and I think that people were impressed, especially if you were standing on guard at a cenotaph or for other things. I wouldn't have missed this experience for the world. I felt like I really did something. I had a good time but I *knew* I was doing something important."

Irena Chavchavadze Lomasney took a more circuitous route to don a Wren's uniform. Born into a noble Georgian family, her father, Prince Boris Chavchavadze was killed during the Russian Revolution just months before she was born. The family then settled in Bavaria after her mother's remarriage to Duke Dimitri von Leuchtenberg de Beauharnais. In September 1939, with another political upheaval looming, Irena, her sister, mother and stepfather were packed and ready to leave Germany in twenty-four hours with the help of the Americans. The family owned a ski chalet in St. Saveur so Montreal was a logical destination. After finding a job as a receptionist at the Royal Victoria Hospital, Irena, who was nineteen years old, joined the Red Cross and was anxious to go to England with that organization. It was not to be. One day, while enjoying a drink with her sister at the Berkeley Hotel on Sherbrooke Street, they were talked into joining the Wrens by the brother of a doctor they knew who realized the potential importance to the war effort of the sisters' language skills: "We grew up speaking four languages and I don't remember learning any of them. We spoke English and French with our governess, Russian with our parents and we lived in Germany. My sister and I were told by friends that the military needed our language skills so we joined the Wrens in 1942. We were sent to Ottawa right away and began working in naval intelligence. My sister censored letters from German POWs. I had to see that information went to the right department and I also checked hard-cover books to see if any escape plans were hidden in them. Once I found an escape plan but my superiors said to let it go as they wanted to capture the prisoners to see how they effected their escape and how they copied ID cards for themselves. I stayed in the Wrens until 1946 when I married an American and moved to the States."

Most military recruits were able to march off to war with their comrades and, if lucky, return with them to live peaceful lives. If they were captured, they could expect that the rules of the Geneva Convention would apply. There were exceptions, of course. In the case of the Canadians captured in Hong Kong and some who were prisoners of the SS, good treatment was a forlorn hope. For most, however, after being told in accented English, "For you the war is over", they could expect to be shipped off to a POW camp to wait out the end of the war. Spies had no such illusions. The men and women who served in clandestine operations had no protection beyond their own resources and the camaraderie and trustworthiness of their fellow spies and contacts. If captured, they knew they would be subjected to extreme torture, and such treatment could go on for long months before they suffered a horrific death in a jail or concentration camp. They lived life in the shadows and had to have the instincts of a feral cat. Every rendezvous they kept and every contact they met could be a setup to capture them since infiltration of cells and treachery by double agents, collaborators and greedy informants was not unusual. They either volunteered or were recruited for MI9, the British agency concerned with training men to return downed Allied flyers and escaping POWs to Britain, or the larger Special Operations Executive (SOE) which had both male and female agents. The SOE agents were told by Churchill to "Set Europe—and later Asia—ablaze", and this they did by countless acts of sabotage behind enemy lines. These agents were multi-talented and in possession of an uncommon courage not granted to many. They had to be, in most cases, fluent speakers of the local language and blend in physically. Since operations were carried out from Europe to the Far East, Canada drew candidates from at least seven ethnic groups but mainly from the French, Chinese, and European communities.

Since the largest base of operations was in France, the language skills of French Canadians, many from Montreal, were much in demand and they rose to the challenge brilliantly. They performed incredible feats which were made possible by their personal bravery, well-honed skills and their ability to speak the language of their French ancestors. Twenty-eight of the agents sent to France came from the Canadian Army but Canada had no female agents.

Before being dropped behind enemy lines, SOE agents underwent rigorous training in England and in many other countries, depending on their field of operations. They were observed to see if they were psychologically and physically up to the task. Besides speaking the language of the country, they had to know its ever-changing wartime regulations and learn the particular gestures and habits of their adopted persona. They were also taught military skills, which included parachute jumping, silent killing and Morse code. Training in evading capture by constant observance of their environment was paramount. When dropped behind enemy lines they operated as saboteurs, radio operators, organizers and instructors. They carried ingenious devices such as silk maps, collar-stud compasses, silent guns, knives, radio equipment and other tools of the trade.

The first Canadian SOE volunteer, and perhaps the best known, was thirty-six-year-old Captain Gustave (Guy) Bieler of the Régiment de Maisonneuve. In September 1940 he kissed his wife Marguerite and two little children, Jean-Louis (John) and Jacqueline good-bye. He left his home at 5439 Earnscliffe Avenue in N.D.G. and headed off to England to become an intelligence officer for his regiment. Born in Paris to a Swiss pastor and his wife, he came to Canada in 1924 at the age of twenty and became a citizen in 1934. Settling in Montreal, he first worked as a teacher in Pointe-aux-Trembles and then as head of the translation department for the Sun Life Assurance Company. The pipe-smoking intellectual, who loved to play the piano, was described by his friends as thoughtful and fun-loving. In England, his language skills, familiarity with France and qualities of character made him a good candidate to join SOE and, with family members still living in France, he had a very personal reason to do so. (His brother, René Maurice was in the Resistance.) His instructors at the SOE training school in Surrey were in awe of the talents and devotion to duty of their oldest student. His reputation was such that he was held up as a model to other aspiring secret agents. His commanding officer described him as "the best student we've had. He is conscientious, keen, intelligent, a sound judge of character, good natured, absolutely reliable, outstandingly thorough, a born organizer."

He was parachuted into France in November 1942 but, unfortunately, suffered a severe and permanent spine injury in the landing. His contacts in the French Resistance wanted him to return to England for treatment but he insisted on staying and carrying on his mission. After a period of recuperation, *le commandant Guy*, as he was known, built up a successful network of twenty-five teams of saboteurs in the area of St. Quentin. They wreaked mighty havoc on the transportation systems and storage facilities but Bieler was always careful to avoid civilian casualties. The Germans were determined to find their nemesis and started a massive manhunt which ended with his arrest by the Gestapo on January 11, 1944.

For the next three months, he was moved from prison to prison and brutally beaten and tortured without divulging any information.

On April 9, 1944, he was sent to the Flossenbürg concentration camp in Bavaria where the torture and solitary confinement continued for another five months. His tormentors were never even to learn his real name. He was executed on September 5, 1944. Impressed by his courage, his SS captors took time off from their grisly work detail to give him a guard of honour when he went, physically broken and emaciated, to his death by firing squad. The heroic Major Bieler is commemorated today on street names and memorials in France, Holland, Germany and Canada. He was the posthumous recipient of eleven medals including the DSO and France's *Croix de Guerre.* There is a Bieler Lake on Baffin Island. In Montreal, a veterans' residence at 1450 Plessis is named "La Maison Bieler". His name can be seen on the war memorial in the entrance to Westmount's Victoria Hall.

His son, John, remembers saying good-bye to his father with a child's innocence. "I was four and a half years old when I waved good-bye to my father at Windsor Station. As the troops were being told to get aboard the train (and between the last-minute hugs, kisses and tears), I shouted out, 'GOOD-BYE, DADDY, HAVE A GOOD TIME!' My Aunt Jane told me this story and says that I broke the tension in the subdued station."

Guy D'Artois was born in Richmond, Quebec and joined the First Special Service Force, the elite Canadian-American unit, before volunteering for SOE. Working with the Free French in the lead-up to D-Day, he commanded 3000 members of the *Maquis* and built what was considered the best communication system in the underground. After D-Day, he was sent to the centre of France where he did everything possible to prevent German reinforcements from reaching Normandy. He met his English wife, nineteen-year-old Sonia (Toni) Butt, described as the most beautiful of all the SOE agents, while doing parachute training in England. Sonia, an adventurous spirit, had been educated in France and spoke the language perfectly. They fell in love and married, which prevented them from working together in France because their mission might be jeopardized if, after capture, one had to watch the other being tortured. Sonia was then assigned as a courier to Christopher Hudson whose "Headmaster" network did heavy damage to the German war machine by training agents to cut telephone lines and blow up crucial installations. She was once detained by two Germans but managed to talk her way out of the situation. After the war, Major Guy D'Artois, DSO, GM, Croix de Guerre and Toni D'Artois, MBE, MiD, settled in a suburb of Montreal and raised a family of six children.

Three other Canadian SOE agents, Frank Pickersgill (brother of politician Jack Pickersgill), John Macalister and Romeo Sabourin (a twenty-one-year-old from the north end of Montreal who left his job as an apprentice mechanic to join the FMR at the age of seventeen), were not so lucky. After being captured, they were savagely beaten and executed in Buchenwald with other SOE agents by being hung on meat hooks and strangled with piano wire. Although wounded, emaciated and physically broken, Pickersgill, with incredible courage, tried to keep up morale to the end by various means. As he walked to his death, he sang songs to encourage the others. A courageous French priest, Father Georges Stenger was able, with the help of one of the guards, to give communion to the Catholics. As they were dying, he reported that their last words were, "*Vive la France!*" "*Vive l'Angleterre*" and "*Vive le Canada!*" An MI9 agent who was imprisoned in Buchenwald at the same time was Georges Rodrigues, a signalman from Montreal. He survived a year of horror in the camp only to die shortly after liberation from illness and maltreatment.

What is not generally known is that Michel Chartrand, the union militant and fiery anti-conscriptionist, had a brother, Gabriel, who was another hero of the Normandy mission. An insurance salesman from Montreal, he joined the Royal Montreal Regiment in 1939 and was sent to England in December of the same year. Dropped behind the lines in 1943, he completed many sabotage operations while cleverly avoiding capture by the Gestapo and returned to Montreal after the war.

Paul-Émile Thibault, a sergeant with the Fusiliers Mont-Royal and a former Golden Gloves boxer, teamed up with another Montrealer, Jacques Taschereau. Of Taschereau, it was said: "He could raise his hands when confronted by an armed man and with a quick twist of his wrist, whip a knife from the back of his shirt collar and strike a target dead centre at a distance of 15 feet." When SOE operations wound down in Europe, these two amazingly adventurous souls then headed to Burma after receiving training in jungle warfare. Accompanying them were eight other veterans of the French mission including Joseph Benoit, an employee of the Montreal Tramway Company, and Jean-Paul Archambault, a Montreal post office inspector who died accidentally in Burma. In the Far East, these men would certainly not blend in but would use their military skills to work alongside guerrilla groups to sabotage Japanese operations.

MI9, the escape and evasion service was organized to evacuate to safety from enemy-occupied countries, downed airment and escaped POWs. It was said that the best people to help plan escape routes were those who had themselves escaped and there were a few such Canadians in France. Everyone knows about the disastrous raid on Dieppe in August 1942. What is less known is that four French-Canadian POWs, Lucien Dumais of St. Jean d'Iberville, Robert Vanier, Conrad LaFleur and Guy Joli, all of Montreal, escaped from the Germans. Vanier, Lafleur and Joli escaped together. Wounded in the raid, they were sent to a German Military hospital and then were placed on a transport headed for Germany. The prospect of being POWs in Germany or Poland did not appeal to the intrepid three so they jumped from the moving train and made their way, with the help of partisans, back to Britain. Dumais, the tough FMR sergeant major, was taken prisoner after tending to his men on the beach. He also jumped from a train but made his way to Britain alone. The four then offered their services to MI9 so they could help future escapees. All but Joli completed the training and the others were sent back to France. Vanier and LaFleur were split up and did valiant work keeping the escape line open. Both narrowly avoided capture by the Gestapo and returned to England. Lucien Dumais teamed up with Raymond Labrosse of Ottawa, who had gone overseas with the Royal Canadian Corps of Signals. Together, they were a formidable team and took part in one of the most successful escape networks of the war in spite of the constant danger of discovery by German radio-detection equipment. They were almost caught one time when they were making their way by bicycle to the Brittany coast and were approached by a German soldier. Since Labrosse was carrying radio equipment in his suitcase, Dumais told him to pedal around the German. This he did without much difficulty leaving Dumais to deal with the situation. When Labrosse turned around he watched Dumais in heated discussion with the German. Pedaling on, he stopped at some point and spent the night on the side of the road. The next morning, with his friend nowhere in sight and expecting the worst, he pedaled on to his destination where he met Dumais waiting for him at a café with two cognacs. He told Labrosse that all the German wanted was his bicycle which he had to relinquish. In a brilliant display of sang-froid he then headed to the nearest German military station and demanded that, because one of their men had stolen his bicycle, they owed him a drive to his destination at Saint-Brieuc—and they obliged! Dumais and Labrosse both returned home to Canada.

Those lucky enough to survive their missions came home weighted down with medals but the secrecy surrounding them continued as few records were kept after the war. Told to forget everything they had learned and get on with their lives, they did. Theirs is a relatively unknown story but the fact that many Allied men and women secret agents underwent torture and death in infamous Nazi concentration camps is a testament to their unwavering courage.

It was not only parents, grandparents, wives, aunts, uncles and cousins who saw recruits off at the railway station. Children, most too young to have formed a concept of war, also got caught up when their fathers went to war. The fathers themselves were to miss many formative years in their children's growth and the children would have to cope with a father they now knew only through letters and postcards. Jacques Boucher tells his story: "We came from the Grand-Mère/Shawinigan area where French-Canadian nationalism was very strong. My father, whose name was Gaston, came to Montreal when he was nineteen. In Montreal people were more open to what was going on. My father was in the navy and one of his brothers was in the army but didn't go overseas. Two of my uncles took off into the woods and worked as lumberjacks for a paper company in La Tuque. These companies needed workers and anytime the army would send men to flush out these guys, some of the company bosses would let them go the day before and they would take off further into the bush until the army was gone and that was it.

"I don't know why my father joined the navy. Usually, for a young man it is an adventure but when he joined in 1939 or '40 he

Alma and Gaston Boucher at the Park Avenue Station.
Courtesy of Jacques Boucher.

was a thirty-year-old man with four kids. I sometimes think that he and his friends were all in the tavern and they double-dared each other to join. He was a stationary engineer and they needed men like this to run the boilers on the ships. I never asked him why he went. It's only when you get older that you want to know. How in hell did you take off with four kids? I don't know what the conversation was with my mother (laughs) but I know he came home one day and said he was in the navy. I was six in September 1939. Claude, Ghislaine and Robert were younger than me. My father was on convoy duty; first the HMCS *Westmount,* the second one was HMCS *St. Francis* and the last one was the *Huron.* He was torpedoed twice and, after the war, he was operated on at the Queen Mary Veterans' Hospital and spent eight months there in a body cast. My father was always proud to have served his country. He always told me that liberty comes with a price."

Beverly Overall Marsh's father enlisted, like many, to escape Depression conditions: "My dad was unemployed and worked for the City of Verdun on projects. I think they paid your rent and gave you a couple of bags of coal as payment. He used to work in the office of a correspondence school until they moved to Halifax. Imagine a man working in an office all those years and then to end up with a pick and shovel picking up after the horses! He came home one afternoon in an army uniform and my mother had a terrible shock. We were all sitting around the table and my father was talking about all the money we were going to get. A man with children was paid more and my brother Sonny and I thought that *we* were going to get this money and be rich! He went over to England in 1940 or '41 with the Service Corps and spent all his time there."

Allen Calderwood saw both his father and brother off to war. "I was ten when the war started. My father and brother joined the Black Watch at the same time. They were both standing in line and John was ahead of my father. My father told John to get the hell home and John told him that if he left the line, they would never see him again. My father knew he meant it because, every summer, John would jump in a boxcar and go out West to try to get a job so

Recruitment advertisement for the Royal Montreal Regiment, June 5, 1941.
Westmount Examiner.

my mother and father wouldn't have to feed him. My father and brother went overseas with the Black Watch. My father was there for quite a while but when they found out he had three kids at home they sent him back to Montreal and then he worked at the Sun Life Building."

So they enlisted, were trained and finally had to leave: the "long and the short and the tall"; the orphans; the adored only sons; the "extra mouth to feed" boys; a few given early release from prison; the embittered; the keen; those with nothing to lose and those with everything to lose; the uneducated; the university graduates; the talented; family-trust boys; poor boys; the brave; the unsure; those leaving with brothers; the young; the not-so-young and the women wanting to serve overseas. The day came when good-byes had to be said at Windsor or Bonaventure Station and perhaps the reality set in. The women who left for overseas were not in the same danger as the men but they still had to cross the Atlantic and, once in Europe, had to face the same risks as the locals. The young men leaving for active duty might have been protected by youthful confidence and a belief in the goodness of destiny at the beginning but some understood quite well that they might never come back. Their parents had memories of another conflict not too long before and tried to hide heavy hearts. Watching a train full of fresh-faced boys waving and smiling with their buddies from the open windows could only have been a source of great anxiety and trepidation for those left behind. As the train slowly moved out, perhaps relatives heard bits of songs like "Roll Out the Barrel" or "You Are My Sunshine". The realization would certainly hit those on the platform that not all the singing voices would return. Family members would then go home with sad hearts to get used to the empty seat (or seats) at the table and hope and pray that a dreaded telegram would never arrive.

Dave McCrindle remembers the day he left. "My parents came to see me off on the train to Halifax. There were lots of tears. My mother was crying. My father wasn't but he didn't look happy. My sister was married by then but she wasn't happy about me leaving either. My father's most important piece of advice to me was to keep my head down."

Stuart Vallières had a happier send-off. "I boarded the train in St. Lambert and it was pretty much a happy occasion for the family because we all figured the war would end soon. My brother was with us and told us that he had just been accepted into the air force and that he was considered a good candidate to become a fighter pilot."

René Héroux went to war with absolutely no fanfare. "When I joined the army I hadn't been further away from home than maybe to Sorel. It was a big thing. You're nineteen, you've never been anywhere and you've got to go to Europe. I did my advance training at Farnham. I used to go home but didn't tell my mother (who was very worried about me) that I had signed active service On my six-day embarkation leave, I didn't tell her that I was going overseas. When I left the house at 6:30 in the morning to get the bus to Farnham, my mother asked me, 'René, are you going to be here next weekend?' I said, 'Oh yeah, I'll get another pass.' When I got to Halifax, I called my brother André and he told my mother. André told me that I fixed him good with that one! The reason I didn't want to tell anyone was because when my brother Roland was transferred to Kingston, you should have seen all the people at Bonaventure Station, cousins, everybody, all waving him off and crying and he was only going 180 miles from the house! I told myself that when I went nobody was going to be at the station."

The dreaded telegrams did arrive and young telegram boys were kept busy pedaling around the city delivering the horrible news. Howard Dearlove remembers those days. "We would be out playing on the street and, all of a sudden, the bikes would show up. You never took it as a joy. Even as a kid, you realized that something was wrong and that a person was missing in action or killed in action. There was a death in my own family. I remember my cousin, Kenneth, leaving. He was about 6 feet tall and was wearing bell bottoms. He was like a son to my father who took him to the station. He was lost when the *Spikenard* was torpedoed south of Iceland. He had three sisters and one brother. There's only one sister left now and we still talk about him on Remembrance Day. My father talked about him until the day he died."

Philip Aspler's brother was killed while serving with the North Shore (New Brunswick Regiment) at the age of nineteen. "I was home on furlough. It was August 17, 1944. We were living in an apartment on St. Catherine Street and Atwater. A small boy—he couldn't have been more than fifteen or sixteen—came up on a C.P. Telegraph bicycle. I rang him in and he said, 'Don't worry. He's only been slightly wounded.' That was to alleviate the shock. Of course, when I opened the telegram I found out that Gerald had been killed at Caen. So I walked the streets for three hours figuring out how I was going to tell my mother who was at work. I happened to run into one of my uncles and told him. He spread it around the family and they brought my mother home from work. I just couldn't tell her. When I got back home she was there. My mother took it pretty hard, I'll tell you that. Gerald was my twin brother. Time heals but it took me a couple of years to get over it."

Madeleine Cloutier Méthot lost her uncle. "My uncle, André Vennat was killed at Dieppe. My aunt, Annette, had rented a small house for the summer in Repentigny and invited my mother, my sisters and me to visit. While we were there a big black limousine arrived and someone asked to speak to Mme Vennat in private. It was awful when they told her the news. She was pregnant and returned to Montreal right away. She rented a house near us and we kept close to her and her small son, Pierre. After a while, she bought property in Outremont and went her own way."

The Bélanger family was a large one. The parents, Orcilia and Philippe had nine children: one boy, Alexandre, and eight girls, Jeannette, Lucienne, Jeannine, Gilberte, Fernande, Rolande and the twins, Andrée and Henriette. Gilberte recounts: "I was eleven years old when the war began. We were living on Boyer Street near Beaubien. My father was a sergeant major with the Fusiliers Mont-Royal and a World War I veteran. My brother, Alexandre, also belonged to this regiment. My father had a job working for a company that sold wood and coal. Things were tough. The Depression was bad for every one and I think that's the reason my father enlisted. My mother was really upset with his decision. My brother signed up first and then my father. My father went first to Iceland, then on to England and he fought in the raid on Dieppe in 1942. He was shot in the back but wasn't taken prisoner because the Maquis rescued him and helped him get back to England. When he came back to Montreal, he spent some time at the Queen Mary Veterans' Hospital. He stayed in the army as an instructor but was never the same. He had trouble with his nerves and we had to have patience with him. I remember the day he came back from the war. My mother always said that *Bonhomme Sept Heures* (the bogeyman) carried a black bag. My father arrived carrying a black bag and one of my sisters who had not seen my father in a long time and didn't recognize him, grabbed another sister and they went straight to bed screaming, "*That's Bonhomme Sept Heures!*" (Author's note: *Bonhomme Sept Heures* is said to visit houses around 7 p.m. to check that all children were in bed.)

"My brother transferred to the Van Doos and was sent to Italy. He was killed at Casa Berardi in the Battle of Ortona on December 16, 1943. My mother had a premonition about my brother's death. She was cooking over a wood stove and suddenly, felt a kiss on her neck. That was how my brother used to greet her when he arrived home. She dropped the heavy lid on the floor and said, 'Dear God! Something's happened to my boy!' She knew something was wrong but carried on as best she could. Four days before Christmas, the telegram arrived telling us he was dead. My mother fainted and we had to call the doctor. I ran to a neighbour's house and told her I needed some cognac because my mother was dying. I was young and shaking so much that the neighbour made her daughter come home with me. My mother had a complete breakdown and stayed in bed for about a month talking to the Blessed Virgin. We all stayed close to her and never left her alone. After a while she was able to function but my brother was always in her thoughts. We called our father who was with the army in Joliette and told him to come home. My father was a good Catholic and felt especially close to Brother André. (It was almost as if Brother André was his own brother!) My father blasphemed and kept saying, 'Why did you let this happen?'

"My brother Alexandre was the only boy in the family and a person who loved to dance and sing. He was a good boxer as well and so good-looking that he had more girlfriends than he could handle. He was twenty-four when he died. He taught the older girls in our family how to dance but the twins, Andrée and Henriette were just babies when he died and don't remember him at all. In our family, we always talked about Alexandre and, every time a new grandson was born, my mother always said that he looked like Alexandre. I have so much sympathy for all the families who suffer losses during any war. In our case, we are a very close family and maybe our brother's death is what helped us to stick together."

Alexandre Bélanger was killed in Italy in 1943.
"My brother had more girlfriends than he could handle."
Courtesy of Gilberte Bélanger.

Carol Lodge, who had four cousins in uniform who all came back unharmed, nonetheless was deeply affected by losing friends and neighbours. "Donald Stuart, a very good-looking boy of twenty, who had been my first teenage crush, was killed overseas in June 1942. This was my first sad reality of war. The Stephenson family who lived at my end of Rushbrooke Street suffered the double loss of their two boys on HMCS *St. Croix* when it was torpedoed on September 20, 1943. I remember that I hardly knew what to say to their younger sister, who was about my age, when I first saw her after the tragedy."

The houses in Griffintown were close to the street which made grieving not the private affair it would be in some other areas of the city. Don Pidgeon: "I remember one family that lived on Murray Street. One of their boys was overseas and I recall that the telegram came. First it was a 'Missing in Action' and then, of course, 'Killed in Action'. I remember being on the street and hearing the crying on the part of the mother and sisters. The windows were open and it was just devastating to hear this wailing. I must have been about five at the time. We were a close-knit community and when one person suffered, we all suffered."

Denise Bernard and her family strive to keep alive the memory of her uncle, Robert Boulanger, FMR, a native of Grand-Mère, Quebec, who was one of over 900 soldiers killed during the raid on Dieppe in August 1942.

"Robert was a young man who couldn't accept injustice and that is why, on September 7, 1940, and without his parents' knowledge, he decided to volunteer for active service in the Canadian Army. He wanted to join those who hoped to bring liberty to France, the beloved country of his ancestors. He was barely sixteen years old but already had the maturity to make this decision. One of ten children, he was always ready to help others. His parents and all the members of his family had a difficult time accepting his decision and were very disturbed as they knew very well what lay ahead of him. In the end, they respected his choice but not without a lot of sadness.

"After undergoing a short training course at Valcartier, he left for

Halifax on June 20, 1941 on his way to the Isle of Wight in England. At the station, just as he was getting on the train, an instructor asked him, 'Are you sure, Robert, that you still want to go?' Looking at his parents with tears in his eyes, he nodded yes. It was a heartbreaking good-bye that they all hoped would be temporary.

"Many letters were exchanged back and forth until the news of the landing at Dieppe on August 19, 1942 filled them all with dread. The morning of August 23, the first telegram was delivered and the family read: REGRETTONS SINCERÈMENT VOUS INFORMER QUE LE SOLDAT ROBERT BOULANGER D114682 OFFICIALMENT PORTÉ DISPARU AU COURS DE L'ATTAQUE. PLUS AMPLES DÉTAILS SUIVRONT SUR RÉCEPTION. These were days of indescribable waiting but hope was always present.

"It was on December 12, 1942 that the second telegram arrived which read: REGRETTONS PROFONDÉMENT VOUS INFORMER QUE LE SOLDAT, ROBERT BOULANGER D114682 ANTÉRIEUREMENT PORTÉ DISPARU AU COMBAT, MAINTENANT OFFICIALLEMENT PORTÉ PAR BERLIN, TUÉ AU COURS DE L'ENGAGEMENT DIX-NEUF AOÛT 1942. PLUS AMPLES DÉTAILS SUIVRONT SUR RÉCEPTION.

"After a wait of more than three months, this was the impersonal and cold announcement which confirmed their worst fears. Their son, who had celebrated his eighteenth birthday six days before the raid, would never be coming home. This was a heartbreaking time and, with the Christmas holidays coming, all the family, his friends and the neighbours in his village were plunged into deep mourning which they never really got over.

"That is why, in honour of Robert, my Aunt Lise and I, as well as his best friend, the veteran Jacques Nadeau FMR, make a special effort to keep his memory alive so that his sacrifice will not have been in vain." [Translated from the French]

Robert Boulanger left a lasting legacy of the determination and bravery of so many of his generation. This letter, written while on his way to the doomed raid on Dieppe with the Fusiliers Mont-

Royal, displays the emotional maturity of a young man which belied his eighteen years. More than seventy years later, it still has incredible emotional power. It was rescued by a friend who put it into a waterproof bag before being taken prisoner. Along with other objects the letter was somehow preserved and returned to the Allies. It was sent to the family by the minister of defence.

Robert Boulanger's Letter

Chers Papa et Maman,

A few minutes ago we were assembled to learn that, finally, we are going to embark to fight the enemy within the next twenty-four hours. Even if I shouted "Hurray!" like the others in the platoon, I don't feel very brave, but, be assured that I will never be a cause of dishonour to the name of the family.

We have been trained with extreme diligence for this day. I have a lot of confidence that we will be victorious in our first engagement so that you will be proud that I was one of the participants.

Since we arrived in England, we have talked with other comrades from all parts of the Empire as well as the English, who are fighting on all fronts. Now, we, the Canadians, it's our turn to join the battle.

In the place where we are now, our colonel, Dollard Ménard, has just confirmed the news and, in secret, told us the place where we will attack the enemy. I am sorry but I can't reveal either the name or the location. We know exactly the situation we are in and it's with confidence that we will attack.

Our chaplain, Padre Sabourin, got together all of us who wanted to receive general absolution and Holy Communion. Nearly everyone went. I want to be at peace with God, in case something happens to me. My good friend, Jacques Nadeau, went too. After receiving detailed instructions from the officers and NCOs, we were invited to participate in a sumptuous meal. We were served by the Women's Auxiliary of the Royal Marines. The tables were covered with white tablecloths and each of us had a complete set of cutlery. It's been a long time since we were treated like this by the military.

I am continuing my letter on board the landing craft which will bring us to our target. We are lucky that the sea is calm and the weather is good. They told us that the engagement with the enemy will take place at 5:30. In the meantime, I'm taking advantage of the time to check my gun and my equipment for the third time, while listening to my comrades discussing different things. Some are telling jokes but you can feel the tension. What's more, I feel it myself. Lieutenant Masson has given us his last instructions before we cast off. Sergeant Lapointe is asking a lot of questions because it is the first time he is in charge of a platoon. Jacques is adjusting his bike and something seems to be bothering him because he's muttering, as usual.

There is enough light for me to continue writing. We've been on the ship for two hours so I must hurry before it gets dark. I want to take advantage of this time to beg your forgiveness for any pain and sorrow that I might have given you, especially because of my enlistment. Roger told me how much grief I caused you and, if I come back alive from this venture at the end of the war, I'll do everything I can to dry your tears, *maman,* and everything in my power to make you forget the anguish I caused you. I hope you received my letter of last week. I know that I celebrated my eighteenth birthday on the 13th and that I didn't have to enlist for active service. But when you hear how bravely I have fought you will forgive me for the worry that I caused you.

Dawn is now appearing on the horizon. During the night I recited all the prayers you taught me and with much more fervour than usual. A few minutes ago, I believe that the action started. On my left, the sound of the guns and the flashes in the sky tell us that it has. Our debarkation group is moving slowly Lieutenant Masson told us that the first attack wave is nearing its objective. It's much brighter now and I can see what I'm writing better and I hope you will be able to read it. Someone told us that we are very close to the French coast. I believe it because we can hear the gunfire and the explosions, even the whistling of the shells which pass over our heads. I finally realize that we are no longer doing an exercise. A landing craft right beside ours has been hit and disintegrated with all aboard. We didn't have time to see too much because in the space of one or two minutes, there was nothing left. Oh my God! Protect us from the same thing. So many comrades and friends that were here two minutes ago are gone forever. It's horrible. Others in our group and other groups have been hit and the same thing has happened to them.

If I am one of the victims, Jacques will let you know what happened because we made a promise that we would do that for each other in case one of us doesn't return.

I love you and tell my brothers and sisters that I love them with all my heart.

Robert
[Translated from the French]

Robert Boulanger.
Courtesy of Denise Bernard.

[CHAPTER FOUR]

A Day in the Life of the Montreal *Gazette*

FRIDAY, FEBRUARY 20, 1942. During the war years Montrealers received their news from the radio, a wide choice of magazines and newspapers, in addition to the latest war newsreel at the movies—a much-appreciated feature in those pre-television days. For the English, the paper with the largest circulation was the mainstream *Montreal Star* which cost three cents. Its sister newspaper was the *Standard,* a feature-oriented weekly. Business people preferred the *Gazette,* a morning paper that sold for five cents. the *Montreal Herald* was a tabloid that served up news, sports and gossip for the working man. There were also many community papers serving different areas of Montreal such as the *Westmount Examiner*, the *Verdun Guardian*, the *Monitor* (serving the West End of the city), and the *Point News* (Point St. Charles). These papers would provide local news and included ads from the Department of National War Service advising people where to bring salvage items such as scrap metal, paper and bones to aid the war effort.

Besides *Le Devoir* and *La Presse*, other popular French newspapers were *Le Petit Journal*, *Photo Journal*, *La Patrie*, *Le Journal de Montreal* and *Montréal-Matin* (known as *L'Illustration* from 1930 to 1936 and *L'Illustration Nouvelle* from 1936 to 1941). It was the first newspaper in tabloid format and it supported the Conservative Party and later the Union Nationale.

In February 1942 Canada and its Allies were nowhere near winning the war. The attack on the American fleet at Pearl Harbor in December 1941 made Canadians worry about the security of their own West coast. The disastrous defeat of the defenders of Hong Kong by the Japanese on Christmas Day 1941, which included soldiers of

Quebec's Royal Rifles of Canada and the Winnipeg Grenadiers, was a demoralizing loss and a preview of the fall of Malaya, a strategically important part of the British Far Eastern Empire. This area supplied nearly half the world's rubber and much of its tin ore. Austria, Czechoslovakia, Poland, Denmark, Norway, Holland, Belgium, Luxembourg, France, the British Channel Islands, Yugoslavia and Greece had been overrun by Hitler's armies. Some of these countries had been defeated in a matter of days. Hungary, Rumania and Bulgaria had fallen under German influence. The German invasion of the Soviet Union (Operation Barbarossa) in June 1941 would be a long, drawn out battle and cost both countries dearly. Italy's entry into the war in June 1940 threatened Britain's interests in the Mediterranean and Middle East, while, in the Far East, the Japanese seemed invincible.

The German attempt to invade Britain was known as Operation Sea Lion. The cliffs of Dover were only twenty-two miles from occupied northern France and the formidable strength of German forces. Hitler's decision to gain command of the air space over England before attempting the difficult crossing of the Channel was met with a stunning defeat. The Allied success of the Battle of Britain in the summer and fall of 1940 was the only ray of light in a bleak scenario of great Allied losses.

Life, however, goes on. The *Gazette* of Friday, February 20, 1942 conveys a good idea of how the people at home combined their working and social lives with waging war on the "Home Front". The three-pronged headline read:

> CRIPPS IN REVAMPED CHURCHILL CABINET. Sir Stafford Cripps entered the British War Cabinet as Lord Privy Seal and Leader of the House of Commons.
>
> U-BOAT ATTACKS SHIPS IN TRINIDAD PORT. A report from Port of Spain said that two vessels were hit by explosions presumably caused by a German submarine. There were no casualties. The fact that American coastal cities were not blacked-out until two months later made it easy for the U-boats to attack targets in the Caribbean.

PORT DARWIN UNDERGOES THIRD BOMBING. The Japanese struck the northern coast of Australia in two attacks causing fifteen deaths and twenty-four injuries.

In other war news, there were communiqués from all theatres of war. The Netherlands Indies Armed Forces, helped by American, Australian and British forces, reported on the ongoing battle with the Japanese in South-East Asia at Surabaya, East and West Java and the continuing action against the enemy at Palembang. The British Burma Army Headquarters said that their troops were battling it out with the Japanese at Bilan. The United States War Department, in its report from the Philippines, stated that the enemy was "increasing pressure on our lines in Batan". The U.S. Navy sank a 5,000 ton cargo ship in the East China Sea. Britain's Bomber Command "laid mines in enemy waters" with the loss of one aircraft. The Royal Navy recorded the loss of the destroyer HMS *Gurkha.* The news from Egypt was that the general situation in Cyrenaica had not changed. The Soviet communiqué read: "During the night of February 18-19, our forces continued active military operations against the German Fascist invaders". On the Axis side, the Italian Command said that bad weather had limited air activity but that a Wellington enemy fighter had been "destroyed in aerial combat in the Central Mediterranean by German fighters". German High Command put a bright spin on the Eastern Front situation: "….. a number of enemy attacks were repulsed", " … the Soviet Air Force lost forty-four aircraft while only one of our planes failed to return". In the waters around Britain and Norway the action was fierce with the German *Luftwaffe* and *Kriegsmarine* claiming to having wreaked havoc on allied shipping. All of the above accounts were enhanced by figures and numbers of damage done and sustained.

In the United States, President Roosevelt had to remind isolationist groups that Germany as well as Japan had to be defeated. Many Americans feared Russia more than Germany and had no interest in propping up England's interests. As far as some isolationists were concerned, the "yellow menace" was more to be feared than a Nazified Europe allied with a Fascist America. In news on a lighter note, a Bronx matrimonial bureau had its problems. While they formerly charged husband-seeking girls a $10 registration fee and $50 when a mate was found for them, the shortage of available men meant that they had to boost their rates to $15 down and $100 upon delivery. Meanwhile, the British were bolstering their air and naval forces in the fight for control of the Mediterranean. We also learned that the Japanese oil reserves were inadequate to meet its needs: "Japan Must Obtain Quickly by Force What She Cannot Import". "With importation impossible and domestic supplies inadequate, much depends on her ability to gain possession of, and make use of, the rich deposit of the East Indies." Information on this score, readers were told, was "obviously a closely kept military secret".

In news closer to home, in Ottawa the ongoing conscription issue rose to the fore with the Conservatives urging immediate mobilization for total war while two Quebec members opposed the imposition of compulsory military service and demanded exemption for certain groups such as farmers, fishermen and war workers. Canadians were warned that the rubber shortage would mean the taking out of service of every non-essential automobile or truck for the duration of the war. In Quebec, plans were made to build an extension to the top of the Gouin Dam on the St. Maurice River in order to supply more hydro power for war industries in the province while, in British Columbia, the Union of Okanagan Municipalities passed a resolution urging the Dominion Government to take immediate steps to stop "infiltration of Japanese into the Okanagan Valley".

With much of the Canadian Army busy training in Britain, the navy and air force were in the forefront of battle. The navy was busy patrolling dangerous waters and transporting goods to England while the young men of the air force were flying mission after mission hoping they wouldn't "buy the farm" on one of them. Families back in Canada were kept up-to-date on losses, injuries and heroic feats. This was brought home on February 20 with the sad announcement that the corvette HMCS *Spikenard* had been torpedoed while on duty "somewhere off the Atlantic Coast". Six young Canadians were reported dead and four missing in an RCAF mission overseas.

On a happy note, there was a picture of a very handsome pilot with the headline, SCARES OFF DORNIER, THOUGH GUNS EMPTY. London: "Pilot Officer George Evans of Montreal, flying with a Spitfire squadron of the Royal Air Force drove off a Dornier-217 which attacked a British convoy off the East Coast yesterday. He is the son of Mrs. R.C. Bulmer of 9 Redpath Place. Evans managed this despite the fact that his guns were unloaded. He made repeated mock dashes at the Dornier until it disappeared in the clouds. A modest youngster of twenty-one, Evans insisted he had done nothing out of the ordinary. 'All I did was dive at him a couple of times and then I didn't see him again,' the pilot said." Happily, it was noted, "the convoy got through unscathed."

As for our army troops, patiently marching and practicing battle drills in Blighty, they enjoyed a six-inch January snowfall in a news item from "somewhere in England". "This is the weather," said the headquarters sentry, muffled up to the ears. "It kind of makes a guy homesick, though." Training went on as vehicles were equipped with chains and ploughed through the snow. Many soldiers somehow found skis and practiced their slaloms. There was also a snowball fight between officers and men "with the former forced to make a strategic withdrawal. Some were chased up trees." The story ended with: "For military reasons, censorship would not permit mention of the snowstorm at the time."

Another bit of news from "somewhere in England" was a letter sent by Capt. B.W. Stevens of the Royal Montreal Regiment to the National Salvage Committee of Montreal thanking Chairman C.T. Russell for the receipt of 15,000 cigarettes which were greatly appreciated by the men. Salvage headquarters reported that the same amount of cigarettes had been despatched to each of the four Montreal regiments stationed in England with the funds coming from local salvage collections.

EATON'S *STORE HOURS: 9 a.m. to 5.30 p.m., Including Saturday.*

"Gee, It's Just Like My Gun at Home!"

Yes, son! But this isn't a toy. It's a 25-pounder that really works, and it costs $25,000. Our soldiers need thousands of them PLUS anti-aircraft guns, PLUS anti-tank guns, PLUS machine guns and rifles and mortars. That means a lot of money.

We must ALL help to pay for them! We CAN and we WILL buy more and more.

VICTORY BONDS!

THE T. EATON Co LIMITED
OF MONTREAL

A Victory Bond advertisement which appeared in the *Gazette*, February 20, 1942.

* * *

For Britons, daily blackouts were a fact of life. Canadians did not face the same immediate danger (although houses were routinely blacked out along the St. Lawrence coast as a precaution against U-boats) but Civil Defence authorities wanted the population to be prepared if the need arose in the uncertain future. German bombers might conceivably be able to reach and bomb Montreal which, with its huge war industry capacity, was a prime target. Strict instructions on how to prepare for an upcoming blackout were stressed by the *Gazette,* and included pointers provided by the Civilian Protection Committe, such as "if you are at home in a house, room or apartment extinguish all exterior lights and all interior lights visible from the outside," and advised "covering all windows and other openings visible from the exterior with some heavy type, dark material through which the rays of light cannot penetrate." The article continued: "If unavoidably outdoors, remain on the sidewalk—do not cross the street or highway; do not smoke or expose lights of any kind; if driving immediately pull over to the right-hand curb of street or highway and turn off lights and motor."

Eaton's (under a picture of Montreal with three black planes flying low over the city) got involved in the educational process and invited everyone, at no charge, to view their "Air Raid Precaution Exhibit" on the sixth floor. With a member of the Women's Volunteer Reserve Corps and one from St. John Ambulance in attendance, visitors would learn "what to do and how to do it, in the event of an air raid or blackout".

An important source of revenue for the war was the money raised in the recurring War Bond Drives. To encourage civilians to invest in their own futures and to fill the war coffers, there were exhortations from all sides to rally to the cause. The government spent more than $30 million in newspaper and radio ads, movie trailers, posters and mailings. About half of the cost of the war was paid for by the sale of War Savings Certificates and Victory Bonds. One could buy Savings Certificates that were sold door-to-door by volunteers as well as at authorized dealers such as banks and post offices. War Savings Stamps cost 25 cents each and their sale was aimed at children who could redeem sixteen stamps for a Certificate. Millions of Canadians were involved in this campaign and it raised a total of $318 million. This amount was only a small part of what was required and the Victory Bond drive filled the gap. There were ten wartime and one post-war Bond Drives. Unlike the Savings Certificates limit of $600, there was no limit to the amount of bonds one could buy. Issued in denominations of $50 to $100,000 and with interest rates ranging from 1.5 per cent (short-term bonds) and 3 per cent (long-term bonds), this drive raised $12.5 billion with businesses accounting for half this amount. These bonds met their goals within hours of being issued. This encouragement to save for future purchases thus freed the manufacturing sector to concentrate on supplying war goods. This enforced saving, as well as price and salary controls and rationing, helped to keep inflation down and the economy healthy.

There was competition among Quebec cities to be the first to reach their objective and the *Gazette* reported that Three Rivers was the leader with 27.5 per cent or $473,000 secured. Large corporations such as the Canadian Celanese Corporation, small businesses, unions, labour groups and individuals all donated generously and had the amounts included in the day's news. The Red Birds Ski Club donated $1,000 and the Lakeshore Lodge, Freemasons subscribed $500. Victory Loan speakers fanned out across the city to spur the population on. One speaker, Edgar Genest was to speak at the Club St. Denis Supper while the Hon. E.L. Patenaude, Cecil T. Medlar and G.J. Jotcham spoke at other venues. The Hon. Louis St. Laurent, the new Canadian minister of justice, was to address a Victory Loan Dinner at the Fusiliers Mont-Royal Armoury.

One could even help the campaign while enjoying an evening out. The Forum advertised a "Victory Loan Sports Parade" to be held the following Tuesday at 8 p.m. The Maroons were to play the Canadiens in a revival hockey match. There were also races, a figure skating revue and a grand finale by air cadets. Tickets ranged from 50 cents for the circle to $1.50 for the boxes. For those who couldn't afford an outing, they could listen to Gracie Fields who arrived in Canada to take part in the Victory Loan drive. She was the star of the CBC Variety Show broadcast from Toronto and heard on CFCF and CBM at 10 p.m. Taking in a movie could also help the cause. The following theatres; Loew's, the Palace, the Capital, the Princess, the Imperial and Newsreel did their bit by stating in their ad that: "The entire receipts in our theatres for this week will be used to purchase Second Victory Loan Bonds."

There was also an invitation to visit Place Viger Station, where the public could visit Canada's fifteen-car long Army Train that had a special Victory Loan preview of an armaments display. "Leaders of church and state, mayors of municipalities and consuls of the United Nations" were invited to the preview on Tuesday night. Business, labour and community leaders were also invited before the public was allowed in on Wednesday and Thursday.

Quebec City welcomed 140 United States army officers and men from Boston who came to help with the city's bond drive. They paraded through the city, were received by Premier Godbout, met Mayor Lucien Borne and took part in two victory beacon fires, one at lower town Jacques Cartier Square and another on the Plains of Abraham. Montreal also had its "Beacon of Fire of Freedom" event. A huge, blazing bonfire on Fletcher's Field was lit by Mayor Adhémar Raynault. Fires all across Canada symbolized a determination that the Victory Loan campaign must succeed.

For women who joined the army, or were thinking about doing so, an article from Ottawa assured them that the Canadian Women's Army Corps was proud of its uniform. This statement was prompted by the criticism from some makers of women's coats and suits (who might have been motivated by sour grapes) who thought the uniform was a sartorial disaster with complaints ranging from "too much shoulder padding" to a "sloppy waistline". Not so, came the rebuttal from Master General of the Ordnance Victor Sifton who stated that, "We haven't heard one word of complaint from a member of the Corps. As a matter of fact, ask officers and ranks of the CWAC and they'll tell you they are Canada's smartest women's service."

While ill-fitting uniforms were a constant joke for many enlisted men, officers in all three services received a clothing allowance and could shop for their own uniforms. Henry Morgan & Co. Limited advertised itself as "Apparel Specialists to Men in the Services", and, we were assured, "conforms rigidly to regulations". There were tunics, slacks, greatcoats, socks, ties, gloves and other necessities. The cost for a greatcoat was $55; tunic and slacks cost $49.50. Both could be had for $100. British quality was omnipresent, from "English barathea" to English melton cloth" A swagger stick in rawhide (sheepskin covered) was available for $1.00 but for those who wanted to "swagger" with a little more authority, a made-in-England-pigskin-covered one would set the army officer back $2.50.

For the man or woman confined to wearing mufti, there were many ads whose hyperbolic descriptions were sure to tempt buyers. Men could step out in elegant splendour by shopping at Simpson's where, again, British quality was stressed. A suit with two trousers cost $37.50. For women, Eaton's had the latest Otto Lucas of London fashion, a hat of ink-blue balibuntal, edged with winking scarlet bugle beads with a matching necklace. The price was $20 and up (depending on material) for a handmade copy and was guaranteed to be "a conversational coup". Women who made their own clothes could, for 20 cents, receive a pattern from the newspaper for a dress and jacket ensemble which was "guaranteed to bring down an avalanche of compliments" to the wearer.

Staying in the city was hardly a sacrifice. Montreal's downtown social life was nothing if not frenetic. The Esquire advertised two shows nightly with a dinner show at 8:45 featuring Nan Blakstone, "The First Lady of Nightlife" with "sophisticated songs and stories".

There was dancing nightly to the music of Buddy Clayton and his orchestra at the 400 Cocktail Lounge on Drummond Street. "No cover charge. No minimum." The Tic Toc at 1258 Stanley Street promised merriment and mischief with: "Shaw & Lee, high moguls of mirth in the zaniest, craziest nutfest of the century. Extra: Stage Attraction, 'How to undress with finesse.' It's a shriek tease with shapely Rolle Rolland." There were two shows nightly and dinner cost $1.50. For those who just wanted to have lunch, the Samovar on Peel Street offered a full-course European lunch which would set one back 50 cents. They had competition from the Hotel de La Salle Grill on Drummond Street which offered a plate lunch for the same price.

Hollywood was in its heyday and the movies of the time were either escapist fantasies or war-based dramas of pluck and heroism. There were usually one or two features, a newsreel and a cartoon. Small movie theatres were often within walking distance of one's home. The large theatres on St. Catherine Street: Loew's, the Palace, the Princess and the Capitol, were gilded entertainment palaces with sweeping staircases, thick rugs and luxurious velvet curtains. The choices that week in February 1942 were *Babes on Broadway* at Loew's. The classic, *How Green was My Valley* was playing at the Palace. The Capitol had *Bahama Passage.* The Princess had two big features: *Call out the Marines* and *Playmates.* Bing Crosby fans could take in *Birth of the Blues* as well as two other features at the Westmount. The small Kent Theatre at Sherbrooke and Hingston in N.D.G. announced that it was "scientifically air-conditioned" but one wonders if that was a drawing card in February. Of more importance was that one of its two feature movies, *Weekend in Havana,* was in Technicolor. The Art Deco Snowdon theatre on Decarie Boulevard, the Monkland, the Imperial and the Orpheum completed the list.

One could get lost in a blizzard of sports news and results, both professional and amateur. There were hockey teams (amateur and school), ladies' and men's curling, skiing, rifle shooting and boxing.

Racing results from Hialeah, New Orleans and Havana and baseball reports from St. Petersburg, Florida completed the list. Many of the participants in sporting events were members of the armed forces. Milt Schmidt, Woody Dumart and Bobby Bauer were known as the "Krauts" and played with the RCAF Flyers hockey team. In hockey-crazy Montreal, there was cause for worry if not despair. The Canadiens were not doing well in their 1942 bid for the Stanley Cup. In fact, they ended up in the cellar, just ahead of the Brooklyn Americans who did not qualify. As it turned out, the team that took home the Cup that April was the Toronto Maple Leafs. The Leafs lost their first three games against the Detroit Red Wings but made an amazing comeback and won the next four games.

In boxing news, Montreal's best welterweight fighter, Maxie Berger, was set to meet Sugar Ray Robinson (a 5 to 1 favourite) in a twelve-round match in Madison Square Garden in the evening of February 20th. Twelve thousand fans were expected to attend and organizers said that, of the $30,000 pulled in, they would donate10 per cent to the National Foundation for Infantile Paralysis, a reminder that polio was still a much feared disease. Montreal was ready. Radio station CHLP promised its listeners "a blow-by-blow description direct from the ringside" at 10 p.m. sponsored by Gillette Safety Razor Co. Berger had his work cut out for him. Robinson had pulverized twenty of his last twenty-five opponents and, in sixteen months of professional boxing, had earned $50,000 but Berger's fans were hoping that his conditioning and longer reach might just do it. It was not to be. After suffering his second knockdown in the second round, Berger rose at the count of four, but was so groggy and weak that the referee refused to allow the fight to continue, giving Robinson victory on a TKO.

In many areas of the city, tenants wishing to move found a new place by word of mouth or seeing a sign on a door. A large number of people simply stayed put in their rentals for years on end and, as the joke went, they paid for the flat or house many times over. For *Gazette* readers (many of whom were well-off) wishing to buy or rent, there were not many choices but all of them seemed very genteel. For the single person, there were ads for room and board in Westmount and downtown. The Gleneagles on Cote des Neiges Road had a choice of six-and-eight-room apartments with garage. Those wishing to buy could visit a seven-room stone and stucco home in the Town of Mount Royal which was available for $13,500. For just a little more, a solid stone residence on Queen Mary Road, (eight rooms, two baths and two open fireplaces was being sacrificed for $14,500). If one had a smaller budget, an eight-room cottage on Addington Avenue in N.D.G. could be had for $6,000 and, in the same area, a duplex on Marcil was $13,500 with an annual revenue of $1,560. There were three small houses in Westmount for sale—small meaning only eight or nine rooms—and all cost under $10,000.

There were other homes higher up the hill in Westmount with real estate descriptions that were nothing less than rapturous. Seventeen rooms with over 34,000 feet of land set in a grove of fine old shade trees and boasting multiple bathrooms, bedrooms, fireplaces and all the rooms necessary in which to live, entertain and house a staff of servants, could be yours for $35,000. Today the West Island is studded with post-war housing but it was once the refuge of well-to-do Montrealers who wanted to escape the city heat and swim in Lake St. Louis. The houses for sale sounded nearly as grand as ones in Westmount with tennis courts, gardens, servants' quarters, and, in one case "building to house several cars." For about $25,000, one could enjoy fine country living close to the city.

The *Gazette* carried the expected crossword puzzle and cartoons such as The Neighbors, L'il Abner and Blondie. Today, one can easily recognize the home of Blondie and Dagwood because their furniture and hairstyles have not changed. What is interesting is that beside the title in the comic strip is the Morse Code symbol for V, (…_) for Victory. Ironically, the V symbol has the same rhythm as the opening bars of Beethoven's Fifth Symphony and was used as the call-sign by the BBC in its foreign language programs beamed to Occupied Europe. This victory symbol was also to be found on the front page of many newspapers and some homeowners marked it on their front doorway.

Just as today, the *Gazette* of 1942 was recycled. A note told readers: PLEASE do not destroy this paper. It is needed in Canada's War Effort. Bundle your old newspapers and give them to your Salvage committee.

[CHAPTER FIVE]

The Home Front

"Use it Up, Wear it Out, Make it Do, and Do Without"

THE LONG YEARS OF THE DEPRESSION meant that Montrealers had to become accustomed to getting by on very little. The war demanded a different sort of sacrifice. With factories, mills, production plants and foundries working at full tilt, the population, while prosperous at last, had to get used to rules and regulations that guided every part of life. They would also be exhorted at every turn to "do their bit". The war would be waged, not only in Europe, the Middle and Far East, but on the home front by everyone from the youngest child to the elderly. Canadians would also become well-documented citizens. The War Measures Act gave the government massive powers to limit certain freedoms in what was considered the best interests of the country. These powers included the right to prevent strikes, outlaw organizations it deemed subversive, incarcerate or deport "undesirables" and confiscate property. The provinces ceded many of their traditional powers to Ottawa which centralized state power and monetary resources. Society became militarized and saw many of its freedoms curtailed. Under the authority of the War Measures Act and the National Resources Mobilization Act (NRMA), between 1940 and 1946 every person sixteen and older, with few exceptions, had to register and carry an identification card at all times with serious penalties for offenders. Upon registration, they were required to fill out a questionnaire providing personal information as well as occupational skills and experience. This information was used by the Department of Labour ostensibly to best mobilize Canada's human resources for the defence and security of the country.

Ruth Swinton, a 1938 McGill graduate, was the newly-married wife of Andrew Stevenson, a navy serviceman posted to Ottawa. A keen volunteer, she did a lot of knitting, secretarial work and helping with blackout duties, but perhaps the most unusual assignment she had was when she agreed to help in this registration: "We were asked to volunteer for everything and, since I liked volunteer work, I signed up to register people at McKenna's Florist on Côte des Neiges. Everyone was supposed to register at that time. There were four or five of us waiting around for people to come in and fill in the questionnaire describing any abilities they had which might help the war effort. We got some very funny answers like the woman who brought down the house when she stated that one of her skills was her ability to do the Dance of the Seven Veils. I don't know what she thought *that* could do for the war effort. My mother told them that she could milk a cow—which not too many people in N.D.G. could—and she was never actually asked to milk one. Not many came, I can assure you. We sat for long hours doing nothing. We were so bored that we were reduced to writing limericks about each other as a way to pass the time."

Travel to the United States was also regulated in 1939 when the US government announced that Canadians would need passports and visas to cross the border. These burgundy-coloured documents (which could be shared by a family) were issued by the Department of External Affairs and required a fingerprint as well as a photograph of the traveller. Censorship (which came under the Defence of Canada Regulations, DOCR) was omnipresent and meant that print, film and radio news reports would be filtered to assist in the successful prosecution of the war. Flaunting these rules meant banning of the offending publication, stiff fines or jail terms. Two examples of punishable offences were holding "defeatist views" or "harming recruitment and the success of His Majesty's forces". More than two-thirds of Quebec households had radios in 1941 and, at a time when Canadians were most hungry for news, they would be fed, not the truth, but governmental wishful thinking. The disastrous raid on Dieppe was one example. While agreeing that losses were high amid "ferocious fighting", the news reports concentrated on the fact that eighty-two German fighter planes were shot down and that "Canadian troops and Canadian tanks were harrying Hun fortifications" (*The Windsor Daily Star*). The Associated Press stated: "....first units of the commando force who had speedily accomplished their mission, returned to a British port in gay spirits." Pejorative terms to describe the enemy were not censored, of course, and "Jerries, Krauts, Huns, Squareheads, Fritz (Germans), Nips, Japs (Japanese) and Eyeties (Italians) became common conversational currency and added a cheeky element to headlines like: "Huns Quit" or "Japs Out".

In spite of censorship, Montrealers glued themselves to the radio to get the latest news from announcers who, although censored, expressed the news with gravitas. Even young children were held captive as their parents tuned in—but they were at least spared the realistic images to which we have become accustomed today. Irene Jones Meikle recalls: "When we came home from school for lunch my mother made us sit at the kitchen table and listen to the BBC News at noon. That was very important to her. Other than that, there was no talk of war at home. I knew that my parents were very upset about the war but they kept a lot away from us."

Naomi Paltiel Lowi got much of her wartime news at school. "In Baron Byng High School, we had a radio in our classroom that was given to us by Mr. Orrin Rexford who was a World War I veteran. At one o'clock every afternoon there was a big news report and the teacher would let us listen. (We also used the radio for dancing at lunch time or after school.) All of life revolved around the war effort. At the beginning the Allies were so ill-prepared that it was frightening so it was important to hear news of things that were actually happening which we found elevating and energizing." Don Pidgeon got much of his news from the print media: "My father (who was raised a francophone) would read the *Montreal Star* to me and I would correct his pronunciation. This is where I got all the war news."

The National Selective Service (NSS) came into effect on September 1, 1942 and was charged with coordinating Canada's manpower resources. Civilian work was designated by a series of priority standards which meant that jobs in war industries were "very high priority" while "low priority" occupations like salesmen, bartenders and taxi drivers could not be filled by healthy males between the ages of seventeen and forty-five. Workers, however unhappy they might have been, were generally not free to move to another job unless they had the approval of the NSS. Employers could not hire or fire any person, man or woman, without its approval under threat of a $500 fine or a jail term. The NSS also had the power to limit strikes in crucial industries. The labour shortage meant that unions gained strength during the war and the government had to make some concessions in this regard such as allowing workers to move from high priority to other jobs. Ambivalent attitudes to women abandoning their domestic role were put to the test as more men were sent to active service. A Women's Division of the NSS which had originally targeted young, single women was forced ito begin registering wives and mothers n 1943. Since teachers were paid a pittance, many left to seek employment in war industries, which led to shortages of staff and school closings. The NSS solution was to classify teaching an "A" priority job, which prevented them from moving to higher-paying war work. Civil service employees also had to remain at their jobs.

The Wartime Prices and Trade Board (WPTB) was set up to ensure scarce commodities were not wasted and inflation controlled. Frequent government advertisements reminded citizens that compliance was a patriotic duty to prevent another Depression as happened after the First World War. Sugar, paper, rubber, alcohol, fabric and gasoline were some of the commodities that fell under its jurisdiction. Limits were set on prices and violators were prosecuted for selling overpriced food or hoarding rationed items. Increases in basic wages, except for cost-of-living bonuses, were banned. In October 1941 Mackenzie King said that these measures, "...represents an experiment hitherto untried on this continent and perhaps having regard to its breadth and variety, hitherto untried by the will and consent of any free people anywhere". Rent prices were difficult to control in a city where the great majority of the population were tenants. The scarcity of new housing and the increased demand caused by the influx of war industry workers into the city meant that many greedy landlords took advantage of the situation. Evicting seniors in favour of more prosperous war workers, demanding "key money" or services and refusing to rent to mothers whose husbands were overseas led to people moving in with relatives or making other arrangements. People had to find shelter in abandoned warehouses, empty stores, garages or dank and dreary hovels, which led to overcrowding and family stress. Many people lucky enough to find any kind of housing would not complain if it were overpriced and even depressingly inadequate.

Clothing was another one of the adjustments that had to be made. With most production of clothing and footwear destined for the military, those at home had to accept the new reality that there would no longer be much choice in colors, sizes and styles in what was available. Another factor was that many women left low-paying jobs in the garment industry to accept better wages in war industries, leaving factories short-staffed. Frivolous clothing intended for fun or glamour had to go—tuxedos, evening dresses, lounging pyjamas, parkas, ski suits all joined a long list of forbidden items. Extra pockets, pleats, pant cuffs, suit vests, shoulder pads, long skirts (any skirt longer than 30 inches) were just a few of the prohibited items. The rubber shortage hit women hard because elastic for underwear, girdles and bathing caps was scarce or nonexistent. The well-known nylon stocking shortage was met by manufacturing a nylon/lisle blend. Women who couldn't find stockings could reach into their medicine cabinets and there, right beside the Carter's Little Liver Pills, would be Duration Leg Do, leg makeup that would never go the duration but turned into a terra cotta horror before the wearer arrived home. A woman with nicely tanned legs could just paint a seam up the backs of her legs before heading out the door. Naomi Paltiel Lowi remembers the nylon stocking shortage. "Before the war, we had to wear lisle stockings but, when nylons did become available, they were hard to get. A rumour would circulate that a certain store on Mount Royal was going to get some so we would line up and, sure enough, at a certain hour, we were allowed in and were able to get one pair, I think was the limit. I don't know where these rumours came from but they were always authentic."

Only a small minority of Montrealers owned cars during the war years, but those who did, were fiercely devoted to their symbol of status, freedom and mobility. There were to be no more carefree Sunday drives or trips to the country or seashore. Car manufacturing was also severely cut back. Both gasoline and rubber had to be imported and once tires wore out, they could only be replaced for driving that was deemed essential. The gasoline shortage that began in 1941 was handled by encouraging motorists to cut back on unnecessary driving. When this proved ineffective, rationing went into effect in April 1942. Drivers were then issued ration books and categorized into "A" to "E" with a separate category for commercial users. Innovative Montrealers saw a way around these onerous regulations and a headline in the *Calgary Herald* of April 10, 1943 read: "Quebec Black Market in Gas Coupons Broken". Human nature being what it is, there was another popular way to get scarce gas. Many a car owner was distressed to find that, while enjoying a movie or an evening outing, his precious supply had been siphoned off. The WPTB also reduced the speed limit to 40 miles an hour and special permits were needed for private trucks to travel more than 35 miles from home. Delivery schedules were cut back and some stores reverted to bicycle and horse and wagon deliveries. Bicycle sales were also restricted. By the end of the war, synthetic rubber was available but businesses had priority so that the average car owner had to wait a bit longer to get back on the road.

Many drivers just gave up and put their cars on blocks for the duration. Howard Dearlove: "Rationing? My father had a '32 Buick. He had to sell it. He couldn't get tires and he couldn't get gas so he sold it to a salesman." Carol Lodge: "Food rationing hardly

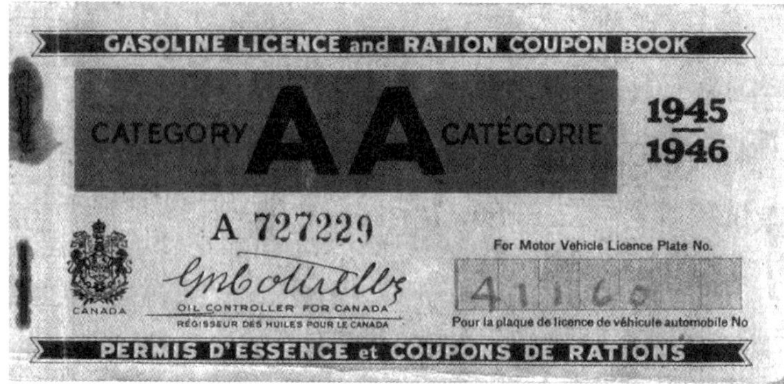
GASOLINE LICENCE and RATION COUPON BOOK
CATEGORY AA CATÉGORIE
1945
1946
A 727229
CANADA
OIL CONTROLLER FOR CANADA
RÉGISSEUR DES HUILES POUR LE CANADA
For Motor Vehicle Licence Plate No.
Pour la plaque de licence de véhicule automobile No
PERMIS D'ESSENCE et COUPONS DE RATIONS

Gasoline ration book.

affected our family at all. The one available item that did upset me was tires for the car. Dad had taught me how to drive when I was seventeen but, about six months later, in 1943, the car needed new tires. My father would not have anything to do with the black market which could provide just about anything—silk clothing, food, gas, etc. By late 1945, what a joy it was driving at last! "

Canada sent so much food overseas that rationing became necessary to ensure that what was left for domestic consumption was equitably shared. The military also required vast and urgent amounts of food. Farm labour was in short supply and schoolchildren were often allowed to skip school to help with the harvest. Meat, butter, tea, coffee and sugar were some of the rationed items. At the beginning, Canadians were asked to manage on half their usual purchases of scarce items but hoarding of goods, especially sugar and flour, made this unfair for the general public. More than 11 million ration books were distributed to Canadians in 1942. While rationing in Canada never reached the levels it did in Britain, it still presented a challenge to housewives, whose lives were already busy enough with war work and taking care of families. They bore the brunt of the responsibility of making food stretch and taste as edible as possible. They also had to keep up with the expiry date of coupons and changing supplies. Families were also expected, if they had the space, to grow a Victory

A rationing scene in Montreal.

garden to provide for some of their food needs.

Trading ration stamps was a common thing as different families had different needs. Mary Prendergast Ebel: "Rationing made it difficult for some newborn babies who could not nurse and were allergic to milk. Once again there was a spirit of, 'we are all in this together' and so other people would give or trade their own corn syrup coupons for the needy baby in the community, so it could be added to formula. I know Mother did not need her butter coupons because she got margarine from a neighbour who went back and forth to Belleville, Ontario each week. She probably traded them for meat coupons for we were big meat eaters." Sometimes, one didn't have to trade coupons. A woman shopping with one or two winsome children in tow might be asked by an elderly widow, "Would you like these coupons, dear. I really don't need them. Take them for the children." Naomi Paltiel Lowi's family did not find rationing onerous at all. "What we noticed in our family was that the rations were quite adequate and we didn't even use all of them. You see, Jews don't mix butter and milk with meat so maybe in general we ate less butter. You know, in all respects, we experienced the war in a much milder way than people in Europe." Families with relatives overseas were also busy sending packages to Britain. Howard Dearlove had a similar situation: "My father had an aunt living in Surrey, England. My mother would send boxes over to Britain with things you couldn't get there like tinned goods, chocolate bars, jams and things like that."

Mothers became expert in making sugarless and butterless desserts with the help of household hints in newspapers and magazines. The government offered ideas such as, "serve meat gravy instead of butter on potatoes" and, "add a small amount of milk when creaming butter for sandwiches". Canned salmon was in short supply as most of it was included in Red Cross packages for POWs but poultry, fish and variety meats were not covered by rationing and were usually available. A good relationship with one's grocer or butcher could sometimes allow for special treatment. Canadians drank more tea at that time so the rationing of tea was often felt more acutely than coffee. Restaurants had meatless Tuesdays and Fridays and chefs at least had the professional skills (and contacts) to rise to the challenge.

Alcohol was also on the ration list and people lined up to get whatever high-priced liquor was available. The black market thrived and bootleggers made as much homebrew as their sugar supply allowed. The WPTB prosecuted many of the offenders but it was a hopeless case as there was always "somebody who knows somebody". Ruth Swinton Stevenson had one experience with the black market. "I didn't find the rationing particularly hard but, during my pregnancy, a wealthy friend asked me if I had any cravings. I told her that I was sorry to disappoint her but I didn't crave anything. She nagged me about it until, finally, I told her that I missed canned pineapple. The next week when I arrived home, there was a huge box full of every kind of canned pineapple at my door. Money would buy you anything, which isn't nice but true."

The proliferation of ubiquitous and brightly-coloured wartime posters was meant to keep up morale at a time of grave sacrifice. The Wartime Information Board (WIB), knew that English and French posters had an immediate and powerful impact on the population. Easily made and distributed, they appealed to every emotion and every situation. "Buy Victory Bonds", "Give to the Canadian Red Cross", "*Enrolôns-Nous*", "Join the Team", "Attack on All Fronts", "Careless Talk Brings Tragedy in Wartime", "Fly and Fight with the R.C.A.F", "*Achetons des OBLIGATIONS de la VICTOIRE*", "LICK THEM over there!", "Become a Blood Donor", "Wanted for Murder. Her *careless talk* costs lives". Adorable children were often used to get the point across. A curly-headed blonde girl plaintively asks: "Oh please do! Daddy. Buy me a Victory Bond". Another poster showed an old and tearful babushka-clad woman with the smoking ruins of her house behind her. The wording read: "...and WE talk about sacrifice. Buy Victory Bonds". A picture was certainly worth a thousand words in these appeals to the national consciousness.

Service groups also utilized graphics to help their campaigns. The Association of Kinsmen Clubs had an ad showing a young British child with a bandage around its head. The wording stated: "Send Milk to Britain. A Dime Sends a Quart". Companies often combined an ad with a patriotic message. In one ad with a pretty, young CWAC, the message says, "*Quand vous achetez* (picture of Christie's Premium Soda Crackers) ...*N'oubliez pas les* (picture of

Wartime posters were meant to keep up morale at a time of grave sacrifice.

War Savings Stamps)".

Neilson's apologized that the supply of Jersey Milk Chocolate bars, "a wonderful energy food", was limited because of rationing and customers were not to blame the dealer because "He is rationed too!" Kleenex warned that, since bleaching ingredients were restricted, customers might find that their tissues were not "Snow White". Coca Cola urged customers to invite sailors to their homes and offer them a Coke to make them "feel at home".

Magazine covers, movies, radio shows, music, cartoons, lapel pins, matchbook covers, children's items (games, toys, books, comics, bubble gum cards and even birthday cards) often carried a war theme which might have led to cynicism or ennui (in the case of adults) but didn't. This was a real war which touched almost every family in Canada in some way. Newspapers, especially after D-Day, published pictures of dead, missing and wounded servicemen along with long lists of casualties so sacrifices at home seemed trivial in comparison. There was also the sense that society was working as one for the greater good.

Montreal's Civilian Protection Committee (CPC) was organized in 1939 and blackouts were held on a regular basis until October 1944, when interest and the threat of invasion began to wane. Many, but not all, volunteer civil defence workers were World War I veterans. The Air Raid Precaution (ARP) wardens had many duties and were issued an ID card, arm band, helmet, flashlight, manual, gas mask and a first aid kit. As well as making sure that the blackout rules were followed, they were trained to act as auxiliary firemen and to direct civilian and military traffic in case of an air attack. At the end of the war they received a certificate thanking them for their help in the "war against the German Reich and the other Axis Powers." They were aided by the Women's Volunteer Reserve Corps and other civic-minded groups. "Blackout Rule is Compulsory" is the heading that appeared over an article in the November 7, 1941 edition of the *Point News*. The article went on to state that the practice set for the following Monday was to start at 9:45 p.m. when the Alert would be given: "warning sirens, factory whistles, locomotives, steamships and radio" until 10:30 p.m. when the All Clear would be sounded. All rules for the exercise were to be obeyed and the newspaper sternly warned that non-compliance could lead to "a fine not exceeding $500 or a year in jail, or both. As an alternative, such person may be prosecuted upon indictment and, if convicted is liable to a fine not exceeding $5,000 or up to five years in a penitentiary or both". In spite of warnings and fines, the population was becoming complacent and more and more violations were noted before the program ended.

Jacques Boucher was a child at the time but remembers: "When we had a blackout, we had to put blankets over the windows before we put the lights on. In our area we had neighbourhood wardens and they made darn sure that we followed the rules. They wore old First World War helmets, an armband and carried flashlights. They also had a whistle to communicate with each other." Howard Dearlove: "We had to put out all the lights in the house and pull the blinds down. Civil Defence people dressed in black uniforms and carrying flashlights went around checking out all the houses. I'd say that this happened a couple of times a year. In Outremont half the streetlamps were covered up all during the war".

The War Bond Drives were an important part of funding the war. Advertisements in newspapers, military displays, national radio variety shows with famous stars, parades, demonstrations, shows, talks by prominent people and sporting events were all intended to make each drive a success. Carol Lodge recalls: "There were terrific concerts at the Forum with outstanding singers, orchestras, and ballet. Some of the performers were internationally famous, like the Russian Cossack Singers—fantastic with their deep voices! We also saw and heard Lily Pons, André Kostelanetz, Gracie Moore (of movie and opera fame) and George Formby, the English comedian."

Some of the ideas generated by the Victory Bond drives were quite innovative. Stanway Signs Ltd. was established in 1918 and, as Enseignes Stanway Signs, is still in business in 2012. The gold lettering on the old Kresge's variety store on St. Catherine Street was one of their projects. Arthur Stanway was a young lad of sixteen attending West Hill High School in N.D.G. when his father's company was contacted by the Victory Bonds office with an unusual request. "My dad was called to the Victory Bonds office every two or three months and his company would make a billboard or banner which would be installed on Phillips Square right across from Morgan's. So this time he came back to the shop and said that they had been asked to make a full-size model of a Messerschmitt 109. I reminded Dad that we were in the sign business but he told me I could do it because I made model aircraft as a hobby. The men in the shop helped me but I had to make the blueprint for the construction. It took us a good week to finish it and all the work was done in the shop. We made a wood frame but, because of the war, we couldn't get good metal to cover the frame so we used cheap black iron which was used for stove pipes at the time. There was no plastic for the coop top so I went to Dawson Brothers Printing, an office supplies store on St. James Street and got some big sheets of celluloid. They were used to keep desk blotters clean. I cut this to fit. The air force gave us a parachute and we borrowed a propeller from Hamilton Standard which had a branch here in Montreal. I was only a sixteen-year-old kid and too young to stay up for the staging but, at midnight of June 3, 1941, my father and two of his workers 'nosedived' the plane in front of the Westmount Library. They dug a hole, put a stake in the ground on an angle and put the plane over it. They hung the parachute from a nearby tree. While they were doing this, two Ferry Command pilots came by on their way from Dorval to downtown and said it looked like the real thing—and they knew aircraft. The next day, the residents of Westmount woke up to see a 'downed Messerschmitt' with a sign: DON'T LET THIS HAPPEN HERE! BUY VICTORY BONDS! A picture appeared in the *Montreal Star* and my dad got paid $350 for this job which was big money in those days."

A little shock value always helped the donations flow in and Montreal staged a mock battle on October 31, 1943 as part of the Fifth Victory Loan campaign to show Montrealers what could happen if the enemy were not kept away from Canada. A fake attack on the city between active army forces from camps in the area and reservists went on throughout the day. The "theatres of battle" were Fletcher's Field, Westmount Park and Lafontaine Park. The city was alive with the noises, smells and actions of battle as smoke screens were laid down and camouflaged troops behind sandbag barricades fought off the "enemy" attack. The demonstration had everything:

The residents of Westmount woke up to see a 'downed Messerschmitt'—
designed and built by Arthur Stanway.
Photo by Conrad Poirier. Fond Conrad Poirier
Bibliothèque et archives nationales du Québec

war correspondents roaring around in jeeps noting the action, careening tanks, Royal Canadian Army Medical Corps men bringing "casualties" to the rear and men of the Signals Corps communicating from units to headquarters. The *Gazette* of November 1 noted: "In the end it was the weight of better equipment that brought victory to the home forces and proved the value of that same equipment when citizens' money provides it for the forces overseas."

Montreal was a magnet for famous and talented entertainers and the downtown scene thrived during the war years. Many well-known figures also came to suppport the war effort. One of them was Paul Robeson, the brilliant intellectual, polyglot, sportsman, actor and singer who was born the son of a slave and whose career as a concert singer and actor was hampered by his work for human rights in the United States and around the world. In May 1942, he came to Montreal at the invitation of the Communist-inspired Quebec Committee for Allied Victory which, while supporting the war effort in all ways, was especially interested in aiding Russia which, at that time, was bravely fighting off the massive Nazi onslaught. Hitler, in a broadcast on March 15, had informed the German people that the Soviet Army would be crushed by the summer. More than 12,000 people welcomed Robeson to the Forum for a benefit concert. He spoke about freedom and his repertoire included spirituals, folk songs and a ballad about the bombing of Madrid in the Spanish Civil—the lyrics were changed to commemorate the courage of Londoners in the Blitz. He received an immense ovation and great reviews that night. Hounded by the American government, this champion of justice for the oppressed paid a heavy price for his ideals.

A few months later, Russia was the object of another fundraising campaign but this time the group organizing it was the Canadian Aid to Russia Fund. In January 1943, the Soviets were engaged in a fight to the death at Stalingrad. On January 19 the packed Forum welcomed Eleanor Roosevelt as part of a drive to raise one million dollars in support of the Russian people. The stage was well decorated for the event with flowers and a colourful backdrop of

The Wartime Information Board (WIB), knew that English and French posters had an immediate and powerful impact on the population.

the red flag of the Soviet Union, the Union Jack and the Stars and Stripes along with the flags of the United Nations. The President's wife was not the only notable present that night. The Danish tenor Lauritz Melchior sang as did Claire Gagnier, the young operatic singer. Military bands boomed and thumped as they always did at these events. One of their offerings was the Russian national anthem, the Internationale. The money raised would provide clothing, medicine and food to a people under siege. There was an interesting roster of speakers with Premier Adélard Godbout leading off. He welcomed Mrs. Roosevelt and mentioned that the enemy presented a real threat, not only to Europe and Asia but also to North America. Next up was Mackenzie King followed by Mrs. Roosevelt who exhorted everyone to give donations, large or small, to help the suffering Russians. She told them that she had recently visited Britain and saw, first hand, what bombs can do to cities. She mentioned that Mrs. Winston Churchill had told her that the British had donated generously after listening to only two of her radio appeals. Mrs. Roosevelt finished her speech by saying: "Today we can rejoice with the Russians that at last the time has come when they have turned the tide of battle and can begin again to reconquer their land".

The pleas for donations worked. A total of $202,363 was raised that night with donations coming from the Bronfman family and corporations like the CPR and the Aluminum Company of Canada. The co-chairman of the event told the happy crowd that a group of "French-Canadian women from the east end" had donated $125. To great applause, Melchior said that he would donate $140 which the Danish community had given him for flowers. Volunteers moved through the audience and, as expected, people gave generously. Quantities of medicine, food and clothing would soon be heading to Russia.

There is nothing like a military parade to fire up patriotic feelings and many were held in Montreal during the war to mark different occasions or just to keep the military profile in front of the public. Irene Jones Meikle remembers her first one: "The first time I remember seeing soldiers parading in the street was on Sherbrooke Street and the corner of Grand Boulevard in N.D.G. They must have gotten off the train at Montreal West Station and were probably marching to the armoury in Westmount. About ten or twelve of us boys and girls were on our way back to Kensington School after lunch. This would have been in 1942 or '43 and I was in grade four or five. It was so exciting to see troops of soldiers all in uniform marching along. They had a marching band, too, and we just decided that we would march along with them. In those days there was very little traffic. We got a little past Girouard Avenue and realized that we would never make it back to school on time so we had to go home and tell our parents what we did. We were spoken to and told not to do it again. Our parents had to write notes for the teachers the next day but, because it was wartime, I think our parents and the teachers excused us."

Howard Dearlove had no choice in the matter: "I used to go to Sunday School at the First Presbyterian Church on the corner of Jeanne Mance. Some of the young girls who taught us had boyfriends in the army and, as soon as we'd finish, they'd drag us down to Sherbrooke Street to watch the soldiers going by. These parades were very long and had various regiments and bands. I think they were marching to get recruits."

Lorne Hamilton, stationed at HMCS Donnacona recalls: "Periodically, the navy would have parades. These were partly designed to keep the naval organization in front of the public but then, on special days, all the units marched with bands—the army, navy and air force. These were beautiful parades, of course, and they were usually for Victory Bonds promotion and so on. They would start from St. Lawrence Main and come west on Sherbrooke Street. They didn't march during the winter but perhaps two or three times during the summer. The navy, as the "Senior Service", always led the parade with two sailors leading Newfoundland dogs which resided at the barracks."

For married women, family life was changed dramatically during the war. The old days of: "Monday, laundry, Tuesday, ironing" must have seemed like a dream compared to their new obligations. Many joined the work force for the first time, which gave them a large pay cheque and a feeling of independence. Volunteers organized daycares allowing mothers to join the work force. For those whose husbands were overseas, there was concern for their safety and time was taken to write letters (always cheery and optimistic) and send parcels overseas. With war talk everywhere, children had to be handled carefully to avoid depression. Women, who usually did the family shopping, had to follow the arcane and changing rules of food rationing and were also expected to act as police officers for the WPTB if the butcher down the street charged too much for ham. They were expected to take part in salvage and War Bond drives; plant Victory gardens (and can and preserve the harvest); do volunteer work; in some cases, replace men on the family farm; run homes with almost everything in short supply; get along with relatives if they had to share housing and follow tips in magazines on how to maintain their "femininity" while doing the work of three men.

Men on the home front of working age were usually involved in essential war jobs and volunteered their time in civil defence or fund raising. Citizens were expected to look out for spies and watch their speech because they knew that "Loose Lips Sink Ships." It was a world of acronyms and initials. A family might have sons in the PPCLI, RMR and RHLI, one of whom got seven days CB after going AWL. Daughters might be serving in the CWACs or WRENs. Father might spend time working for the CPC and the DNWS while mother took a job at DIL while volunteering for the IODE (Imperial Order of the Daughters of the Empire). Aunt Ethel might be a member of the MSWL while working at the DND after applying to the NSS for permission to change jobs.

Children and teenagers played a big role in the war effort. Many boys, some of whom had not yet shaved, were serving and dying overseas (according to Veterans Affairs Canada, about 700,000 boys under the age of twenty-one served in uniform). Many children worked on farms to help with the food supply and the government lowered the legal driving age to fourteen so teenagers could operate farm vehicles. Even young siblings at home were militarized and often played at war. The boys learned to identify plane silhouettes while the girls played "Red Cross nurse". Cadet corps were popular in many high schools. Those old enough to understand the reality of war and who had fathers overseas prayed and worried. Children became scavengers and collected scrap material, some even giving away their toys. Millions of dollars were contributed by children in the Victory Loan Drives. Boy Scouts and Girl Guides, with their large numbers, were able to pool their resources and contribute impressively to the war effort. Junior members of the IODE and the Red Cross, the Canadian Girls in Training (CGIT) all did stalwart service doing things like selling calendars; collecting books; knitting; holding toy, bake and rummage sales and sorting clothes destined for overseas.

The atmosphere at home could, at times, be scary for young children. Howard Dearlove: "We never heard much against the Germans or Italians because the only time I was really frightened was when the Japs bombed Pearl Harbor. I was six years old and didn't know what was coming off except that the atmosphere really scared us and I used to get goose bumps. My grandmother had a Japanese dish and she was so angry that she threw it across the room. (laughs) We were sending men up to the Aleutians and the war wasn't going too well for us in North Africa and those places until the Americans got in and we really started to push ahead. We didn't realize until after the war what we had done to Japanese Canadians. I remember the Tanaka family. They had been interned and we went to school with them when they moved to Montreal." Mary Prendergast Ebel was a young observer who remembers a united community. "There were so many family generations that would come together to live during those years. It provided company and solace, especially for those who had some member serving overseas. I remember a family up the street who always had a Union Jack flying from the porch and during the warm seasons the grandmother and the mother and maybe an aunt would sit outside and knit socks. It was one of those pictures a photographer forgot to take. It could be eerie at times because I remember sometimes watching to see if there was some type of black ribbon over a door because then you knew there was a death in the family." Don Pidgeon recalls his parents taking time out from their war routine to enjoy a simple pleasure: "On Saturday nights we would listen to the various bands at the Waldorf Astoria Hotel in New York City. My parents would put the table aside, turn out all the lights and dance with only the dial of the radio lit up."

For those children whose fathers were overseas, there were special adjustments that had to be made. Jacques Boucher: "I saw my father maybe four times from 1939 to November of 1946 when he got out of the navy. I got belted many times by my mother because I was the eldest and should have known better. 'You should take care of your brothers and sisters. You should....You should...' I was helping my mother do the cooking, the washing and the ironing. *I'm seven years old!* I went to St-Jean-de-la-Croix School on the corner of St. Zotique and St. Lawrence. In those days the teachers were brothers and nuns and their way of thinking was the same as the Church's hierarchy. A lot of times I got into fights with some of the kids at school who wanted to know why my father was fighting for the English. I would punch them and give them a bloody nose and then, hopefully, I wouldn't get the crap beaten out of me. I didn't know anybody else in my school whose father was serving. I didn't meet anyone who served in the war until I went to high school and had a teacher who had been in the army." Jacques also remembers the social times when his father's friends visited. "Every night was party time at our place. My father had a lot of buddies in the service so our house was like a drop-in place for when they would come to town and have no place to stay. Sailors would bring food from the ships' stores and I remember a lot of music and drinking."

Living in Verdun protected Beverly Overall Marsh from peer hostility but there were definite changes to family life with her father away. "We lived on Second Avenue which was strictly English and French and, I think, more English in those days. Grandpa lived with us and I had a brother, Sonny. I went to Bannantyne School. We were all pretty much the same but I was the only one of my friends whose father was away at war. One of my dad's brothers was manager of the A & P and, since Mom got her cheque only once a month, he would put stuff away for her until the money arrived. Mom worked for a short time at DIL (Defence Industries Limited) but she didn't stay there because it was shift work and she worried about us being alone at home with Grandpa who was becoming forgetful."

The families of German, Japanese or Italian background were often under suspicion in spite of the fact that many had sons and daughters in the service. Those with family members interned had to suffer family dislocation and financial hardship. Many in the Jewish community had known from the beginning what was happening to the Jews of Europe. Many Jewish servicemen had no illusions about Germans and, in case they might be taken prisoner, some asked to have their ID tags changed to indicate that they were Christian. While the community gave the war effort its all, it also had the stress of trying to keep track of relatives in danger. Naomi Paltiel had two brothers serving, Ephrom in the merchant marines and Daniel in the navy, but remembers her family worrying about relatives in Europe. "We heard through normal channels during the thirties that there were restrictive laws in Germany against Jews so we already knew the Jews were in trouble. The thirties were hard times for all kinds of reasons so there was a lot of anxiety in the community with the news and the economy. We had English relatives from Manchester who lived in Montreal for part of the war and I remember one of them talking to my father about some distant relatives in Rumania. My father had left Rumania in 1901 and this relative's family went to England at around that time as well so they didn't keep in regular touch. During the war when there were rumours of Jewish people being in trouble in Europe, this relative and my father sent a letter to Rumania which came back with a stamp, "Address Unknown", or something to that effect."

Paper, empty toothpaste or shaving cream tubes, pots and pans, old fur coats, coat hangers, rubber, cooking fat, glass, rags, scrap metal and even the bone pried from Fido's mouth were all needed for the war effort. These would be turned into everything from tanks to togs for servicemen. Rubber, especially, was in very short supply and, if Granny couldn't part with her hot-water bottle, she had to lovingly conserve it as there would be no replacement. The National Salvage Campaign was launched in April 1941 by the Department of National War Services (DNWS). Organized by municipalities as well as service groups and children's organizations like the Boy Scouts and Girl Guides, almost everyone could get involved and almost everyone did. Even a ten-year-old child pulling a wagon and collecting old newspapers was "doing his bit". Quebec had over 200 local salvage committees in 1942. The fact that many Montrealers moved on May 1 helped the growing piles of salvage when old trophies and other bits and pieces were donated. Collection centres were set up all over the city but schools also functioned as depots, which made it easy for children to donate.

Allen Calderwood remembers: "I went to Gilson School on Harvard just above St. James. We collected paper, toothpaste tubes, pots and pans. You brought them to school and everything was piled up near the principal's office." Joan Byers Mullins: "As kids, we all collected tinfoil from cigarette packages as part of our war effort at Willingdon School in N.D.G. We picked up all we could from family, adult friends and neighbours and had a class competition as to how much we collected each week. The winners were listed on a big poster in the classroom. Our school sent 'ditty bags' to our armed forces overseas consisting of toilet articles, chocolate bars sometimes but *always* cigarettes, I'm ashamed to say." Howard Dearlove: "I started school in 1941 and we had to bring pennies for the Red Cross every day. We also had to bring our old toothpaste containers which had a lot of lead in them in those days. We lived on Ducharme Street and there was a woman in our neighbourhood (which was a mix of Jewish, English and French

Allen Calderwood: "I went to Gilson School on Harvard just above St. James. We collected paper, toothpaste tubes, pots and pans."

Canadians) who was very interested in helping Russia. We were all collecting clothes for Russia and they were piled up almost to the ceiling in our school. The Outremont School Board also donated an ambulance to the Red Cross."

Due to the costs associated with transportation and sorting, it wasn't possible to turn all the savaged material into useful items. The program did serve a few important purposes however—it involved a huge number of citizens, made people feel good, which helped morale and, as a side effect, probably resulted in many basements and back sheds being tidied up.

Volunteering was a huge aspect of the successful outcome of the war. Across the country, millions of women freely gave their time, energy and talents to do whatever they could to alleviate wartime suffering and deprivation. It was something that middle-and upper-class women had always done and, with wartime austerity, it was also a guilt-free way to socialize by organizing teas and card parties as benefits. These women were also ideally placed to take in a child evacuee from Britain. It was not only privileged women who volunteered. Many who had not previously been part of a volunteer group also pitched in with great alacrity while members of church and social groups redirected their efforts for the duration. Many organizations were divided along religious, class, financial and linguistic lines from the somewhat elitist IODE to the "*dames auxiliares*" of French-speaking regiments. Among other services, women were involved in knitting projects and the staggeringly high numbers of items sent overseas were indicative of their devotion and gener-osity. Women who, before the war, might have spent leisurely hours knitting themselves an angora pullover or cardigan in soft pastel colours now spent hurried days and evenings making man-sized articles out of coarse wool known as "service weight". Much of the knitting was done in groups and articles turned out included socks, scarves, balaclavas and sweaters.

The all-encompassing Red Cross had its own membership but also coordinated the efforts of large numbers of volunteers affiliated with groups such as the National Council of Women and the Federated Women's Institute. Red Cross volunteers did everything from taking home-nursing classes to organizing blood drives. The Royal Victoria Hospital nurses' alumnae association produced 6,000 surgical dressings each week in their Red Cross room. As well as sending socks, sweaters and sea boot stockings overseas, they also included amputation covers.

Women also made pillows, sheets and flannel shirts for the soldiers and baby layettes for children. They raised money, gathered scrap materials for salvage, prepared overseas parcels, arranged for servicemen to be invited into homes for a meal, organized daycares, took part in entertainment for servicemen, provided clothes for refugees, and packaged "ditty bags" for servicemen with items like chocolate, sewing kits, razor blades and the ubiquitous package of cigarettes. In an era when cigarettes were described as "mild", "slow-burning" and endorsed by doctors and famous actors and actresses, the amount sent to the troops was astounding. The Red Cross alone sent 25 million cigarettes in the first three years of the war. At $1.90 for 1,000 cigarettes, they were affordable and families were able to send a steady supply overseas through authorized dealers. All kinds of organizations from regimental associations to service groups were kept busy raising money for "cigarette funds". Canadian cigarettes were a precious commodity and, while the donors could imagine that these gifts eased the stress of battle or were a treat for airmen as they lifted a pint in a pub in England, the Catholic Women's League and other organizations might have been shocked to learn that some of the more than seven million cigarettes they sent to the boys would be traded for sex.

One important service performed by the Canadian Red Cross was sending food packages to Commonwealth POWs. A Montreal depot opened in 1942 and volunteers spent countless hours putting together these packages. For a cost of about $2, a POW would receive a package containing biscuits, tinned meat and fish, chocolate, cigarettes, butter, cheese, jam and other items.

Unfortunately, packages sent to POWs in Japan were often pilfered by guards but many former POWs in prison camps in Europe say that the only reason they survived was because of these packages. Again, cigarettes were bartered with the guards for bread, sugar, boots or other items. In some camps, twenty cigarettes was the price of obtaining bread.

Phyllis Eperson: "There was a place in Côte St. Paul which we called the Babies' Home. It was where they took in destitute children. All the women from the church guilds in the neighbourhood would go there once or twice a week and knit socks and do this and that for the war effort." Joan Byers Mullins: "The Junior Red Cross at school provided yarn to make caps, mittens, scarves and gloves for members of the armed forces. The socks for members of the navy required special waterproof yarn. The gloves for the air force gunners were knitted with the index finger free so they could operate the trigger of the gun. The heavy yarn was in army, navy or air force colours and not too exciting to work with. My mother and I knitted like crazy while we listened to *Lux Theatre* or *Fibber McGee and Molly* on the radio in the evenings."

Madeleine Cloutier Methot: "We formed a group, *Les Dames auxiliares*, to help needy families of servicemen. I was the secretary and my aunt, Mme André Vennat (Annette) was the president. We were associated with the Régiment de Châteauguay and our office was on Pine Avenue near the Fusiliers Mont-Royal armoury. We went every Monday and tried to do something nice for the people. We didn't have uniforms. The English had uniforms and I liked that idea. We had many volunteers who knitted toques, mittens and scarves for these families. We also organized tombolas, concerts and suppers. When soldiers returned on leave for the weekend, the mothers all made *sucre à la crème* (fudge) so they could bring it back to camp as a treat for all the soldiers."

Some volunteering took a different form. Lucille "Lou" Pacaud remembers getting an unusual request one day. "The Red Cross asked if we could come on duty for one whole day without telling anyone what we were going to do. I asked my boss at Dominion

Textile if I could have the day off and, with his permission, off I went in my uniform. The other volunteers and I went down to Bonaventure Station where we were to meet a prison train with German POWs passing through Montreal. We had to scrub the place—which was filthy—and then make coffee and sandwiches. The German soldiers were a happy bunch, singing and very cheerful and we were quite cheerful ourselves. I think they were happy to be out of danger. We said hello and passed the sandwiches which apparently were very good or else the soldiers hadn't eaten in a long time. I remember being pleased just to take part in the war and having to keep quiet about this made us all feel a little bit important."

Beverly Overall Marsh remembers what young girls did to be helpful and involved. "A gang of us would get together and sell lemonade or fudge. We had to go to get permission from the mayor of Verdun to do this and we would give the money that we collected to the Red Cross."

Many talented and attractive young women took time out from regular jobs to volunteer to entertain servicemen. One of them was Peggy Ford Stanway, in her early twenties, from Verdun. By days a secretary for the Robert Hampson & Sons Insurance Company, she was a dancer for the YMCA's TNT Revue in her spare time. "A bunch of us girls got involved. Somebody knew somebody who knew somebody and that's how you got started. I stayed with the group until the end of the war. We had rehearsals once a week at the downtown Y where we practiced dances like the can-can. Later on, I remember we did a Russian dance. Molly Usher-Jones was our teacher and came with us to all the shows. The Y (or someone) provided the costumes and they were very nice. A couple of the girls sang so there was also singing at our shows. We went to army camps in Huntingdon, Cowansville and Valcartier near Quebec City. When we went to Valcartier, we'd go for the weekend and stay in the barracks. It was very secret, you know. I don't think my mother told anyone what I did. My parents were never bothered about the shows. As long as I kept out of trouble, that was the main thing. We did our shows during the week. The Y supplied a bus—not an "Uncle Harry" bus—a *nice* bus and Molly would take about twenty of us. We would sing songs all the way there, army songs or popular songs of the day. The army would provide a stage and we did our routine. I think they served refreshments after but I can't remember. We just had a good time and maybe we'd stay and dance with the boys when the show was over. The boys seemed to like our shows. I guess their officer told them they had to like it or else! We'd sometimes get home at 2 or 3 o'clock in the morning and then I'd have to get up and go to work the next day. The Y gave us $5 to take a taxi home. There were a couple of girls who also lived in Verdun and we'd take a taxi together. I was the last one out and I used to hate that, being the last one with the taxi driver. I was scared stiff, although Montreal was very safe at that time. Nobody bothered us when we walked downtown."

One woman who could not be called a volunteer but who nevertheless provided a "home away from home" for young people who lived in the area was "Ma" Heller. She and her husband ran a snack bar on Sherbrooke Street near Marcil. As well as writing to young boys serving overseas, "Ma" would often send them packages. Irene Jones Meikle: "Ma Heller's was a kids' hangout. We all used to go there for hot chocolate after skating in N.D.G. Park. She got the name "Ma" Heller because she was so good to the troops. She knew a lot of the boys from the area who went overseas because, as kids, they spent a lot of time there. She wrote to them and they wrote back to her. She had a wall of letters, I remember."

While there was much work to do, both voluntary and paid, and morale to be maintained, there was a full menu of things Montrealers could do to keep up spirits. Besides the theatres, clubs and restaurants, the Forum was a popular destination for politicians, entertainers and shows of all kinds during the war. Lily Pons, Gracie Fields, Broadway composer Sigmund Romberg and Jeannette MacDonald were some of the well-known stars of the day who played to appreciative audiences. Frank Sinatra performed at the Forum twice during the war. In May 1942 he made his debut

Dancers at the Johnny Holmes weekly Saturday Night Dance,
Victoria Hall, Westmount, 1942
Fonds Johnny Holmes, Concordia University Archives.

as a featured vocalist with the orchestra of Tommy Dorsey and he returned again in 1944 headlining his own show. He wowed the teenagers but shocked the city by playing on a Sunday. Tickets for that show started at $1.25 with boxes going for $4. For those who loved hockey, Dick Irvin Sr. coached the Canadiens for the first time as they played Boston to a 1-1 tie in November 1940. Maurice Richard scored all five goals in the Canadiens' 5-1 playoff victory over Toronto in March 1944. In the same month, the "Habs" beat the Maple Leafs 11-0 in a semi-final game which was the largest shutout margin in playoff history. Gluttons for glory, the Canadiens beat Chicago 5-4 winning their fifth Stanley Cup. At all of these games, the Forum would be filled with men wearing overcoats and fedoras while the women kept warm in fur coats and church-going hats.

Dances were held every Saturday night all over Montreal at places like the YMCA and Victoria Hall in Westmount. His Majesty's Theatre was the site of the wonderfully entertaining RCN show with an entire navy personnel, "Meet the Navy" in May 1944. "Cast of 135—40 Beautiful Women—30 Piece Orchestra". Prices for that show ranged from 75 cents to $2.50 (no tax). One could combine a sense of patriotism as well as have a good time by supporting war fundraisers such as the three-night show put on by Montreal High students in 1943 with The Montreal Victory Serenaders band that included Oscar Peterson on piano and Maynard Ferguson on trumpet.

The music of the war years was the glue that connected military personnel and civilians together. It served to unite, inspire, cheer and encourage people while giving them a bit of an escape from reality. It could also be unbearably sad if it brought back memories of loss or heartbreak. This music was enjoyed by servicemen at shows held wherever troops fought, as well as by families back home. Glen Miller, Count Basie, Guy Lombardo and his Royal Canadians, Benny Goodman, Duke Ellington and others brought the big band sound to dance halls and homes and provided an upbeat note when it was needed. An endless list of popular singers like Perry Como, Ella

Fitzgerald, the Andrews Sisters, Vera Lynn, Bing Crosby, Doris Day, Gracie Fields, George Formby and Frank Sinatra appealed to every emotion. There were patriotic songs: "We're Gonna Hang out the Washing on the Siegfried Line" and "We Must All Stick Together". Upbeat songs: "Boogie Woogie Bugle Boy", "This is the Army Mr. Jones" and "Kiss Me Goodnight Sergeant Major". Songs of almost unbearable poignancy: "The White Cliffs of Dover" and "We'll Meet Again". Romantic songs: "Who's Taking You Home Tonight" and "I'll Be Seeing You". Songs of hope: "There'll Always Be an England" and "I'll Be With You In Apple Blossom Time". Sing-along songs: "You Are My Sunshine", "Mairzy Doats and Dozy Doats" and "Roll Out the Barrel". Many of the ribald songs sung by servicemen got into the popular repertoire and were always good for a shot of rebellious fun by young people. These included: "The North Atlantic Squadron", "Roll Me Over in the Clover" and the mocking song about the testicular deficiencies of the Nazi leaders which was sung to the tune of the "Colonel Bogey March".

Hitler..........has only got one ball.
Goering........has two but they are small.
Himmler.......has something sim'lar,
But poor old Goebbels
Has no balls at all.

Canada was always looking for heroes to bolster support for the war effort and they found a perfect one in George Beurling of Verdun. In Serge Durflinger's book, *Fighting from Home, The Second World War in Verdun, Quebec*, he describes the massive contribution of Verdunites during both World Wars and explains that support for these wars was due to the predominantly British population and a very supportive French group of citizens working together in a closely-knit community. Verdun, a suburb of Montreal on the St. Lawrence River, was a separate city until 2002 when it merged with Montreal. During the war years it pursued its own initiatives to support the war effort. The navy was the service of choice for many men from Verdun, which could be attributed to two factors; the first being the British connection to the Senior Service and the second, the city's proximity to the St. Lawrence River and the many boating clubs in the area. (Interestingly, the opposite seems to be true of the many Prairie boys who also had a propensity for the navy, despite having never seen much water in their lives!)

There were not too many boys from Verdun who joined the air force due to the strict educational standards required at the beginning of the war, but one who did became the pride of his city which honoured him by naming a street, a school and a park after him. Pilot Officer George Frederick Beurling DSO, DFC, DFM & Bar, the most successful of all Canadian Fighter pilots in World War II, was a brilliant eccentric. He had more nicknames than medals: "Buzz", "Screwball", "The Falcon of Malta", "Knight of Malta" and the "Verdun Ace". There were also many adjectives that were used to describe his singular personality—troubled, reclusive, eccentric, antisocial, complicated, intelligent and tough were some of them.

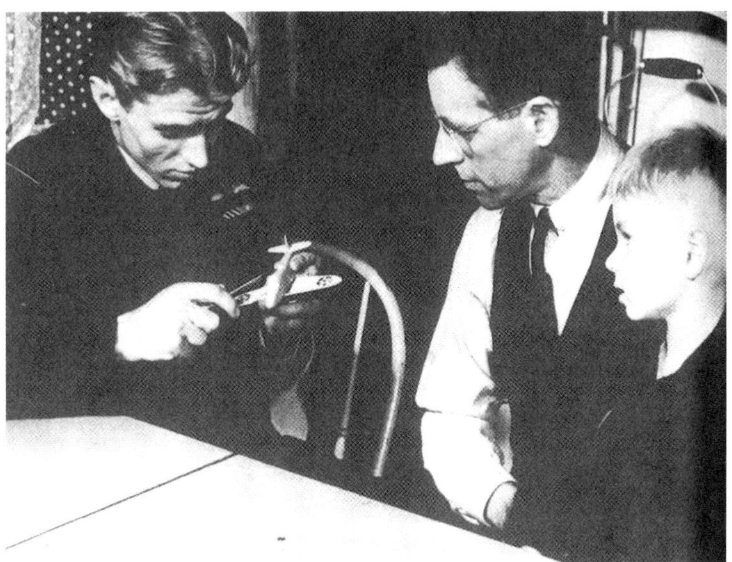

Canada's flying ace George Beurling at home in Verdun.
Department of National Defence.

His eyes, his most startling physical trait, were described as piercing blue and unnerving in their coldness. Born into a fundamentalist Christian family, it was his parents' wish that George go to university but he was not terribly interested in school and left in grade nine. Planes were his obsession. He started by making models as a child and graduated to hanging around airports and pilots, discussing tactics and paying for his own flying lessons as a young teen. He took his first plane ride at the age of nine and was flying solo at age sixteen. His was a natural talent which he endlessly perfected to an art. His perfect eyesight, well-honed skills in deflection shooting and ability to manoeuvre made him nearly invincible in combat.

At the beginning of the war, his lack of education made the RCAF reject his application. He flirted with the idea of joining the air forces of China or Finland but those plans came to naught so he headed to England in a convoy to join the RAF. He had forgotten to bring his birth certificate and had to come back to Canada to retrieve it. Making a safe return trip on the U-boat-infested seas, he was accepted by the RAF as a pilot and took part in a few missions. However, his lone-wolf tactics, while successful, did not earn him many points with his peers and superiors. He was never a team player, preferred to fly solo and certainly was not over burdened with humility. He was then posted overseas to the beleaguered island of Malta where he joined No. 249 Squadron and became an ace in just four days with five kills. He shot down a total of twenty-nine planes and, at the age of twenty, was a celebrated Canadian war hero. The stress of battle and health problems forced him to spend almost two months recuperating. Shot down and wounded in October 1942, he spent some time in hospital before returning to Canada at Ottawa's request to take part in a cross-country Victory Loan Drive tour promoting the sale of war bonds. He was lionized all across the country but Montreal and Verdun gave him a special welcome.

Beurling arrived in Montreal on November 10 and was welcomed by massive crowds as his motorcade made its way through the downtown streets before arriving at the Verdun Auditorium for a ceremony. The lavishly-decorated auditorium was packed with thousands of well-wishers from all elements of the population, from military figures and politicians to cheering locals. The shy hero brought down the house with his comment, "This is no place for me….I'm a fighter pilot." It was probably Verdun's proudest moment. Carol Lodge remembers that day. "George Beurling, Canada's war ace, was a Verdun boy who appeared at the Verdun Auditorium and we all went wild. A real killer! Of such are war heroes made. I also remember skipping class to see him come down McTavish sitting in the back of a Cadillac convertible the afternoon before his appearance in Verdun."

He was never comfortable in public and his comments on being a fighter pilot shocked many of his colleagues who believed that he appeared to take an unseemly enjoyment in killing. He transferred to the RCAF in late 1943 but his maverick behaviour was a bad fit, which led to his being given an honourable discharge in October 1944. One month later, in the presence of two witnesses, he married Diana Whittall, a debutante from British Columbia, in St. George's Anglican Church in Montreal. The marriage was short-lived. He ended his career with a total score of thirty-one kills with one shared and nine damaged planes. In 1948, at the age of twenty-six, Beurling died in the crash of his Noorduyn Norseman plane in Rome while on his way to join the Israeli Air Force.

It almost goes without saying that Beurling was never interested in team sports but he loved to swim and that is how Penny Pentland Gélineau got to meet him. "I met George Beurling at the Verdun Natatorium towards the end of the war when I was fourteen years old. There was a very large shallow pool and, one day, I noticed a young chap with the bluest of eyes standing by himself. We started talking and he asked me if I could swim underwater. I said I could and we decided to have a contest to see who could swim the farthest. I swam to the end of the pool and saw that he had already come up and was shaking the water off his head like a puppy. To this day I do not know if he let me win or if I really beat him. We had this contest a few more times and I didn't always win. It was just a fun thing. I had no idea who he was but he was extremely kind, a lot of fun and very decent to a young teenager. He was always smiling and charming and a genuinely nice person. When he came to the pool, he always left early. Maybe he didn't want to be recognized. When he was killed I recall that I felt very sad for his family because he was so young."

When it became obvious that British civilians would certainly be a target of German bombing raids, the government started planning for the formal evacuation of women and children as early as 1938. The upper classes had only to send their children off to their country estates or make private arrangements with friends or relatives in Canada, the United States, Australia, New Zealand or South Africa. Many mothers, accompanied by nannies, left with their children. Working people were advised to send their children to friends, relatives or foster parents in the countryside. The quality of foster care was uneven and some children had lifelong bad memories of being fed table scraps and having to eat wild berries to stave off hunger. Others had wonderful experiences with caring adults with whom they kept in touch as long as possible.

With the threat of a possible German invasion, plans were made to send the children overseas and many countries were keen to take part in an organized evacuation. Prime Minister Churchill was against the plan and the country had the example of the King and Queen who refused to leave England or send the Princesses Elizabeth and Margaret away to safety. In spite of this, private schools, corporations, service clubs and societies began to transport children to Canada. The establishment of the Children's Overseas Reception Board (CORB) allowed children between the ages of five and sixteen from mixed-class backgrounds to go abroad. Parents registering their children with CORB had to make weekly payments based on family income. Almost 6,000 came to Canada by the end of 1940. They arrived generally during the summer so they could start school in September and most stayed for the duration of the war. William Massey Birks became the chairman of the Montreal Council for

Overseas Children. The plan, however, was short-lived. Two events brought the operation to a shuddering halt. In September 1940 the *Volendam*, which carried more than 300 CORB evacuees, was torpedoed. Only one Dutch naval officer was drowned while trying to lower the lifeboats and there was no other loss of life. However, only two weeks later the *City of Benares* was also torpedoed with a loss of more than seventy CORB children on their way to Canada. Ironically, two of the children lost on the *Benares* were *Volendam* survivors.

While British parents were saddened to see their sons and daughters leave home, Canada was certainly ready to welcome them. There were specifications and quotas consistent with the prejudices of the time to be dealt with. Many provinces wanted a majority of Protestant children while Quebec was willing to take up to 65 per cent Roman Catholic. Jewish children were not welcome although there were homes waiting for them and absolutely not a single "coloured" child was to be accepted. Foster parents in the plan were offered a tax break equal to $50 to $80 per child which was not offered to those in private arrangements. The medical and dental problems which arose were often taken care of by family doctors volunteering their services.

When the children arrived, they were met at the docks in Halifax and Montreal, and later at train stations along the way, with cheering crowds, candies, gifts and applause. Settling into their new homes, they had to adjust to a new way of life and a school system in which many of them seemed one or two years ahead of the other students. They were generally welcomed by Canadian children and teachers and tried to make the best of the separation from their families. The sad reality was that "the duration" meant that in their formative years these children were away for four or five years and memories of home began to fade as did their accents. Many became more attached to their Canadian families and never made a successful reintegration to their families after the war.

Adults old enough to remember Halloween during the war say that they never gave up the custom of going door-to-door and asking

Wartime colouring book.

for "Charity please!" Many remember not only getting pennies and apples but fudge and candy as well. Christmas presented a bigger challenge. Children still wrote letters to Santa—the *real* and *only* one at Eaton's—with their Christmas wish lists and went to see the Santa Claus Parade. After visiting Santa, they also enjoyed a ride on the Toyville Train, but these were the only constants in the war years. Even though many parents were making good money in war industries, the supply of toys was sparse due to the lack of metal and rubber. Those that were available had a war theme such as toy tanks, planes and ships for boys and dolls in Red Cross outfits for the girls. Books with a war theme, such as, *Wings Over England*, were especially popular with boys. There was also a colouring book entitled *Your Daddy and Mine* with pictures of men in all services pictured "in action". If a new doll were not available, many mothers could make doll clothes for the old one. Rag dolls could also be appreciated by very young children. Used toys would also be spruced up and clever fathers or grandfathers could make wooden toys like cars, and doll houses. Later in the war, toy companies manufactured toys made of plastic or wood.

The government encouraged the giving of War Savings Stamps in special Christmas envelopes. Irene Meikle remembers getting such a gift. "Our parents and grandparents would buy us Victory Bonds for Christmas and our birthdays. They might have been five-or ten-dollar Bonds. They were not big amounts because, at that time, rents on our street in N.D.G were about thirty-six dollars a month." Gifts for adults were also hard to get as war production pushed aside consumer goods like radios and toasters. Clothes were not uniformly available and jewellery was taxed almost out of reach. Parents thinking of setting out an idealized Victorian feast had to contend with the usual shortages of food and liquor. Turkey was hard, but not impossible, to get as most of the supply was sent to the armed forces. Christmas trees were plentiful and, for the thrifty-minded, could be had for as little as ten cents close to the big day. Montrealers planning a weekend holiday ski excursion to the Laurentians on the very popular *P'tit Train du Nord* would be disappointed when the service was banned in 1943 as an austerity measure.

While shortages could be managed, those suffering bereavement were under a heavy burden to carry on. As the war dragged on, casualties mounted and many sons, fathers, brothers, cousins and friends had been killed. Thousands were suffering in POW camps and those away at the front were a constant source of worry. Young children who could barely remember their fathers or who were born after he left for duty were a special concern. Religion helped to console and encourage and churches were packed with parishioners praying with perhaps more than the usual fervour. Most servicemen stationed in Montreal at Christmas were able to get leave to go home to their families. Those who couldn't, especially airmen from Europe, Australia or New Zealand, had no trouble being invited into private homes for the festivities as there was a surfeit of willing hosts. By late 1944, wounded men were being returned from Europe and filling local hospitals. Ogilvy's set up a Christmas tree and Montrealers were able to bring gifts to be distributed to these patients.

Much effort was spent in sending gifts to family members either living or serving overseas but this had to be done as early as late summer. Many downtown stores were happy to oblige. Ye Olde English Cheese on Stanley Street offered to send packages to "H.M. Forces and Civilians Overseas." The *Gazette* had a half-page ad for the Henry Morgan & Co. Limited on August 17, 1944 which showed a smiling serviceman sitting under a tree in the Middle East and enjoying his gift. "And Christmas parcels for our lads and lassies are something Morgan's Epicure Shop knows down to the last raisin in a fruit cake." The cheapest package, the Number 1, included 1 package Oxo cubes, 1 package hot chocolate, 1 tin sardines, 1 fruit cake, 1 tin pork and beans, ½ lb. toffee, 1 package soda biscuits, 1 writing pad and envelopes, and 1 package snack tabs. The total came to $3.25 including postage.

A deluxe edition, the Number 4, included many of the above items but chicken replaced the sardines and the following items were added: 1 tin Paris Pate, 1 tin Chox, 1 lb. Toffee, 1 Colgate's Kit, 1 playing cards, 1 pocket edition book. Contents and shipping came to $7.17. Packages for women serving overseas, "The Lassies", were available in Numbers 1 or 2. The more expensive Number 2 included 2 bars of face soap, 1 lipstick, 1 jar cold cream, 1 box face powder, 1 box dusting powder, 1 shampoo, 1 deodorant, 6 packages bouillon powder, 1 20-oz tin of chicken, 1 tin Paris Pate, 1 tin meat, 1 tin Chox, 1 fruit cake, 1 shortbread and 1 lb of toffee for a total cost of $8.22.

Christmas parcels for POWs were a special concern of Morgan's. They also had a list of suggested items for POW parcels to help the prisoners pass the long hours which included: Games (cards, cribbage boards and a variety of a dozen other games), Sports Equipment (ping pong sets, baseballs, running shoes, etc.), Educational Supplies (sketch books, pencils, paint boxes, note paper, etc.), Gramophone records and needles, books of selected authors "We have the approved list." Not to be outdone, on the same day Eaton's also had a huge ad telling people to send parcels for POWs "as soon after Sept. 1st as possible!" Eaton's warned its customers that thousands of parcels were damaged and delayed because of improper packing and "Remember that parcels shipped from Eaton's War Services depot meets all the specifications and have the best chance of safe arrival for Christmas."

When war was declared it was thought, as in World War I, that it would be over by Christmas. There were to be six wartime Christmases beginning in 1939 and, with each one, Montrealers could only hope wistfully.... "Maybe next year."

[CHAPTER SIX]

War Industries

The Canadian Army is a dagger pointed at the heart of Berlin.
–Lt. Gen. Andrew McNaughton

HOPING TO AVOID THE DIVISIVE problem of conscription, in 1939 Mackenzie King had agreed to allow Canada to be part of the massive and expensive Commonwealth Air Training Plan that would train Allied pilots in Canada. As European countries fell like dominos to Hitler's divisions, it became obvious that this would not be enough. Canada would need not only very sharp daggers but also aircraft, ships, tanks and weapons of all types. With the creation of the Department of Munitions and Supply in 1940 the country was to change from being an exporter of raw materials to an industrial powerhouse. The government had to build production plants and oversee a newly-trained force of workers while controlling wages and managing labour disputes. Not only did Canada supply its own forces, it sent war materials to other Allied countries like Britain and Russia. Britain was in a particularly dire situation because of the loss of 75,000 military vehicles (out of a total of 80,000 with which it had entered the war) abandoned at Dunkirk in 1940. Nearly 40 per cent of Canadian tank production was to go to the British.

With its factories safe from bombing attacks, Canada became, as Mackenzie King had promised, the arsenal of the Allies. The total value of Canada's wartime production was nearly $10 billion which, in today's money would be $100 billion. Out of a total population of 11.3 million, 1,049,876 Canadians worked in war industries with more than two million more working full time in essential services such as farming, communications and food processing.

Unemployment was to virtually disappear in a country just staggering out of a bleak Depression. The amount of Canadian war production was enormous. According to Canadian War Museum figures, the list included: 815,000 military vehicles, 50,000 tanks and armoured gun carriers, 9,000 boats and ships, 43,000 heavy guns, 16,000 aircraft (10,000 of which were sent directly to Britain), 1,700,000 small arms, 2 million tonnes of explosives, anti-tank and field artillery, naval guns, small arms and automatic weapons, radar sets and electronics, synthetic rubber and uranium for the Manhattan Project. By 1945, Canada's war production was fourth among the Allied nations. Canada lent money interest-free to Britain and gave it a gift of war supplies in 1942 as well as donating war surplus production to the Allies through the Canadian Mutual Aid Board.

The man in charge of this massive output was the powerful, dynamic and efficient C.D. Howe, the head of the Department of Munitions and Supply. A graduate engineer from Massachusetts, he came to Nova Scotia as a young man to teach at Dalhousie University and later became wealthy running his own construction business. He served continuously from 1935 to 1957 under both Mackenzie King and Louis St. Laurent and was responsible for the industrialization of the Canadian economy. During the war, his department created twenty-eight Crown corporations and coordinated all purchases made in Canada by Allied governments for military materials. Under Howe's leadership and with his ability to attract competent "dollar-a-year men", even tiny businesses such as bicycle shops were transformed into makers of armaments.

Quebec and Ontario, the two major industrial centres, benefited from wartime contracts but Montreal, Canada's largest city and the transportation hub of the country, was particularly well-placed to take on the challenge. Much of wartime aircraft construction took place in Montreal. Noorduyn Aircraft of Ville St. Laurent manufactured Harvard trainers for the RCAF, Mosquito fighter bombers as well as the famous Noorduyn Norseman. By 1943, its 12,000 workers in five factories were completing more than three planes a day. Fairchild Aircraft which was based in Longueuil had 7,000 employees. They produced Bristol and Bolingbroke bombers as well as Cornells and Helldivers for the Americans. Pratt and Whitney, also in Longueuil, made aircraft engines for all types of planes from Catalina flying boats to Harvard trainers. They also became involved in manufacturing by opening Canadian Propeller Ltd. Canadian Car and Foundry produced airplane propellers and wings for Ansons and Hurricanes as well as large-calibre shells.

At Canadian Vickers, an aircraft and shipbuilding company on Notre Dame Street East in the Maisonneuve district, they were busy building corvettes, frigates, freighters and minesweepers for the navy and merchant marine. Their industrial wing produced steam engines, boilers and steam generators. In 1941 the government awarded Vickers the contract to build PBV-1 "Canso" amphibians (a version of the Consolidated PBY Catalina flying boat). A new manufacturing facility to produce the Canso was built at Cartierville Airport in Ville St. Laurent and Vickers managed this plant for the government until 1944 when it decided to concentrate on ship production. Ottawa then signed a deal with the new Canadair Limited, whose executives were former Vickers employees, to continue aircraft design and production. United Shipyards, located in Old Montreal where the Bickerdike Pier is today, produced ten-thousand ton freighters as well as landing craft. Montreal Drydocks Limited produced Norton-Class tugs as well as diesel barges and ammunition lighters.

The Canadian Pacific Railway (CPR) Angus shops in the east end of Montreal produced the Valentine tank, so called, some say, because it was approved on February 14, 1940. The workforce at Angus numbered 3,500 and they produced 1,420 tanks costing $90,000 each. Forty thousand parts were required for each of these tanks whose top speed was 25 mph. All but thirty of the tanks produced in Montreal went to the Russians.

The Montreal Locomotive Works produced Ram and Sexton tanks as well as engines for the navy.

Defence Industries Limited (DIL) was a subsidiary of CIL which, by 1943 employed 32,500 people across Canada. The Verdun facility alone employed nearly 7,000 workers. There were plants in and around Montreal. The facilities in the north-central area of Villeray, Verdun and Brownsburg, north of Montreal, produced small-arms ammunition. The factories in St. Paul l'Hermite and St. Thérèse filled shells while Shawinigan and Beloeil produced explosives.

Dominion Textiles employed thousands of workers in the production of fabric for uniforms and cloth for items from tents to surgical dressings. Clothing factories turned out uniforms by the thousands. RCA Victor, Northern Electric, Merck Chemical, General Steel Wares Ltd. and the National Railways Munitions Ltd. produced everything from portable radios and transmitters to penicillin and naval guns. While enjoying decent salaries and happy to be productive again, increased income tax rates and taxes on many consumer goods somewhat dimmed the euphoria of workers who now had to pay more for everything from radios to movie tickets. Many accepted this new burden with patriotic tolerance while government appeals for understanding attempted to convince the balkers.

Small companies were often given a share of war contracts. One of them was the Martin Kiely Company Limited of Griffintown. A family-owned machine shop that had produced shells in World War I, it suffered, as many businesses did, during the Depression but survived to take on war contracts in 1939. James Kiely, in his 1984 oral history of the company recalls the war years. "In 1939, of course, the war broke out and we had to assume more war work. In this period we ran two shifts. I was acting as general foreman but had a sub foreman under me. I was called frequently during the night and slept with the telephone beside my bed during the whole period. There were always problems coming up.

"We were doing a lot of work for the merchant marine, heavy castings, steel plates, etc. which we were machining. This work was very good and we became accustomed for it. We had to jig up for the work and did, I think, a very credible job. The other part of the naval program consisted of the Chadbourne Telegraph System. It was the communication device between the bridge of the ship and the engine room. It consisted of a series of heavy tubing and bronze castings used to turn the tubing and run the enunciators on the bridge and in the engine room. All of this was fairly precise work and we made thousands of these parts. We also did some work for the aircraft companies but it consisted of mostly aluminum, cutting and moulding of pieces to be fitted into some part of the aircraft. It was precise and it was annoying. We didn't particularly like it nor did we make much money at it.

"Incidentally, it must be remembered that all the prices on these things were fixed. There was no question, at least on our level, of profiteering. At the same time, the men's salaries were fixed, too. You were assigned to a shop and if you were acceptable and could do the work you remained there."

Another small company with an interesting history was Wartime Services Limited, a machine tool repair shop. A Crown corporation, it gave work to more than one hundred German and Austrian men from internment camps who had tool-making skills. These men had been rounded up as suspected Nazis in Britain and sent to Canada. They were, in fact, fleeing from Fascism and would see their status change from "enemy aliens" to "friendly aliens" and, finally, to "refugees". Located in two factory halls in Ville LaSalle near Seagram's Distillery, Alan Bronfman treated these men as Seagram's employees and arranged for them to buy reasonably-priced meals at his cafeteria. These released refugees ran the business under the supervision of one army captain. In 1945 Helmut Pokorny, the supervisor, went into partnership with the French-Canadian manager with whom he had worked. What started out as a three-man operation making die casting machines grew to number 400 men by the time Pokorny retired in 1970.

While the war lasted, these industries offered a good living for many family men. Don Pidgeon remembers: "My dad worked for Norduyn, an armaments factory which was up in Ville St. Laurent. He worked very long hours and sometimes did double shifts. He was a butcher by trade but, with four children and a wife, working at Noorduyn meant a better living for all of us. After the war he went back to butchering." Howard Dearlove: "My dad had a milk route, a car and a property. He lost it all during the Depression and was out of work for two years. He managed, somehow or other and we were able to stay in the same house. Don't ask me how he did it. I was too young to realize everything. During the war, my dad got a job at Canadian Propeller. He made the washers for the propellers. After the war, my dad suffered again. All the boys came back from overseas so he was out of work again and he did everything—drove a taxi, slung beef and all different kinds of work. He was born in 1892 so he was older then, too."

During the Depression there was little home construction in Canada and after 1939 the situation continued with the dearth of building materials and manpower. This led to an acute housing shortage which lasted for years. With construction of war industries taking precedence over building homes for wage earners, Canadians were told to "double up". This was easier said than done. It is estimated that 85 per cent of Montrealers were tenants during the war years. Some areas, like Westmount and Outremont, had a fairly high home-ownership rate but in Verdun the percentage of tenants was over 90 per cent.

The duplex and triplex style of housing, with the owner generally living in the bottom flat while renting out the upstairs unit(s), was unique to the city. While families might take in other family members, it was more difficult for a single worker and almost imposible for families to find a place to board. The more than 250,000 war industry workers who crammed into a city with an almost zero vacancy rate were desperate to find accommodation.

The Toronto situation was eased somewhat by the fact that many war industries were located in outlying suburbs, but Montreal's major employers were in the city or within easy commuting distance.The City Improvement League stated that 51,000 new dwellings were desperately immediately. This, of course, did not happen. Workers with an annual income of about $1,200 were prepared to pay $25 a month rent, which was considered average. But where were they to find places to live?

Wartime Housing Limited (WHL) was created in February 1941 to address this problem and 4,172 emergency wartime houses were built in Quebec. Those in Ville St. Laurent were built for the workers at Canadair. There were similar projects in Snowdon and Montreal East. Originally intended to be torn down after the war, with the materials being salvaged, the post-war housing shortage gave them new life. Small and serviceable, they were erected on cedar piles, had space heaters and rented for $22 to $30 a month. After the war, many tenants bought these houses for under $3,000 and immediately went to work using their "do-it-yourself" skills to make them more liveable. The first thing most of them did was to dig out a basement, just in time for the "rec" room era in the 1950s. They added bedrooms, updated kitchens, enlarged living spaces, added garages, changed the façade and, today, these houses are hardly recognizable from the basic units they were. "Mudville" was the name given at first to the Ville St. Laurent project as new tenants coped with wooden sidewalks and runny ditches. The appeal of these houses was that each family had a backyard and private space, unlike the cramped neighbourhoods of duplexes and triplexes. Returning soldiers were also offered a chance to buy these houses. With war workers or veterans, these homes proved popular and many owners stayed and raised families in them.

While the WHL plan was a good one, it did not nearly begin to ease the housing requirements of the city, which meant that many workers were left to live in third-world conditions, often in hovels with no proper bathrooms.

At the beginning of the work week in March 1943, Montrealers could not get to work, go to a movie, visit a sick relative or go shopping due to the tramway strike. There were not too many cars on the road at that time and those that were still running were much in demand. With the streetcar and bus strike, walking or hitchhiking (always easier for young, attractive ladies) was the order of the day. Some companies arranged bus and truck pickups at central points to enable their workers to come in. Bicycles were another way to get around. The *Gazette* reported: "Homeward-bound on Dorchester west, a well-dressed gentleman of about 50—complete with homburg and cane—pedalled sedately on a brand-new bicycle, so new, in fact, that the sales tag was still attached to the handlebars across which the executive-looking gentleman had carefully placed his cane." Another adventurous spirit hitched three dogs to a buggy and drove in from Montreal North to get to work at the Pepsi-Cola Company.

What Montreal did not need was an illegal transit strike right in the middle of the war and in the snowy month of March, since war industries absolutely depended on workers being able to get to work. The strike at the Montreal Tramways Commission (MTC) lasted just forty-eight hours. It was a dispute over which union would represent the workers. An affiliate of the American Federation of Labour had an understanding with the MTC but there was competition from the popular Canadian Brotherhood of Railway Employees.

Some had no patience with this disruption in service and wanted the War Measures Act imposed suggesting that perhaps a few armed veterans would hurry the solution along and get the men back to work. Ottawa solved the problem by flying in labour lawyer H. Carl Goldenberg who solved the dispute overnight by applying a band-aid solution to get the economy moving again. The CBRE was declared the victor because, as Goldberg said, "In a democracy, the will of the majority must prevail". The subject of wages was not dealt with and, in December of the same year, Montreal was to experience another transit strike that lasted eleven days. These strikes were occurences in a year that seemed biblical in retrospect. There were cold waves, record snowfalls and epidemics of flu and scarlet fever, which sometimes closed a number of schools.

The Montreal Tramways strike was only one of many during the war. In 1942-43 workers walked at Vickers, Fairchild Aircraft, Noorduyn the Angus shops and Canadair. It was not only war-industry workers who were unhappy. Factory workers, distillery workers, bank tellers, shipyard workers, police, firemen and blue-collar workers all had grievances. Some were unhappy with wage freezes, higher taxes (both on income and goods) and the mobility restrictions of the NSS. Montreal workers resented the fact that wages were higher in Ontario. Absenteeism rose when employees realized that overtime pay would be eaten away by taxes. They were also, encouraged, cajoled, "guilted" and sometimes even bullied into buying War Bonds and contributing to other wartime charities, which cut into their net income.

It is strange to realize that with full employment and good salaries, there was so much labour unrest in all parts of Canada during the war. This reached a peak in 1943 when one out of every three trade union members was involved in strikes. On the face of it, it doesn't appear that workers had much to complain about. Between 1939 and 1943, the average salary rose from $956 to $1,525 so that, even with higher taxes, workers enjoyed a high standard of living and many were able to propel themselves into the middle class. The antagonism between labour and business was caused by wage controls and the deficiencies of the 1907 Industrial Disputes Investigation Act which did not compel union recognition and only asked for a "cooling off" period before a strike while compulsory negotiations took place with labour, business and government representatives. The unions demanded collective bargaining not only to raise wages but to improve working conditions and gain status for union members to participate in decision making. The labour shortage provided the unions with a good bargaining position, which they didn't have during the Depression, and membership more than doubled during the war. This increased union activity led to many confrontations. In 1941 in Arvida, a wildcat strike by 10,000 workers at the Aluminum Company of Canada led to the occupation of the plant and troops were sent in. The workers did not back down and won a pay raise along with increased rights to speak French on the job. There were also strikes at National Steel Car in Hamilton and at Kirkland Lake mines. It was only in 1944 that Mackenzie King provided a legal mechanism for union recognition and between February 1944 and March 1945 the new Wartime Relations Board certified 133 new union locals.

These strikes did not sit well with the public who thought that striking during wartime was self-serving and unpatriotic. It was also thought to lower the morale of Canadian fighting men who—sitting in a trench, doing convoy duty or scrambling for another mission—did not have the same option. There were some who considered that strike action was fomented by enemy agents.

The number of working women in Canada doubled during the war from 600,000 to 1,200,000. They worked not only in the traditional occupations such as teaching, nursing and office work, but rolled up their sleeves, donned turbans and became riveters, ammunition workers, drivers, mechanics and aircraft assemblers. Over 30,000 worked in factories doing "men's jobs". One became a pioneer. Elsie Gregory McGill, the world's first female aircraft designer from British Columbia started work at Fairchild Aviation in Longueuil but in 1938 moved to Fort William, Ontario to became the chief aeronautical engineer at Canadian Car and Foundry. In the two years 1943-44, the number of women working in the service sector was 439,000. The manufacturing sector had the second largest number with 373,000 while 4,000 worked in construction. They had the heady feeling of earning a good salary and contributing in a very real way to victory. While their salaries might have been good, they did not equal what men were making. During the war, men saw average annual salaries increase from $1,055 to $1,761. Women in certain industries, such as aircraft production, did quite well but the average salary for women only increased from $594 to $1,051. As well as being paid less than men doing the same work, they often had to tolerate disrespectful behaviour from their male co-workers. They worked to help the war effort, to augment the family income or merely to avoid boredom. Married women had to combine working with normal home responsibilities which, if their husbands were overseas, often included mastering new skills like plumbing repairs, painting and handling finances for the first time. In Quebec, they had to contend with the Church's disapproval of women working outside the home which, it believed, would have dire consequences for family life and might cause grave harm to children. Catholic unions and the Catholic Women's League of Canada joined the chorus and, as a result, married women and mothers in Quebec were underrepresented in the workforce. It was not only Quebec that frowned on married women working. Across Canada, women's place was generally thought to be in the home.

The problem of daycare for young children was addressed in June 1942 when the government created the Dominion-Provincial Wartime Day Nursery Program involving Ontario and Quebec, the major centres of war industry, that would provide care for children aged two to five. School-age children up to sixteen would be supervised at lunchtime and after school. The provinces shared the cost of day-care facilities. The lack of day care meant that working mothers often had a high absentee rate. Quebec was suspicious of these government day care centres and only six were opened in Quebec while Ontario had twenty-eight. The spaces available didn't come close to meeting the needs and the care of children generally fell to family members or community volunteers. Desperate mothers sometimes left their children poorly supervised and were blamed for the rise in juvenile delinquency rates.

Lucille "Lou" Pacaud's job did not come to an end after the war. She had a long career at Dominion Textiles, only retiring in 1983 after forty years of service. She describes her wartime experience: "Dominion Textiles made material for the armed forces and one of my jobs was to keep track of the greige material. We would tell the government how many yards would be available to them. There was a room that had many telephone lines to the different departments of the military in Ottawa and that impressed me very much. They would tell us how many yards they needed of each colour and then it would go through the dying process."

The prospect of finding a job brought Rita Melanson to Montreal from Campbellton, New Brunswick in 1942. "My sister and my dad were already in Montreal and Dad (who was working as a blacksmith for Wonder Bread) sent me the fare to come up here. I was seventeen years old and had tried to join the service when I was sixteen. They told me to go home, that I was too young to join anything. Coming in from New Brunswick for a city job—that was something! We all lived in a boarding house in the east end near Adam Street. My sister was working in a war plant and she told me that it was a good job so that's where I went. I told them I was eighteen and I got the job right away because they needed people. It was an ammunition factory run by C.I.L. at St. Paul l'Hermite. I took the train to work every day. It was a two-car special train for the employees; one car for the men and the other for the girls. It left from the east end so I could walk to the train. There were three shifts. I hated the 3-to-11 shift because your afternoon was gone and so was your evening. The pay was 70 cents an hour. When I became a supervisor I think I got 80-85 cents. How did I get to be supervisor? Well, I could speak English and French and my foreman was French. (laughs)

"I worked in high explosives. My sister didn't want me to work in that section but I liked it. It was a big, big outfit which was fenced in. There were different sections and we called each section by a badge colour—"blue badge", "red badge" and "yellow badge". The "blue badges" were high explosives and we worked in a building closest to the gate. My sister worked further away in the "yellow badges". When you arrived, they checked to make sure you had your badge and then you had to go to a special room, take off your street clothes, hang them up and put on a blue uniform and a bandana which covered all your hair. We also had to wear heavy brown shoes that wouldn't make sparks. Then we had to go through a second gate. There were two women there and they would say, 'You, you.... Go to the.....' It was a little house on the side like a guard house. Those who were picked would be searched. If you had cigarettes, lighters, matches, things like that, they would take them off you. If you were caught in the workplace with anything like that, you had to go to the courthouse in Joliette to pay a fine. There were many who paid a fine. They would also come to the door while we were working and ask for two or three women to go and be frisked.

"The powder for the ammunition is so fine that it flies all over the place. We had men to clean the pipes and we had to make sure that we didn't make sparks on the wooden floor. When I had to go and get the powder in the powder room, I walked with a thick leather case with two handles on it. A girl would walk ahead of me holding a red flag. Nobody could touch me. *Nobody!* When we got there, a man would put the powder in the little box, put it back in my leather case and I would follow the same girl back to my department.

"I was never in an accident but there were a lot I've seen and heard about. The girls who worked on the detonators would sometimes touch a hot dish and burn their hands a little and we'd send them to the nurse. We were never allowed to put the powder into just anything. If there was any left over, we had to drop it very, very slowly into a special pail with oil. One man didn't do his homework. He would put the leftover powder in the sink. One morning when I came in someone said, 'Hi Rita. Did you hear what happened last night? One man who worked in the powder room was washing his hands after his shift and the sink blew in his face and he died.' Another man was with him. He didn't get hurt but he went absolutely out of his mind to see his friend with practically no face. He had a nervous breakdown and couldn't work anymore. We had big dryers with shelves where we put the detonators to dry. There was a man who was taking care of the temperature dial and he put the heat up too high and it exploded and he got killed. I heard it was a mess—his hair was on the wall—it was a mess. Many people were killed but I don't know how many. I also heard (I don't know if it's true or not) that a young girl lit a cigarette in the toilet and caught fire. She started to scream and scream and scream but they had to hold the door closed because, if she got out, she would have run all over the place. They had to leave her there and she died. Everybody was talking about it when I got to work. The shock wears off when things like that happen.

"I worked there for three years, eight days, four hours and fifteen minutes. I don't know why I counted the time like that. I left on August 29, 1945. I was never scared working there. If it's going to happen, it's going to happen."

Women working in a Montreal munitions plant.
Library and Archives Canada.

"Jo" started working in the same factory as Rita Melanson and has similar memories but had to quit and find another job. "When the war started I wanted to join the army but they told me to go home and grow up. So I went to work at the Royal Victoria Hospital. I didn't stay long because then I got a job in a munitions factory in St. Paul l'Hermite. I took a train down to Montreal East to get there. There were a lot of women working there. The men were mostly the higher-ups. There were very few young men working there. It was a good job but very dangerous. I only stayed there for six months because the powder they used made me break out in hives. I'm allergic to milk and you had to drink milk if you worked there because of the poison. I had to get a doctor's paper to quit that job.

"My next job was working as a riveter and fitter for Fairchild's (Fairchild Aircraft Ltd.). The pay was 90 cents an hour. The men got paid more for the same job. They always did and they always will! Fairchild's built planes and they were in Longueuil. We travelled by train from St. Henri Station. I was only five feet tall so they made me a bench to stand on. Our department made the ailerons and gun turrets. Sometimes I had to drill the holes before I put in the rivets and sometimes I just did the riveting. It wasn't hard physical work. Different-sized rivets needed different-sized dollies and you would just put them in the gun. I was there for three years and enjoyed it. I didn't save any money because I had two kid sisters and I used to spend a lot of money on them.

"I never went out during the week. I got up a five o'clock and started work at eight. We finished at about 4:30 and it was after seven by the time I got home. I was very happy when the war ended but not happy when I lost my job. About a couple of thousand of us were laid off in one day. My next job was at Morgan's and I didn't ask about the pay. When I got my first pay which was $11 a week I said, 'Hey, I paid that in income tax in my last job!'"

Wars, as terrible as they are, often leave a legacy that improves living conditions and advances scientific knowledge. While workers were busy producing the materials of war, scientists were at work improving those weapons as well as doing research in food preservation and medicine. The research done by Canadian scientists through The National Research Council, Crown corporations and the armed forces led to many innovations. Designing Arctic clothing for the military led to the invention of artificial fur. The use of nylon for parachutes was developed by the National Research Council. The Council was also responsible for inventing processes to manufacture powdered eggs, milk and preserved bacon. Originally intended to ease the food shortage in Britain by aiding food transportation, some of the condensed and powdered foods are still used today. Modern winter air travel is made safer by the wartime development of electro-thermal de-icers for aircraft propellers.

Research on magnetism to learn how to "degauss" (demagnetize) ships to protect them from certain types of mines and to detect submerged submarines led to the ability to detect bodies of ore from the air for mining purposes. Many ships were saved by the Canadian Anti-Acoustic Torpedo (CAT) gear which was used as a counter measure to enemy acoustic torpedoes. To protect ships' hulls against salt-water corrosion, a technique of cathodic protection was developed during the war and is still used today, saving millions of dollars in ship damage. Anti-fog windshield liquids developed for transport vehicles were also a Canadian invention.

The rubber shortage that caused such deprivation for civilians would be eased by the end of the war with the development of a synthetic product that was 90 per cent made from wheat derivatives. An all- synthetic rubber product was not invented until after the war and Canada played a leading role in its development. Nuclear energy research in Montreal led to the development of the Chalk River atomic energy facilities and the eventual development of the CANDU nuclear power generator by the Atomic Energy Commission.

George J. Klein, was one of Canada's most productive inventors. Born in Hamilton, Ontario, he worked for forty years as a mechanical engineer at the National Research Council laboratories in Ottawa. During the war he developed aiming systems for artillery and anti-submarine mortars as well as a technique to test and quantify snow conditions. He conducted research on high velocity projectiles and their fuses and developed an anti-roll stabilizer for an anti-submarine weapon. Among his many later inventions were the electric wheelchair for quadriplegics and the microsurgical staple gun. In 1995 he was inducted into the Canadian Science and Engineering Hall of Fame.

In microwave radar development Canadian scientists developed the plan position indicator which is still used today. Canada provided to the Allies 9,000 radar sets worth hundreds of millions of dollars. Many Canadian radar personnel worked on British warships. Medical breakthroughs were no less impressive. Mass production of penicillin became a reality and work done by Dr. C.H. Best of the University of Toronto made blood serum available. Studies on seasickness and motion sickness led to drugs being developed to help the symptoms. Research on night vision led to red lightning being used by the Royal Canadian Navy, the Royal Navy and for some aircraft of the United States Navy. The Banting Institute built the first decompression chamber in North America, invented the "Anti-G-suit" (still used by pilots of some aircraft) and built a human centrifuge. They also made improvements to aircrew equipment like oxygen masks and conducted research into the effects of cold and fatigue.

These stellar achievements of Canadian scientists were made by men often as young as those fighting overseas. In 1944 and 1945, the average age of the three hundred men working on radar research at the National Research Council was twenty-six.

[CHAPTER SEVEN]

Montreal
A Helluva Town

QUEBEC WAS THE MOST RELUCTANT province to join the Prohibition movement in Canada. Its brief flirtation with the banning of alcohol was implemented in 1919 and repealed in 1921 due to public protest. In the United States, however, Prohibition (1920-1933) was a national movement that spawned a great increase in criminal behaviour and makeshift measures to skirt its restrictions. Montreal soon became the destination of choice for thirsty North Americans who flocked to the city in great numbers not only for the legal booze and great entertainment but also for gambling and prostitution. Montreal became known as Sin City and lived up to its title with typical *joie de vivre.* There were many after-hours drinking spots and closing hours in regular bars could also be quite elastic. If a club had to close on Sunday—not a problem—the management would be happy to provide a show at a minute past midnight on Monday morning. While horse racing was legal and very popular, the city had about two hundred illegal gambling dens that offered craps, roulette, blackjack, chemin de fer and the popular dice game of *barbotte,* a Montreal specialty. In some places, patrons could also bet on sporting events and horse races. These establishments ranged from the grand to the grotty and were patronized by everyone from doctors to dockworkers. One particularly plush one was Harry Ship's casino on Côte St. Luc Road, which also offered excellent food and fine whiskey to its upper-crust denizens. To appease the disapproving public, the police would occasionally conduct staged raids. The raids followed a set pattern. The police would thunder in, seize a telephone or some other piece of "evidence" and then affix a padlock to a door—any door—a bathroom or cupboard door would do. Fines would then be paid by the owner, or his fall guy, and, within hours, it was back to business as usual. The fines contributed to the city's bottom line and the thousands of dollars made in payoffs every week to police and municipal officials kept almost everyone happy.

Montreal's entertainment heyday, generally considered to have been between the mid 1920s to the mid 1950s, offered wonderful diversion for locals and visitors to the city. American "headliners" like Frank Sinatra, Dean Martin and Jerry Lewis, Red Skelton, Milton Berle and Sammy Davis Jr. regularly came to town. French audiences could enjoy *vedettes* like Charles Trenet, Edith Piaf, and Charles Aznavour. While establishments changed and adapted to shifting tastes and economic realities, during the war years there were hundreds of taverns, clubs, lounges, bars, cafés, theatres and restaurants that catered to all layers of society and where one was guaranteed a good time. The night club scene included clubs and lounges that only served drinks. Others offered fine dining, dancing, floorshows and superb entertainment provided by local musicians and dancers as well as imported acts that played the North American and Europe circuit. These acts ranged from soon-forgotten performers from New York to entertainment icons like Sophie Tucker, "The Last of the Red Hot Mamas", who was a popular visitor to Montreal from the vaudeville days at Loew's until her final appearance at the El Morocco in 1963. Radio was in its golden age—listeners at home could hear the latest dance bands and variety shows beamed live from local hotels like the Mount Royal's Normandie Roof and hotels and studios in other major cities. Montrealers could also tune in to Guy Lombardo and His Royal Canadians, who played for years at the Roosevelt Grill in the Roosevelt Hotel in New York City. The Waldorf Astoria was another New York hotel that beamed out the big band sound to war-weary Montrealers.

There were three major downtown areas of the city which provided entertainment for all tastes. The black community district of Little Burgundy was home to Rockhead's Paradise, a club at the corner of St. Antoine and Mountain, owned by the personable

Rufus Rockhead, a former railway porter and liquor smuggler. It became famous for its first-rate black entertainers, many of whom were from New York's Harlem district, and house bands that provided music for dancing. Café St. Michel, a jazz hot spot, was just across the street at 770 Mountain Street and Duke Ellington and Oscar Peterson were frequent visitors to this legendary club. The Terminal Club on St. Antoine opposite Windsor Station featured black entertainers and became an after-hours jamming venue for musicians. The Alberta Lounge near Windsor Station completed the list of what were known as the "downtown clubs" that provided black entertainment but welcomed a mixed audience.

Many of the "east end" clubs were mainly centred in the red-light district around St. Lawrence Boulevard and St. Catherine Street. Connie's Inn, at 1417 St. Lawrence above St. Catherine was billed as "Featuring the highest calibre of colored divertissement direct from the World Famous Harlem". Connie's Inn, the Montmartre, at 59 St. Catherine just west of St. Lawrence, and Club Hollywood were typical of east end clubs in that they featured black entertainers who played to white audiences and often had a French clientele. Further east was the Lion d'Or on Ontario East at Papineau. A cabaret, it featured local and visiting entertainers. Today, it looks much as it did when it opened in 1930 and is used for special events.

The "uptown" clubs and theatres were in the area now known as "downtown". Most were on or near St. Catherine Street in an area stretching from Atwater to Bleury. The Top Hat Café across from Eaton's and the Maroon Club across from Simpson's were just two of the many places to celebrate. Others were the Samovar on Peel, the Copacabana, the Savoy, the small and always crowded Clover Café, the posh 400 Cocktail Lounge on Drummond and the Esquire on Stanley, which opened in 1940 as an unlicensed supper and dance club and quickly became popular with servicemen and their dates. Sharing the west side of Stanley Street with the Esquire was Club Lido, a leading supper club with an Art Deco exterior, elegant decor, top-rated floorshows and fine food. On the ground

Ruth and Andrew Stevenson at the Normandie Roof, 1940.
Courtesy of Ruth Stevenson.

floor of the same building was the Tic Toc Club offering dinner and two shows nightly. The Palais d'Or just down the street was another lively and popular dance spot offering the Big Band and Dixieland Jazz sound. The Auditorium was a licensed dancehall on Ontario near Bleury that would become the site of the Bellevue Casino in the late forties. Although racial discrimination was not as blatant in Montreal as in some other cities, the uptown clubs catered to white audiences and generally featured white performers.

Chez Maurice was a popular club at an upstairs location at 1244 St. Catherine near Mountain. Offering dinner, dancing and three floorshows nightly, it became the unlicensed Chez Maurice Danceland during the war as the number of licensed clubs was reduced. Meals and floorshows were a thing of the past and gone was the long list of cocktails and mixed drinks. Instead, customers often brought their own liquor in flasks. Eager teenagers were

The Normandie Roof atop the Mount Royal Hotel 1937.
Joe Bell Scrapbook. Concordia University Archives.

welcome and jived to American bands led by Jimmy Dorsey, Duke Ellington and Cab Calloway with his trademark phrase, "Hi-de-hi-de-hi-de-ho". Hungry dancers could always pop downstairs to Dinty Moore's Restaurant which was located in the same building. Noted for its corned beef and cabbage, it was named after the comic strip "Bringing up Father", which recounted the ups and downs in the life of Maggie and Jiggs, a *nouveau riche* Irish-American family.

The Normandie Roof on the top of the Mount Royal Hotel on Peel Street was the destination of choice for many revellers. In a setting reminiscent of a Hollywood movie set, it featured fine dining as well as dancing and entertainment. Ruth Swinton Stevenson remembers it fondly: "The Normandie Roof in the Mount Royal Hotel was very expensive. My husband and I didn't go very often but sometimes we figured that we might as well eat, drink and be merry. The meals were very good but I think many people also went for the drinks. They had a full-sized orchestra for dancing and we thought it was wonderful, although I didn't have much to compare it with."

The Piccadilly Lounge, "the Pic", on the ground floor of the same hotel was a popular bar for airmen and also for the dashing, daring and extremely well-paid civilian pilots of Ferry Command who at first flew out of St. Hubert Airport until Dorval opened in 1941. For many upper- and middle-class girls, the Pic was rated one of the better hangouts and to snag a date with one of these heroes was considered a real social plus. For young ladies who wanted to dance with their new friends, the Music Box in the lower level of the hotel was the place to go as, unlike the "Pic", it offered dance music.

The Ritz Café in the Ritz-Carlton Hotel on Sherbrooke Street was probably the most prestigious spot of all and was known as a place for the moneyed classes to unwind. Regular folk on a budget knew that they would always be welcomed and have a good time at the more reasonable Berkeley Hotel which was down the street near Drummond. The El Morocco at 1410 Metcalfe and St. Catherine was considered one of the best clubs in Montreal with fine dining, dancing and floorshows.

The theatre scene was also lively. His Majesty's Theatre on Guy Street was a venue for the best in live theatre and musical performances. Some of the most famous performers of the time like Helen Hayes, Alexander Woollcott and Tallulah Bankhead played there until it was demolished in 1963 to be replaced by Place des Arts. The grand chandelier which once graced the 1,750-seat theatre can now be seen on the main floor of Ogilvy's department store. The Stork Club, just north of the theatre, boasted a long bar and dancing with a band but no floorshows. It was a popular after-theatre destination for those who had just seen an opera, concert, ballet or recital. The Monument National, built by the St. Jean Baptiste Society as their headquarters and opened in 1893, was intended to present a showcase of French-Canadian progress and talent but, due to financial considerations, it became necessary to rent the space to other groups. It became a multicultural venue for plays and concerts not only in French but English and Yiddish as well. Irish Montrealers were also involved and St. Ann's Parish in Griffintown always managed to fill the hall with their annual St. Patrick's concert. It was one of the theatres where the internationally-famous singer and recording star, Alys Robi from Quebec City, often performed.

Close to many nightclubs, the Chic'n Coop Restaurant was located on St. Catherine between Drummond and Stanley in the former Montreal home of Thomas D'Arcy McGee, one of the Fathers of Confederation. It was a major attraction for shoppers and office workers during the day and a late-night gathering place for prominent entertainers passing through Montreal. The Indian Room upstairs was a dining and dancing place and decorated with paintings of the Blackfoot nation.

There were many great restaurants operating at that time with their chefs creatively trying to maintain standards with wartime rationing. Among them were Café Martin on Mountain, considered by many to be the best, Chez Stein, Aux Delices, Chez Son Père among others. It was not uncommon for busboys and waitresses to offer their unused liquor coupons to restaurant owners so thirsty clients could be accommodated.

Another big wartime attraction were the dances held every Saturday night at Victoria Hall in Westmount which, for many young people, was just a short ride away on Sherbrooke Street's Number 3 streetcar. For the young girls at the time, not being invited to the dance at Victoria Hall on Saturday night was a painful social slight. The Johnny Holmes Orchestra featured singers like Wally Aspell and Lorraine McAllister with the soon-to-be-famous Oscar Peterson on piano. What many remember is that Peterson would often play on alone after the dance ended while young people gathered around the stage to listen in awe to music they thought was "fantastic". It was unusual for a black musician to play with a white band and when Holmes was booked to play at a dance at the Ritz-Carlton Hotel, the manager informed him that Peterson was not wanted. Bravely, Holmes stood his ground and told the manager that advertisements would be placed in the city's English

The Johnny Homes Orchestra on stage at Victoria, Hall, 1943.
News Pictures of Canada, Johnny Holmes Fonds.
Concordia University Archives.

newspaper advising the public that the Johnny Holmes Orchestra would never again play at the Ritz because of their racist stance. The manager caved in and Peterson was prominently featured by Holmes the night of the dance. Maynard Ferguson, a trumpet player from Verdun, also played with the band before he formed his own orchestra at the tender age of sixteen and moved on to play at the Verdun Pavilion. Ferguson eventually left Canada and had an outstanding career as a jazz musician in England and the United States. Dances at the downtown YMCA and YWCA were also popular and, during the war, welcomed all branches of the service.

The Gayety, on the southeast corner of St. Catherine and St. Urbain, was a burlesque theatre that became famous with the arrival of Lili St. Cyr in 1944. Her voluptuous figure and blonde Nordic beauty made her a household name and helped put Montreal on the map. In her heyday, between 1944 and 1951 she was the bane of the Morality Squad and the Catholic clergy which, at the time, disapproved even of social dancing. A Jesuit priest, in a vitriolic attack on her, said that whenever she plays "the theatre is made to stink with the foul odour of sexual frenzy". Middle-class women might admire her stunning beauty but her life was so far removed from their own that she was merely a curiosity to them. Those who did attend her performances were very often impressed and did not seem overly shocked. She never completely disrobed and sometimes even did a reverse striptease by adding clothes as the routine progressed. The artistry of her shows certainly seduced the men and boys at the Gayety who packed the premises night after night to see their "Goddess of Love". Lili loved Montreal as much as Montreal loved her and she was often seen after her shows at the El Morocco or some other bar socializing with athletes, reporters, gangsters, moguls and millionaires. Indefatigable, when the regular bars closed, she would then move on with her entourage to one of the city's many blind pigs that sold alcoholic beverages illegally.

Montreal's red-light district—St. Lawrence Boulevard at St. Catherine and neighbouring streets—was another attraction for locals, visitors and the thousands of young servicemen who swarmed into the city to train at HMCS Donnacona or to pass time between sailings, take courses at the Air Force Training School on Queen Mary Road or Manning Depot in Lachine or await their next flight at Ferry Command. Brothels served a varied clientele from government ministers who could afford the best to those that served men and curious teenagers on a restricted budget. It was no secret that the police took bribes from brothel owners, the proprietor of the largest one even employing seventy-five women just doors away from the No. 4 police station on Ontario Street. When, from time to time, a clean-up of the district was demanded, the usual routine would be followed. The police would swoop in, perform the "padlock ceremony" and take the girls into custody. The well-dressed owner of the bawdy house (or houses) would then sail into court, pay a fine and leave until the next visit. One of the most successful and carefree was the mink-coat-wearing Mme Beauchamp who owned at least twenty-four houses and always arrived at court in a chauffeur-driven Cadillac, exchanging *bons mots* with all in her perfumed path. The relationship between the police and the brothel owners was a long, profitable and cozy one. One advantage of this arrangement was that the madam could always call on the police who would, for a tip or a "freebie", break up the fights that occasionally happened with intoxicated patrons. Certain members of the public wanted a crackdown on "disorderly houses" but many city officials and others considered the brothels to be a safety valve. So the system continued, with the courts getting the fines, the police lining their pockets and moralists and the Catholic Church fuming and fretting.

Arthur Fraser remembers what it was like for a young schoolboy living in that area. "I lived on Sanguinet Street between de Montigny and Ontario. It was the red-light district and there were also night clubs, gambling places, taverns and blind pigs. I went to École St-Jacques which was on my street so I didn't pass any of these places going to school. There were two brothels on Ontario Street close together. A little restaurant on Emery and Sanguinet streets served meals for 25 cents—that included soup, the main dish, dessert and coffee. When the girls ordered their meals, the owner would come out and ask anybody who was there on the street if they wanted to deliver the food. We always said yes. (laughs) The first one there got the chance. I used to put on an apron and deliver the meals. There was always a girl in the window who would open the door. The meal cost 25 cents and they always gave me 25 cents tip.

"On St. Dominique, De Bullion and Berger there were three or four places on each side of the street. They had shutters and the girls would open them and ask if we wanted to have some fun. At the time, it cost one dollar. We all knew where these places were but we didn't pay too much attention. Some of the girls wore a two-piece outfit like a bathing suit with short pants. Once I saw a woman on the second floor with her breasts exposed. When a man passed by, she would open the shutters. Many of these places were duplexes with two front doors close together. When the police came and made a raid, they would put a lock on one door. They would take the girls down to the police station and when they let them go they would go back and enter by the upstairs door."

Roger (not his real name) was a young sailor from a small town who spent a short time training in Montreal in the summer of 1941. It wasn't long before the charms of Montreal were made apparent to this wide-eyed eighteen-year old. "Montreal was the biggest city in Canada at the time and it was really something. People had a different attitude and, of course, I had to try out the red-light district. At that age, you try everything. The first time, I went with another fellow. We wore our uniforms because, being in uniform, you thought you were a man. Before that we were kinda shy and our uniform changed our way of thinking. Funny when you think about that. We went to a place on Ontario Street. The madam let us in and then seven or eight girls started parading and we made our choice. At eighteen that was really something!"

One veteran training in Montreal remembers that even official exercises could be executed in the area. "The sergeant major at the Viger Barracks (who probably liked the ladies), always took his young recruits up De Bullion Street on their regular long-route marches. When passing the brothels, the mostly young and innocent boys would be treated to a show of flapping shutters, waving arms and winks from the scantily-clad girls."

The party came to an end in 1944 when the Canadian army, overwhelmed by the alarming increase in venereal diseases among its soldiers in Quebec (which had the highest rate in Canada), demanded that Montreal brothels be padlocked permanently. There was a war to be won and soldiers *hors de combat* with VD were not the ones to win it. If the City would not agree, the army would declare Montreal out of bounds to servicemen thus endangering the massive profits they brought into local businesses. The City complied and, in February, the girls had to don their snow boots and hit the icy pavement to drum up business. It was a temporary civic success, however, and swinging shutters and tempting voices could still be heard from many houses in the area.

While military officers, well-paid war workers and black marketeers might be able to afford Montreal's night life, it was different for the servicemen training or passing through the city. Many had very little money and socialized at regimental armouries or air force and navy organizations. As early as November 1939, the government declared that four groups; the Young Men's Christian Association (YMCA), the Knights of Columbus, the Salvation Army and the Canadian Legion would be designated as official auxiliaries to the military and they were given millions of dollars to fulfill this mandate. These organizations were to provide for the physical needs of servicemen at home and overseas. They were to be managed so that duplication of services was to be avoided but the main concern of all was making the lives of servicemen and women easier. In "army huts" overseas (Nissen huts that were semicircular military shelters made of corrugated steel) or in social centres in Canada, the aim was to provide a "home away from home" in a friendly and non-official manner. All of these groups had a long history of service to Canada during times of war and peace and were prepared, once again, to do what was needed.

Tea vans and canteens operated by these groups were rather a straightforward operation—most servicemen and women like tea, biscuits and doughnuts—but more ingenuity was needed in providing entertainment and education services to the mixed bag of personalities that made up the armed services. They ranged from the illliterate to the university educated; from the man of simple interests to the urban sophisticate; from the soldier who thought an evening of hymn singing was "just swell" to the fellow who preferred burlesque. Thus, a variety of movies, concerts, discussion groups, talent nights, poetry and essay contests, live entertainment, dances, crafts, educational and sporting activities were organized which were meant to keep up morale and provide physical activity. Personal advice was also given to the men overseas who needed individual help in something as simple as arranging for a telegram to be sent home or making sure that a man's family in Canada had enough coal in the winter. Soldiers could also write a letter home on donated stationery, read a newspaper, enjoy a meal and buy needed items like cigarettes and toiletries at a modest price. These groups often provided hostels where soldiers on leave could stay at extremely reasonable prices.

At the Red Triangle Club on Philips Square which was run by the YMCA, more than 1,000 women volunteers helped to make this recreational centre a homey place for the thousands of servicemen who passed through Montreal. There they could play games, enjoy a singsong, dance and socialize. The "Y", through Sir George Williams College, allowed servicemen to attend free university classes. Typing, shorthand and mathematics classes had the effect of training clerks, signallers and artillery men not only for the war but for the postwar years.

The Knights of Columbus offered recreational and practical help to servicemen and servicewomen overseas and on Monday, November 4, 1940, they officially opened the Knights of Columbus Army Hut at 1191 Mountain Street. Geared mainly but not exclusively to Catholics, dances were held and refreshments and meals were served by dedicated volunteers.

The Salvation Army set up Red Shield Service Centres at five military locations in Quebec, including Lachine and Valcartier. In Montreal, the Army operated a large hostel where soldiers could spend the night as well as offering assistance to the families of men serving overseas. Besides providing creature comforts wherever they set up services in war-torn areas, there would always be a person available to offer gentle counselling to a burnt-out airman or battle-scarred soldier or sailor. While grateful for the support services given to them by all organizations, the Salvation Army holds a special place in the hearts of veterans who remember that they were always present offering help and friendship with kindness and generosity. General Harry Crerar had this to say about them, "It would be easier to forget one's name than fail to remember the times without number when the Salvation Army was, in truth, our comforter and friend."

For the young Jewish servicemen passing through the city, the impressive YMHA (Young Men's Hebrew Association) building at Mount Royal and Park Avenue operated an Active Service Centre

Y.W.H.A. HOSTESSES ENTERTAIN VETERANS

The Y.W.H.A. hostesses of the Y.M.H.A. Active Service Centre took on the task Sunday of entertaining more than 90 veterans of the fighting in Italy and Normandy who were stranded in the city all day while waiting for trains to carry them to homes reaching as far west as Vancouver Island. They took the men to the Y.M.H.A. for showers and letter writing and then to Windsor Beach for a picnic, followed by a banquet at Central Station. In the above picture age gets the choice. All the men in the above picture are over 40 years old—some by a long way. Right to left the men are, **PTE. A. D. McMASTER**, Moosejaw; **CPL. T. THOMAS**, Calgary; **SGT. G. W. BINKS**, Trail, B.C.; **BDR. H. A. WONNACOTT**, Winnipeg; **TPR. T. J. "POP" TAYLOR**, and **TPR. A. TODEI**, Saskatoon. All these men were in both the Sicilian and Italian campaigns and have been sent home because they were far over the age limit.

Photo by R. Hirsch.

On August 20, 1944, hostesses of the YWHA entertained 90 veterans of the Italian and Normandy campaigns. Montreal *Gazette,* August 22, 1944. *Jewish Public Library Archives.*

where service personnel could attend a dance, get a meal or take a shower. Hostesses from the Young Women's Hebrew Association (YWHA) could be counted on to cheer up these lonely servicemen and would often invite them home for Friday night dinner. In one unusual case, in August of 1944, these young ladies entertained over ninety veterans from the Italian and Normandy campaigns who were sent home from the front because they were far over the age limit. (One of them, Trooper "Pop" Todie of Saskatoon, was fifty years old.) Stranded in Montreal on a Sunday while waiting to be shipped back to homes all across Canada, Capt. Paul Lanctôt, the Railway Transport Officer of Military District 4, turned to this group for help and got it in spades. First the girls took the superannuated warriors to the YMHA so they could freshen up and write letters home. Then they took them to Windsor Beach for a picnic, which was followed by a banquet at Central Station. For these men who had been away from Canada for up to four years spending much of the time living in slit trenches or manoeuvring tanks over unfriendly terrain, it was a grand day and a wonderful welcome back to Canada. This type of activity reflected the willingness and generosity of spirit that guided so many home front volunteers at the time.

While many young women spent their time volunteering in traditional ways, others practiced their tap dancing, acting and singing skills to prepare for the many shows put on to provide wholesome entertainment for servicemen. These energetic personalities often worked during the day and performed at night and on weekends, sometimes travelling for hours to get to their destination. The Bell Telephone Company had its Blue Bell Bullets, "Blue Bells"; the Sun Life Assurance Company had its "Eager Beavers" and the YMCA had its TNT Revue. The Evans Sisters Revue was another in a long list. If the girls arrived at work the next morning bleary-eyed with fatigue, they at least knew that they had cheered up many young servicemen while having fun themselves.

Hilda Galt was a professional dancer who recruited volunteers to provide shows in Montreal and parts of Quebec and Ontario. Through the entertainment committee of the Montreal War Services council, she organized more than 300 shows for departing and returning soldiers. The Royal Canadian Legion provided buses with a banner on the side that read: "Canadian Legion All Stars—A Show for Servicemen." Doris Bourque was one of those young women who gave of her time and energy in the Hilda Galt Revue. In an interview with the *Gazette* after her death in 2000, her daughter, Caroline Wiley, recalled that her mother got involved because, "She really felt sorry for the men….So many of them wouldn't come home and she wanted to do her part." She continued, "Mom used to talk about how, after the performances, they would dance with the soldiers and the Legion people were there to make sure the men never got too close, so nothing inappropriate ever happened."

Martha Allan was born a child of privilege at Ravenscrag, her family's Square Mile home, which later became part of the Royal Victoria Hospital. Sir Montague Allan and his wife Marguerite had four children but outlived them all. The First World War exacted a high price of this family when Martha's two younger teenage sisters, Gwen and Anna, were lost in the sinking of the *Lusitania* in 1915. Two years later, her brother Hugh was shot down over the English Channel while serving with the Royal Naval Air Service. Martha, the eldest, went overseas after training as a nurse and was injured while driving an ambulance in France. Back in Montreal, this confident, talented and dynamic woman, who had acting in her blood, used her energy, money and contacts to advance the cause of theatre in the city. She started the Theatre Guild of Montreal (later changed to the Montreal Repertory Theatre). The MRT could boast of many talented cast members, such as Christopher Plummer, Gratien Gélinas, Denise Pelletier and Hume Cronyn. At the outbreak of war in 1939, it was thought that the MRT should disband but Allan created the Tin Hat Revue (the forerunner of the Army Show). which entertained soldiers with skits, dances and music. Allan died in 1942 at the young age of forty-seven, which forced the MRT to carry on with new leadership.

Young women tried to carry on a social life against the backdrop of worrying about brothers or boyfriends serving overseas. The many eligible young servicemen in the city provided opportunities for socializing at all levels. From the unsophisticated country boys in the army and navy to their suave officers and the generally better-educated air force recruits, there were fellows for all tastes. Naomi Paltiel Lowi was very young when the war started. "In 1939 I was thirteen. I was at the earliest stage of dating so there wasn't too much of it. We lived on Esplanade Street facing Fletcher's Field. There was an army camp with big tents there during the war. I never was inside the camp but you could see it from the street. At

Betty Burland Jennings (right)served as bridesmaid at her friend Jean Morrison's wedding to Bob McBride at the Church of St. James the Apostle, May 31, 1941,. *Courtesy of Betty Burland Jennings and the McBride family.*

that time in the community, Jews did not date non-Jews (laughs), or they shouldn't have, and although I don't recall my family saying don't, I had already incorporated this limitation for myself so I would sort of sneak looks into the camp but I had no direct contact with the people in the camp. I had a little job during the war working in a book store and a soldier came in. I served him and then he walked me home. (He was Jewish!) I have a very clear memory of feeling *so proud* that I was with a guy in uniform with all the kids on the street seeing this. So that was my experience dating a soldier. I think we corresponded when he was in Shediac and I met him later at university."

For many young women, the boys of the air force were their first choice. One good place to meet the flyers was at Air Force House on Sherbrooke Street where they could go and apply to be hostesses. If found socially acceptable and pleasant-looking, they would go on a Saturday evening and participate in social activities such as chatting with the young men or singing around the piano. Dances were held in the basement and it was every girl's dream to dance with an officer. The young men would often escort the girls home and sometimes be invited home for Sunday dinner. Carol Lodge remembers those years. "Great dances, usually at Navy House, sports clubs, churches and the "Y" where we met mainly air force boys, many late teenagers and scarcely older than ourselves. Airmen, indeed! My best friend and I also went to Air Force House at the northeast corner of Sherbrooke and Mountain Street. By this time, I was close to eighteen. Girls were given approval by a group of ladies to attend and we danced with the boys, played cards, table tennis and also chatted. We also served Cokes, coffee and light snacks—great fun and the source of many light-hearted romances. Sometimes the boys were invited to Sunday dinners at our homes. They were more than happy to come and it gave our parents a chance to 'check them out'. We were all keen to get keepsakes, like the insignia from their caps or a button from their uniform. Of course, they would have been in a lot of trouble if they did this but we still tried and sometimes succeeded."

Young women from Westmount had a busy social life before the war and it only got busier as they pitched in to "do their bit". They and their mothers also had a strong tradition of volunteering with such organizations as the IODE and the Red Cross. Betty Burland Jennings was an attractive and fun-loving young woman in her early twenties when many of her male friends from Westmount joined the service. The prewar years were an idyllic time of house parties, skiing at the Alpine Inn, debutante dances, dinners and parties at the Badminton and Squash Club. Unable to enlist due to a bad knee, she helped to entertain the many servicemen who passed through Montreal. Another duty was acting as bridesmaid at the numerous wartime weddings. "You just went along with the war and, if there was anything you could do, you did it. My aunt and uncle had a big house on Aberdeen Avenue and sometimes they would invite servicemen for Sunday dinner. They obtained their names from a church or somewhere and would invite me over to chat with them. My friend Hally was in the navy down in Halifax and would send me some of his navy friends. There were often parties at the Badminton Club so I'd haul them along and entertain them there. I had my own friends and wasn't really interested in them but that was the one thing you could do—give your time to entertain the boys."

Lucille Pecaud also grew up in Westmount and attended Trafalgar School for Girls and Kings Hall Compton. She recalls the war years: "I joined the Hillside Tennis Club in 1927 which makes me the oldest living member today (2008). When the war started we only had about twenty men left at the club. These were mostly men who had important jobs in Ottawa. We used to have dinner at the club every night with all of us sitting at one big table and, half the time we had to make it ourselves. The dinner would cost 40 cents and each member would sign a chit so they would be billed later. The British RAF officers were allowed the courtesy of the club so there were a lot of very nice and attractive men around. A few of my Hillside friends became widows during the war. There were a few men who weren't killed but who didn't go back to their wives. They weren't married very long and it was natural that, after being separated for four or five years, this would happen."

Madeleine Cloutier Méthot, when not busy with volunteer work, was lucky enough to be able to spend time with her steady boyfriend. "My boyfriend, Guy Méthot, joined the air force but didn't go overseas. I had known him since I was about seven years old because we were in the same parish and our families knew each other. He had one weekend off every month and we used to go to movies at the Rex which was on St. Denis Street not far from my house. My mother loved Guy and always made a big fuss when he visited."

For the young and inexperienced boys spending time in

Canada's metropolis, it was a heady time of training with time off to savour the delights of downtown. Kenneth Delamater from Edmonton arrived in Montreal on a snowy day in December 1941. His air force training began in Calgary and continued at the No. 1 Wireless School on Queen Mary Road in a building that was a converted school for the deaf and which later became the Queen Mary Veterans' Hospital. He was joined by airmen from Australia and New Zealand and spent a total of four months here during that winter. "Our favourite restaurant was the Chick'n Coop on St. Catherine Street. Many of us also spent time at the Piccadilly Lounge which was a large bar and considered one of the best in Montreal. It was always full on Saturday nights and there were always tables of girls. There were two night clubs that had really good entertainment. One was Rockhead's Paradise, which had a good floor show with jokes, musicians and entertainers. It was considered the best and always filled up quickly so, if you couldn't get in, you went across the street to Café St. Michel which also had good shows."

Stuart Vallières remembers spending time at the Air Force Club. "There was entertainment with singing and cribbage. It was on the north side of Sherbrooke Street near the Ritz Carlton. They also had a bar. We were told that we were not to be 'forward' with the ladies or they would bounce us from the place. We all hoped to meet someone, be invited home for dinner and get lucky but that rarely happened. Why did so many girls seem to prefer fellows in the air force? Churchill mentioned the 'boys of the navy', the 'men of the army' and the 'gentlemen of the air force'. The educational levels of the air force were high and I guess that mothers felt safer if their daughters went out with gentlemen."

Roger (not his real name) and many of his fellow navy recruits had to balance a strict training routine with drinking sessions in local taverns and bars. "We lived on Drummond Street next to the YMCA. It was a big, old house and several of us rented the living room. Since we were living outside the barracks, we had to get up on our own in the morning to go to Donnacona. Most of the time, we weren't getting up early enough—especially when we had been drinking—and the Shore Patrol would come and get us out of bed and we'd be in trouble. When I started to drink, I didn't feel like getting up at all. Then we'd get No. 11 punishment: they'd put a pack on your back with something heavy in it and you had to run and run in the back alleyway. I guess that was one of the worst punishments, especially on a hot day. The gunnery officer who was with us would hold a rifle by the bottom of the barrel and turn it first to the right and then to the left without losing control and he told us that anybody who could do that didn't have to do the punishment. I got so much punishment that, after a while, I was able to do it." (laughs)

The officers at Donnacona often had their hands full with their spirited charges. Lorne Hamilton remembers: "No question that sailors sometimes got into trouble. Many of them were away from home and drinking was readily available in Montreal. They went to those cheap places on lower Stanley—everywhere they shouldn't go, including Ontario Street in the east end."

It was inevitable that some servicemen found true love while in Montreal. That is exactly what happened to Ken Delamater. "We got out on Saturdays and Sundays and would go downtown. One Saturday I was waiting for my friend George in the Music Box Bar in the Mount Royal Hotel. I waited and waited but he never showed up. At about 7 o'clock another airman arrived and asked me if I wanted to go to a party on Souvenir Street. A girl named Marjorie Walker had organized the party for air force fellows at her house. I guess she must have liked me because, while I was talking and dancing with another girl, she came along and said, 'Come and dance with me'. She never let go of me after that. (laughs) When I was sent to Dartmouth, we wrote to each other and before I went overseas, Marjorie told me that she wanted to get married. I asked her why she wanted to get married as the only money I had was what the air force gave me. She said, 'Never mind that. Some Englishwoman will get a hold of you and I'll lose out so I want to get married before you go'. I got leave from Dartmouth and we were married in St. Stephen's Anglican Church in 1943. She really should have given me more credit for being able to say no to the English girls!"(laughs)

Apart from the regular melees involving servicemen and zoot suiters, there were constant bar fights which were fuelled bylinguistic reasons, jealousy or just the result of the mix of youthful testosterone and beer. Jacques Boucher: "The air force and navy guys hated each others' guts. Once, at the Beaver Club on the corner of St. Catherine and Bleury, my father got into a fight with some air force guys and he got punched from the top floor, down two sets of stairs and landed on St. Catherine Street without a scratch on him."

Philip Aspler spent the war years in Montreal and remembers one "boys will be boys" melee in particular. "There was a club near St. Matthew Street called the Madeline. There were a lot of fights there. It was unbelievable. One night I was there with two fellows, Dougie Martin and Bob Parker, whose family owned the Parker House Hotel where the Château Champlain is now. They both went to the bathroom and a fight erupted at the next table to me. I got up to protect the quarts of beer and, as soon as I stood up, this fellow took a running dive at me and knocked me over. I went back and my chair hit the radiator so I stuck up my two feet and let him have it in the stomach and he went back about four tables. (laughs) Then the fight started! I was lucky. I would have been killed except that Alfie Bryant from St. Ann's Ball Team was there with two or three fellows that I knew and they came rushing down. They realized that I didn't start the fight so the waiters threw out the gang that had started it."

Stuart Vallières remembers the rivalry between his air force buddies and sailors all vying for the attention of the girls they met downtown. "Yeah, there were a few free-for-alls for no particular reason. If an air force guy went to the Music Box with a nice-looking girl he was the target for the navy who figured how did he get so lucky? It usually started off kinda friendly but it usually ended up a bit physical but with no hard feelings. We had pride in uniform and, if the air force were lucky one weekend, well, the navy made sure they had enough reinforcements there the next weekend. (laughs) It always ended up with the Shore Patrol showing up Saturday nights."

During the war, troop trains replaced tourist trains as Canada sent its young men to war. Windsor Station, ca 1940.
Canadian Pacific Archives.

[CHAPTER EIGHT]

Enemy Aliens

Wrong Place, Wrong Time

HINDSIGHT, WHICH CAN BE ACUTELY embarrassing to history, now tells us that the internment of selected elements of the Canadian and immigrant population was an exercise in overkill. However, the actions of the government must be put in the context of the times. The first duty of a country in wartime is to protect its borders and interests. Even if 98 per cent of the internees were innocent, a lot of damage could have been done by small groups numbering only four or five. The fact that there was no fifth-column sabotage is a debated topic. Was it because no danger ever existed or was it because the potential saboteurs were safely under guard? Fifth columnists had already wreaked havoc in Holland and France. The Canadian population had been asked to sacrifice another generation to total war and very few had patience with radicals marching in blue, brown or black shirts and insignia. They demanded protection from the "enemies within" and many burned up the telephone lines to various RCMP offices helpfully offering up names of neighbours and co-workers they suspected.

When the uneasy peace of the late thirties was shattered by war, Canada sprang into action and again invoked the War Measures Act as it had in World War I. An order-in-council was passed in 1940 that defined as enemy aliens "all persons of German or Italian racial origin who have become naturalized British subjects since September 1, 1922." Twenty-six internment camps were set up across Canada to house these potential saboteurs. After the bombing of Pearl Harbor, the government proceeded to act against the Japanese population which was mostly based in British Columbia. The three ethnic groups that were targeted for surveillance, the Germans, Italians and Japanese differed in two respects—for the Germans it was a déjà-vu experience that their community had experienced in World War I. As Japan and Italy had been our allies in that conflict, these communities were facing wartime hostility and sanctions for the first time. Another important distinction was that Germans and Italians were treated on a case-by-case basis with opportunities for appeal while the entire Japanese community (which included Japanese nationals, naturalized Canadian citizens as well as those born in Canada) was treated especially harshly.

You are living in British Columbia. Pearl Harbor has been attacked and the Canadians have suffered their first cruel losses of the war in Hong Kong. Living along the coast of your province are thousands of Japanese Canadians, in fact, 95 per cent of the 23,000 people of Japanese origin living in Canada. And—you never know—these people have flashlights, binoculars, mirrors, radios, fuel, cameras and they speak the language of the enemy. In case of an invasion, they might willingly or, through coercion, decide to become a fifth column. These people are Japs and can't be trusted.

You are a Japanese Canadian living in one of the many communities that had been set up on the West Coast since the arrival of Manzo Nagano in 1877—the first Japanese person to officially immigrate to Canada. Your first name is Ken, Dorothy, Frank or Eileen. You are a Nisei (Canadian born) and love swing music, baseball, corny jokes, playing cards and flirting. Gosh, you even like all things British, having had that bred into you at school. There has always been a lot of discrimination against your people. Your father, who is a Japanese national, sometimes talks of returning to Japan and buying a small piece of land. You are sure that you and your siblings can talk him out of it. You love this country. It's the only one you know.

In the late 1930s news of Japan's invasion of China and its barbarous behaviour in Nanking did not help the already precarious status of the disenfranchised Japanese living mainly on the west coast of Canada. the *Toronto Star* quoted Archdeacon F.G.

Scott who had it "on good authority" that Japanese naval officers in disguise were manning fishing boats equipped with 16-inch guns ready to fire on British Columbia should Japan declare war. A 16-inch gun on a fishing boat is as logical to imagine as a scrawny five-year-old boy trying to toss a caber at a Highland Games competition but reality had no place in the hyperbolic rhetoric of the times. Statements like these found a ready audience for those prepared to think the worst of their Japanese compatriots.

The attack on Pearl Harbor in 1941 and the defeat of two Canadian battalions in Hong Kong on Christmas Day of the same year meant that, with Canada now at war with Japan, people of Japanese origin were to be considered enemy aliens. Previous demands for economic sanctions on Japan were now replaced by demands from B.C. politicians for the establishment of ghettos, identification cards, the transferring of this community to other provinces and even deportation to Japan. Saner voices noted that these stipulations were more in tune with Hitler's Germany than Canada's tradition of fairness. Mackenzie King said that the great majority of people of "Oriental racial origin" were loyal to Canada but privately agreed with their compulsory registration. The prime minister had to walk a fine line between appeasing the fears of British Columbians and also, of not offending the Japanese government that had the power to exact reprisals against Canadian POWs. Meanwhile, the beleaguered community complied with the escalating demands and hardships forced on them with a forbearance that was rare and unique. They asked themselves: Why us? What have we done and where will it all end? Will we be allowed to return to our normal lives after the war?

The Japanese of British Columbia were hard-working, self-sufficient and family-oriented, with a crime rate that would have been the envy of a Mennonite community. These good qualities inspired, in equal measure, grudging respect and jealousy among many of the locals. The community watched and listened with great trepidation as political events unfolded around them. Although there were many political and editorial pleas for tolerance, sulphurous political verbiage won the day and the Japanese community found itself facing unbearable economic consequences and isolation. Twelve hundred fishing boats were impounded putting 1,800 fishermen out of work. Businesses lost their white clientele and had their windows broken. Many lost their jobs. Insurance companies rushed to cancel policies. German and Italian aliens already had to report regularly to the Registrar of Enemy Aliens but the registration of the Japanese which was begun in March, 1941 included *all* persons of Japanese origin, regardless of citizenship. The nervous community could only stand by and hope that Canadian decency and British fair play would protect them in the end.

But Canadian decency and British fair play were in short supply for the Japanese. With the exception of members of the CCF Party, civil liberties groups, certain newspapers and some church groups, they faced an angry chorus of censure from British Columbian and federal politicians. More than 21,000 Japanese Canadians, of whom 75 per cent were Canadian citizens, were taken from their homes and sent to eight internment camps in B.C. to live in primitive conditions. Family separation, confiscation of property with little or no recompense, forced labour and sometimes years of numbing boredom would follow the implementation of the War Measures Act of February, 1942.

In World War I and, with Japan an ally, 196 Issei (first generation) enlisted for service, fought brilliantly and suffered high losses. Japanese-Canadian soldiers were present at the Battle of Vimy, one of the defining events in our history. In spite of their small numbers, it was only in 1931 that these veterans got the vote, a right that did not extend to their wives or children. Wartime service to Canada did not keep these veterans out of internment camps later on, either.

It is astounding to realize that, with all these attacks on their community, so many Japanese Canadians wanted to demonstrate their loyalty to Canada and went to extraordinary lengths to do so. In 1939 the Japanese Canadian Citizens League sent a wire to Prime Minister King pledging their support and loyalty. Hundreds of thousands of dollars flowed into the war coffers of the Department of National Defence. The Nisei were even prepared to fight against Japan if necessary but signing up was made difficult for them. There was silent discrimination against their enlistment in B.C. It was thought that they could not be trusted and their inclusion in general ranks would cause dissent in the training camps. It was also realized that, by allowing them to serve, it would have been difficult to keep on denying them the right to vote. In January of 1945 a few of them were recruited for their language skills (some of them shaky indeed) to help the Intelligence arm of the British Army deal with Japanese POWs. How frustrating it must have been for these potentially fine warriors to be given non-combat jobs that did not allow them to prove their mettle on the battleground. It must also be noted that many young men who tried to enlist were angrily told they were an embarrassment to their displaced and dispossessed families. We now know that there was not a single act of sabotage or disloyalty among the ranks of Japanese Canadians during the war. The few trouble makers were known to the RCMP and rounded up early on. To be sure, there were some in the community who hoped for a victorious Japan and many others, embittered by their experience, began to wonder just how much loyalty they owed Canada. Japanese language schools (proudly flying the white and red *Hinomaru*) had operated for many years in the province and had taught young children to revere all things Japanese. In an unwelcoming province, Issei parents often contemplated returning to Japan and wanted their children to be equipped for this eventuality.

The Japanese living in Montreal at the beginning of the war were a miniscule minority. The census of 1931 indicates a population of twenty-six souls. Their small numbers did not make them immune to discrimination, however. Mr. Nisuke Tomahara, in an interview with the *Gazette* in 1988 recalled that being Japanese in Montreal during the '20s and '30s meant that he couldn't enter movie theatres and had to avoid certain neighbourhoods. Finding a job and a place to live were also painful ordeals. Their small numbers meant that, when war came, they were not considered a huge threat but nonetheless, were subject to the constraints of the War Measures Act. In spite of this, the Tsubota family of Lacombe Avenue in Montreal answered the call to arms by having two members enlist. The father, James Jitsuei, a Vimy Ridge veteran, became a language instructor for the British Army. David, born in 1921, signed up to serve in the Royal Canadian Navy in 1940. Discharged after only three months for racist reasons, he then joined the Black Watch, fought at the fateful raid on Dieppe and was captured, spending the next two and a half years as a POW in Stalag 8B. One of the permanent reminders of his time as a guest of the Reich was the scar on his wrist from the shackles that these prisoners had to wear for more than a year.

Betty Kobayashi Issenman was also part of this tiny group. The Kobayashi family consisted of her father Shinsuke from Japan, her mother Mary Campbell Jamieson from Glasgow, her sister Mary Campbell (born in Calgary in 1919), Betty (born in Winnipeg in 1921)and her younger brother Gordon Robert (born in Winnipeg in 1925). Shinsuke began to be known as Harry and saw action in the First World War in the trenches of France and Belgium while serving as a sniper with the Edmonton 49th Battalion. After the war he worked for Mr. Ichiro Hayakawa who owned the Mikado Company which imported dry goods, small toys and decorative items from Japan. It had branches in three Canadian cities. In 1926 Harry accepted Ichiro Hayakawa's offer to help manage the Montreal store on St. Lawrence Boulevard (in which he eventually became a partner). The enterprise later gave up the retail side of the business concentrating on wholesale dealings with hundreds of retailers in Montreal such as Kresge's, Eaton's, Simpson's and Metropolitan Stores. The family's first home was on Delormier Street in the east end of Montreal with a population that was predominantly Roman Catholic and French speaking. Betty and her siblings had to listen to urchins in a sing-song voice recite: "Chinky, chinky Chinaman, wash my pants. Put them in the boiler and make them dance." More appalling and frightening were the French-speaking boys

[Top] The Kobayashi children (left to right): Gordon, Mary and Betty.
[Bottom] The Mikado Company on St. Lawrence Boulevard, 1930.
Harry Kobayashi is second from the right in the first row.
Courtesy of Betty Kobayashi Issenman.

who would chase Betty and tell her that they planned to kill her. When she came home crying, her father, a devout Christian convert, consoled her with the admonition to "turn the other cheek and do good to them that hate you". In later years, she commented that "the small torments thrust on me have encouraged me to champion the underdog, be it in the field of human rights, poverty, saving our planet from environmental or military destruction, or improving our health and educational systems".

A move to the supposedly more enlightened and English-speaking area of N.D.G. did not end the taunting and name-calling. The Board of Wesley United Church even held a meeting to decide whether a Japanese family should be admitted to the congregation. The response was positive and the church with its friendly and helpful parishioners became the centre of the family's activities.

A precocious, popular and, according to her teachers, "adorable" student, Betty began school at five. Her memories of Willingdon School and West Hill High School were especially happy ones in which she participated in many sports and other activities.

Being at McGill during the turbulent late 1930s meant deep immersion in political activities. As vice-president of the Women's Union and a member of the Student Christian Movement that promoted Christian socialism, she championed the causes of the International Brigade in Spain (whose annihilation devastated her) and Chinese Student Relief. To protest Japanese aggression in China, she, along with some of her classmates, foreswore silk, convinced that they were striking fear into the Japanese militarists with their actions. It was an awkward family situation, of course, because her father imported these same goods. It was at McGill that she met her future husband and kindred spirit, Arnold Issenman, a McGill activist who had served as news editor of the *McGill Daily.* Betty Kobayashi graduated from McGill in 1940 (BA Honours Sociology and Anthropology). With her Diploma, equivalent MSW, from the Montreal School of Social Work granted in 1942, and an MA in *Service Sociale* (Community Organization and Urban Planning) from the University of Montreal she was ready to take on the world.

"I had a ton of friends and acquaintances when the war started and their attitude didn't change. In fact we became closer as the war we had tried to prevent burst upon us. I was first employed in 1942 by the Family Welfare Association, then the Children's Aid Society, the Women's Directory (for unmarried mothers) and in the Public Service of Canada (Department of Veterans Affairs). I had the most cordial relations with everyone I worked with, although the head of DVA may have had to confer with his superiors about my Japanese background.

"When the War Measures Act was invoked, I, my sister Mary and brother Gordon were notified that we were enemy aliens and had to report to the RCMP once a month with a card that had our fingerprints on it. I can still envisage what I went through; I can see and feel the huge, hairy hand of the monstrous, sneering official as it pressed down each of my fingers first on to an ink pad, then on to a paper. My feelings then, as at this moment, were of shame and anger. Naively (I was only twenty-one) I tried to point out that I had been actively campaigning against the Japanese Government, but he looked at me with contempt. I am still reduced to tears when I think of that event. It was only later when I learned about what had happened to the Japanese Canadians of British Columbia that I realized what had happened to me and my siblings was very little in comparison. We were not interned although the business my father (a Canadian citizen) co-owned was seized by the Custodian of Enemy Alien Property. My father had gone to Japan on a buying trip in 1941 and was caught there. He was not only decreed to be an enemy alien in Canada, even though he had fought for Canada in World War I, but the Japanese Government as well declared him to be an enemy alien. With my father away and many of the Japanese in Montreal dispersed, I had no contact with any Japanese for many years.

"It was when I tried to join the army that it hit me how racist were our government policies. I applied to the Canadian Women's Army Corps in 1942 and was refused entry. Then when the army was recruiting social workers I applied in 1943 and again in 1944. When I finally was granted an appointment with an officer, he informed me that my application was refused. I was floored when he advised me that, since I would be admitted as a lieutenant, other ranks would be required to salute me which they would be loath to do toward a Japanese. A further insulting reason for the refusal was that I would be eating in the Officers' Mess and these officers would not want an Oriental to be present. I think I staggered from the room and had to sit outside in the corridor to recover.

"My sister Mary Hecht suffered more through her treatment by the RCMP which forced her dismissal from her job as the public health nurse at Canadian Vickers. My brother Gordon seemed to fare somewhat better than we did. He applied to join the air force when he graduated from high school at age sixteen but was told to wait a year. Although persons of Japanese heritage were barred from the armed forces, he was admitted when he was seventeen almost by a fluke, the recruiting officer being a former teacher of Gordon's.

"In January 1945 I received a letter from the RCMP (Japanese Registration, 'E' Division) stating that I was now classified as a Eurasian and no longer considered an enemy alien and therefore not subject to the terms of the War Measures Act. Despite the insults already dealt out by the army, I reapplied in March 1945 to Social Service, National Defence Headquarters, enclosing this letter and asked that they reconsider my application. I said that I could not accept their refusal on grounds of race. Even though the lieutenant set up appointments, she would cancel at the last minute and I never heard from them again.

"In 1949, my husband and I hired a lawyer to recover something of my father's property. The lawyer charged us a bare minimum in fees, but the Custodian of Enemy Alien Property imposed a substantial amount for keeping and selling the business. The resulting small amount the family received, which my father divided between himself and my mother meant that we children had been done out of our financial heritage."

At war's end Betty's father, in his mid-fifties by then and with his successful business in Montreal gone, remained in Japan and worked for a while for the American Army of Occupation. In 1948 he wrote home saying, "I certainly want to return to Canada with all speed possible, where I can restart my work again." This never happened. To support his family in Montreal, he started an export business in Japan and died there in 1988, one of the last surviving Japanese-Canadian WW I veterans. Gordon, his son, relocated to the warmer climate of Vancouver in 1976 and always participated in the Remembrance Day Ceremony at the Japanese-Canadian Memorial in Stanley Park. On this memorial is carved the name of Harry Shinsuke Kobayashi, the man who had fought for "King and Country".

The end of the war brought to light the bitter reality that not only was their property confiscated and sold, the government passed and then rescinded an order for the deportation of Japanese Canadians. Four thousand left anyway and, in Japan, a foreign country to many, they faced the same nightmare of non-acceptance. "Voluntary repatriation" to Japan was sought by the Canadian government for those not willing to prove their loyalty by scattering across Canada. Many left because they were too old and disheartened to start over in another province. It was only in 1949 that Japanese Canadians were allowed to return to British Columbia. By that time, most were settled in other parts of Canada and were busy restarting their lives.

In all bad situations a rainbow must be found. In the case of Japanese Canadians it was that they were forced to spread out to other provinces, which hastened their total integration into Canadian society. They experienced different levels of pain, dislocation and frustration; with one extreme being the older people who lost everything and had neither heart nor energy to start over, to the young people for whom life in the camps was a bit of a lark. One example of the latter group is Lois Nakashima Hashimoto of Laval, who spent time in Slocan internment camp with her family. Her father, another World War I veteran, had fought in the trenches of France and was grateful that Lois's eighteen-year-old brother, Kats, was "exempted" from answering the call to the colours. Lois has fond memories of that time: "It was difficult to feel that we were being treated badly. Slocan is located in the beautiful Kootenay Valley. We hiked up the mountains and swam in the lake. We picnicked by the river. We attended dances and concerts, and most importantly, school. Our parents planted beautiful, bountiful gardens. We visited friends from other internment camps miles away. It was a strangely fairy-tale kind of existence when you consider that the rest of the world was in turmoil." In the scope of the terrible suffering and loss of young Canadian soldiers and, in fact, of people all over the world, Lois feels that the dislocation of her family was a negligible inconvenience. For many others, however, those years of internment scarred their lives and tested their resolve.

On September 22, 1988 each Japanese person affected by the internment policy was awarded $21,000 in compensation. For many, who might have lost valuable property in booming British Columbia which today might be worth millions, it was enough to perhaps replace a few windows on their bungalow in Dorval or buy a new car.

In the Battle of Hong Kong in December 1941 every Canadian soldier was killed, wounded or taken prisoner. The nearly 1,700 POWs were to suffer cruelty to an unimaginable dimension for almost four years with 276 dying in captivity. In December 1998 the Canadian government agreed to give each Canadian Hong Kong POW a payment of $23, 940 in compensation for forty-four months of maltreatment by the Japanese government based on the rate of $18 a day. This followed other smaller payments given to them after the war by the government when Japanese assets in Canada were sold. Another small payment was awarded to them by the Japanese government at the Peace Treaty in San Francisco in 1952. Canada finally got an official apology from the Japanese seventy years after the fact in December 2011. Its lateness made it seem a bit tepid and, for the remaining thirty or so surviving victims, probably did not mean much.

Japanese Canadians, however bad they may feel about the treatment of the POWs, make a clear distinction between the two situations: many of the Japanese who were interned were either Canadian-born or naturalized citizens while the Canadian veterans were at war with a hostile nation.

Unlike the Japanese, the Germans in Canada were not a homogenous group. Small numbers landed in New France and settled in Quebec before 1759. Many others came with the British army as mercenaries and took part in the early battles that shaped Canada. They fought with the British in the American War of Independence and stayed here to become an integral part of the Canadian mosaic as United Empire Loyalists. Others settled here after spending years in the United States. Many of the later arrivals came from outside the boundaries of present-day Germany, such as Rumania, Poland, Russia and other German-speaking areas of Europe. They are one of the largest and most assimilated ethnic groups in Canada. This assimilation was helped along by the hostility of the Canadian population to them during World War I. Many started to speak English on a daily basis and a simple name change from *Schmidt* to Smith facilitated acceptance. It was also an easy segue to go from *Deutsch* to Dutch. Intermarriage was also common and hastened the loosening of ethnic ties.

In 1931 the number of Germans living in Canada was almost half a million. Of the 6,068 German-speaking people in Montreal, 2,254 were German-born. At the onset of World War II the police wasted no time in scooping up about seventy Montreal members of the Nazi Party and confiscated a wireless set, incriminating documents, framed photographs of Hitler and many swastika banners. Most German Canadians, however, were willing to support Canada's war effort, with many enlisting in the armed services and giving generous financial support. (Naturalized German Canadians were permitted to enlist only in 1943.) By 1941, out of the total population, only 16,000 ethnic Germans were not Canadian citizens. Citizens or not, those who entered Canada after 1922 had to register as enemy aliens and more than 800 were interned. Most were released by 1941 but the eighty-nine enemy aliens remaining in internment camps probably posed a real threat to Canadian security. These Nazis were mostly disaffected, financially marginal, recent immigrants who found a home in the *Deutscher Bund Canada.* This pro-Nazi group moved its headquarters from Kitchener to Montreal in order to maximize the influence of the German consul general and his contacts with Nazi Germany. This was done in spite of the fact that the target population, was not a large one and not too receptive to its propaganda which had some success among the newly-arrived farmers in the Prairies but not among the general population.

In Montreal, very few of the 170 members who joined the *Bund* belonged to the Nazi Party. The leadership of the *Bund,* Hitler supporters to a man until most of them left the group to form their own Nazi organizations, stated that their goals were social and cultural, not political. Their unstated goal was to create a core group of German-Aryan members who would spread the word of German attitudes and solidarity to the community at large. Their high-handed methods meant that they were often in conflict with older, established German clubs in Montreal, such as *Deutscher Verein Teutonia.* In 1936 the Montreal branch of the *Deutsche Arbeitsfront* (German Workers Front or DAF) was organized. Composed of a few dedicated Nazis, it never had the influence of the *Bund.* The German-Canadian press had subscribers numbering in the thousands across Canada and, out of seven newspapers, only two were not sympathetic to Hitler at the beginning of the war.

German-Canadian opposition to the Nazis was, of course, strong among the communists. Another organization formed to counter Nazi propaganda was the German-Canadian League, which was formed in 1934. More than 500 members of the League passed a resolution condemning Nazi philosophy and subversive activities in Canada at a rally held on April 20, 1939 (ironically, Hitler's birthday) at the Montreal Forum. The overt hostility of many Canadians to Germany, became stronger as the 1930s wore on, and led many former pro-Nazis to modify their tone, go underground, or return to Germany if they no longer felt comfortable in what they perceived was a hostile Anglo-Saxon world.

Although there were members of the German community living in all parts of the Montreal area in the 1930s, the largest concentration was in the downtown area around St. Lawrence Boulevard in the district now known as the Plateau. The recent immigrants who lived there had to concentrate on making a life for themselves in a new country and had little time for the luxury of political debate or Nazi mischief. Most either belonged to St. John's Lutheran Church or to St. Boniface Catholic Church.

The German Society of Montreal (*Deutsche Gesellschaft zu Montreal*) was founded in 1835. The community also provided musical, theatrical and sports groups as well as social clubs that catered to different groups of ethnic Germans, such as the Hungarian-Germans (*Verein der Ungarn-Deutschen*). Public attitudes to them were less hostile than during the First World War but there were still many anti-German incidents reported at the beginning of the war. The Hofbrau, a German restaurant on St. Catherine Street West had its windows smashed and the office of the German consul-general, also on St. Catherine Street, was given police protection. Margaret Neville remembers an event involving a Mrs. Brown of Papineau Avenue who had two sons serving overseas. One day she came out of her house carrying a German flag and set it afire to a chorus of cheers from the onlookers.

Rosalie Eberwein Stoss, an ethnic German, was born in Rumania in 1921 and came to Canada in 1930 with her mother and younger brother and sister. Her father, as was often the case, came ahead of the family in 1928 and, after finding no work in Saskatchewan, in 1929 rode the rails to Montreal where he knew he would find some support from fellow *Donauschwaben* (Danube Swabians). The normal problems of cultural adjustment and financial worries were complicated when Rosalie's mother died at the end of 1930. Her father's second marriage in 1932 and the birth of a half-brother meant another adjustment for the family.

"My father had been a bricklayer in Rumania but he worked for Seagram's repairing their ovens when he came to Montreal. They were a very good company to work for and took care of their people but, during the Depression, you didn't always have work. The men would go to Seagram's in LaSalle in the morning and there would be a line-up of many, many men. Only a few would be hired and the rest would go back home. The next morning, it would start all over again. He worked for the Bronfman's until he died in 1937 of peritonitis following a work accident. He was forty-one. In hindsight it was a terrible time. Our stepmother wanted to send us back to Rumania but they were no better off in Rumania than we were here. You could almost say that we children became the breadwinners. The Jewish people gave us 85 per cent support in every which way. Yiddish is similar to German and we could always make ourselves understood. They always gave us jobs babysitting or lighting their stoves on the weekend. They paid a penny a house and we each had our customers. The men were always given little jobs in tailor shops or factories. If it hadn't been for the Jewish people I think we would have perished and this didn't change when the war started. We first lived in Verdun and it was traumatic to be here without a mother and not knowing the language. Verdun was

A 1932 First Communion class of St. Boniface Parish. Rosalie Eberwein Stoss is the girl on the top right.
Courtesy of Rosalie Eberwein Stoss.

all English and they were very apt to make fun of you but when we moved to Montreal it was so much better because the French were always more receptive to immigrants than the English. But God looks after all of us. I married my husband, who was from the same community, when I was seventeen and he was twenty-three. We both needed a home and it worked out really, really well for us. We had three children and were married for almost sixty-nine years. My brother and sister had a home with us and our stepmother kept our half-brother.

"As children we didn't know anything about politics nor did we care about politics. What we thought about was our next meal and whether we were going to school or not. We were just young and concentrating on making a future for ourselves. I think the whole community felt the same way. Maybe the older generation or those who came from Germany were thinking of war overseas but not us. First of all, how many of us had a radio in the 1930s? And, if you had a radio, did you care to listen? Our parents couldn't speak English or French anyway so they couldn't understand anything that was being said on the radio. We were also well assimilated and got along well with our neighbours, whether they were Polish, Russian or Jewish and so on.

"We had our little theatre groups and social groups and there was one group (*Deutscher Bund*) that was good for teenagers because they had a summer camp like the Boy Scouts or the Girl Guides. It was described as a pro-Nazi organization. My friends who belonged to that, what did they really know about being pro-Nazi? They only knew they could sing songs and go to camp for two weeks every summer, which their parents couldn't afford. When the war started, suddenly we were enemy aliens—even my sister who was two years old when she came to Canada. We had to go down to be fingerprinted. We were supposed to report on a regular basis but, after a while, they decided it was too much trouble and told us not to come back. My husband did not have to enlist in the armed services (although he went down to register) because he was a foreman in a factory that made coats for the air force.

"We don't like to talk about the war because, basically, it was not our fault although many people treated us as if it were. Since we lived in our own community, we were not exposed to too much but, if you had an English teacher, you might have been her favourite on Wednesday and then, on Thursday you became a German and her bitter enemy. You always had that in you—don't talk about it. Some mothers didn't want their children playing with 'that German'. How could you explain that you weren't 'that German' but were as Canadian as they were. That was a terrible time for the young people because we didn't start the war."

Fred is another ethnic German who came to Canada in 1930 at the age of nine.

"We lived in the Plateau area and my family was very involved with the German church of St. John's Lutheran on Jeanne Mance. My father had the intention of coming to Canada and earning enough money to go back to Europe. He worked for a year at Seagram's and then opened his own painting business which grew and grew. I went to Aberdeen School and then to Strathearn High School and considered myself a Canadian. I belonged to a United Church Boy Scout group and went to Camp Tamaracouta in the summer. I played sports with all kinds of boys. I used to play soccer with Jewish boys in Fletcher's Field. They knew I was of German background and I never had any problems. When the war started, we were not Canadian citizens. I was considered an enemy alien and didn't have to go into the army. I was fingerprinted and had to carry a card. I didn't have to report to the RCMP every month and was never asked to show my card all during the war. If I were Japanese it might have been different but, as a young man, I had blond hair and blue eyes so I guess that was an advantage. My father wasn't interested in politics. He was thinking of his job and the work he had to do. He didn't want to have anything to do with uniforms. He said that he had had enough of that. Both my parents lost family members in the two world wars. We didn't even know who Hitler was in the beginning. He didn't do Germany any favours. They were paying for his desire to rule and he forgot that we are all human beings.

"We had a neighbour who was also a church member. He was interned during the war and whenever my family went to market we always bought things like a sack of potatoes for his family. During the war there were always one or two RCMPs sitting at the back of our church during services. They understood German and were listening to make sure there was no propaganda. Reverend Peters' sermons were not political and most of the church members felt themselves very fortunate to be in Canada and out of Europe.

"My first job was with the Robert Simpson Company. I was a trained pattern maker for men's clothing and traveled with my job. During the war, I was in more army, navy and air force camps than any soldier. I took measurements of the generals, admirals—you name it—not the rank and file who just lined up to get their uniforms. These people were the *crème de la crème* of Montreal and when I opened my own business after the war, they became my clients. We have services in English now and the German service is not well attended. I'm still a member of St. John's. I kept my enemy alien card for many years but then decided to throw it away."

Another life-long member of St. John's Lutheran Church remembers that, as a young girl heading to German classes during the war years, she had to carry German books which were carefully hidden under a sweater that she wore no matter how warm the day. Being called Nazi by classmates and friends was not fun either but, as she recalls: "I didn't know what the word meant and I'm sure they didn't either and we all remained friends".

The Earl of Athlone arrived in Canada in 1940 with his wife, the Princess Alice, to be installed as the sixteenth governor general of Canada. They were not the only arrivals from England that year—the British government had decided to send interned aliens and POWs to Canada to prevent their becoming a fifth column in case of a German invasion, which was considered a distinct possibility. The Canadian government geared up for the arrival of these fearsome Nazi crack troops and evil-intentioned spies who would be held in internment camps along with our own internees. The irony was that many of the internees from Britain were German Jews and political refugees who were themselves fleeing Nazi oppression. Canada was to play host to 2,290 of these men who resented the term "enemy alien' or even "friendly alien" and wished to be acknowledged as political refugees. The German and Italian POWs (Class A) were lumped in with these civilian internees. (Class B and C) with some predictable friction. Divisions were made to separate the two groups with the result that some camps eventually had a political refugee majority. Many of these men who remained in Canada after the war went on to become a veritable "Who's Who" of Canadian and Montreal life, among them Dr. Max Stern who established the Dominion Gallery in Montreal and Dr. Gregory Baum (the former Catholic priest who was born into a Jewish/Protestant family) who became one of Canada's best-known theologians. Dr. Baum taught at McGill University's Faculty of Religious Studies from 1986 to 1995.

The Veterans' Guard troops and members of the Provost Corps girded their loins when told of the imminent arrival of these battle-hardened and fanatical Nazi POWs. With determined expressions and fixed bayonets at the ready, they couldn't believe it when they saw what the train disgorged: lads as young as sixteen and men in their sixties, bespectacled intellectuals, pale rabbinical students with ear locks, Catholic priests wearing cassocks, sensitive musicians along with some well-muscled farmers and metal workers as well as sullen and defiant POWs. A few aristocrats enhanced the list, among them: Prince Friedrich of Prussia, the handsome, charismatic and anti-Nazi grandson of the Kaiser who was interned at Farnham and Baron Egon Ernst Ketschendorf who was sent to New Brunswick. Montrealer Edgar (Eddie) Lion was one of the young Jewish men who arrived in Canada after being interned on the Isle of Man while studying at the University of Edinburgh. He was born in Vienna in 1920, the only son of a prominent family.

"My father was a highly-decorated and popular World War I officer of the *Deutschmeister* Regiment. I mention this because I think it was because of his military contacts that he was saved from a concentration camp after being arrested twice after the *Anschluss* of 1938. He was also a corporate lawyer with many government and business clients. When the Germans marched into Austria, I was a student at the Theresianum Academy, a very famous and exclusive boarding school run along military lines. It was quite a sacrifice for my parents to send me there. I was one of only three Jews in a class of thirty six boys but was popular with my classmates. The Germans annexed the first and second floors of my school and, since they had nothing much to do then, their pastime was to collect so-called undesirables—Jews, priests, communists and so on and torture them. I remember one incident well: we all looked out of the school window and saw, downstairs in the garden, a group of Nazis standing in a circle and wielding wooden clubs. A big fellow, obviously Jewish, was in the middle. One fellow would hit him and, as he staggered back and forth, he was hit repeatedly until he collapsed in a pool of blood and was carried out to the street where he lay all day, bleeding profusely. Not a single person came to help him. At the end of the day, he recovered enough to

Eddie Lion with his parents and great-aunt in Vienna, 1935.
"I stayed up for three nights talking to my parents because we all felt that we may not see each other again."
Courtesy of Eddie Lion.

crawl away on all fours, leaving a dark streak of blood in his wake. That experience will stay with me for the rest of my life.

"One day a bunch of Nazi hoodlums came to our apartment and took my mother away with some other people and made her wash the sidewalk with water laced with acid. When my father came home and saw what that had done to her arms, he wanted to kill them; even knowing that it would have meant he wouldn't have survived. This was another example of people turning into animals."

Realizing that things were only going to get worse, in 1938 Eddie's parents arranged (with much difficulty) for him to study engineering at the University of Edinburgh and they themselves left Austria for Britain on work permits one year later, just before war was declared.

"I stayed up for three nights talking to my parents because we all felt that we may not see each other again. At the airport, I had to strip to prove I was not smuggling money out of the country. They even cut a cake of soap into small pieces to check it. In London, the immigration official thought I looked suspicious and, since I didn't have my university registration papers, I was in danger of being sent back, which would have meant a concentration camp. They gave me a week to prove I was a student, which I did. In Edinburgh I led a typical student's life—studying, lots of fun and extra-curricular activities."

In 1940 things changed. Britain's Home Secretary, Sir John Anderson, decided to intern all German and Austrian males. On May 12, 1940, Eddie was picked up as he prepared to go for a bicycle ride with friends. A police car drove up and the officers politely asked him to bring a toothbrush and pajamas and to go with them just to answer a few questions.

"In a thrilling ride, with the police car going 80 mph and the siren wailing full blast we arrived at police headquarters. There were no questions at all. My fellow refugees and I were herded into a room and kept there all day. At night we had to sleep on the floor. There was no food for us and we were kept incommunicado. There were some dyed-in-the-wool Nazis among us but even they couldn't have been spies (perhaps they were just tourists who were caught up) because they bragged about being Nazis and they told us they would cut our throats after Hitler won the war."

For the next year and a half, Eddie Lion was pinballed around from camps in Liverpool, the Isle of Man and, after arriving in Canada (on an overcrowded ship with German and Italian POWs as shipmates), Three Rivers, Quebec, Ripples in New Brunswick (ten miles from Minto) and finally Sherbrooke, Quebec.

"The ship landed in Quebec City in the fall of 1940 and we had to walk through the city. The people were shouting, cursing, throwing stones and spitting at us. We were insulted in both English and French! They thought we were German POWs. It was pretty miserable. We were taken to an old exhibition hall in Three Rivers. In protest against our arrival, the German POWs set fire to the camp, with minimal success. They were sent out West within days. After a while, we were put on a train which belonged to a long-gone era. The windows were nailed shut to prevent escape—although nobody would have known where to escape to—and it was bloody hot. On arrival in New Brunswick we were met by the Veterans' Guard and soldiers (many past their prime) with machine guns. At the time it all looked impressive. We were later told that when the camp commandant saw how young many of us were, he wept. We marched in the heat and the dust to a half-finished, barbed-wire compound. All of a sudden, there was a downpour. We threw off our clothes and enjoyed the warm rain—an instant nudist colony with about 800 members!"

The inmates were issued the standard POW garb, a pair of blue denim pants with a red stripe down the leg and a jacket with a big red circle on the back to provide a target in case of escape. Eddie spent his days cutting down trees at the munificent rate of 20 cents a day which was later raised to 30 cents a day. It was, for Eddie, the period of his life when he was the healthiest he has ever been. The hard work also allowed him to sleep well at night and not dwell on his uncertain future. He also did a lot of reading and gave courses in algebra and geometry to the young boys in the camp who hadn't finished high school. Occasionally being part of the "truck party", he got to drive to the nearby train station to pick up camp supplies. As a secular Jew, he noted that the Orthodox Jews had many dietary and other restrictions that were eventually respected by the military but which he did not share.

"Life continued in Camp B until the fall of 1941 when many of us were transferred to a camp in Sherbrooke. It wasn't a camp at all, it was a filthy railroad shed surrounded by barbed wire. Our double bunks were placed between the train tracks. There was gravel on the ground and we had no place to put our things. There was mind-numbing work to do, like making nets or working on a sock machine. However, in a matter of weeks, some people came and told me they were my distant cousins from Montreal. I was released late in November into their custody and in 1945 I graduated as a civil engineer from McGill."

There was great excitement in the Italian community on the morning of Friday, July 14, 1933. Those attending the big event got dressed *alla fascista* or in their best Sunday clothes and headed for Longueuil to greet the arrival of the handsome and dashing Air Force Marshall Italo Balbo and his twenty-four Savoia Marchetti S.55X flying boats (each with a four-man crew) that were on their way to the World's Fair in Chicago. The flight started in Rome and included six stopovers. The crowd at St. Hubert Airport numbered in the thousands and was filled with pride at this amazing achievement. Many in the Italian community needed this boost. With the exception of a few entrepreneurs and small businessmen, most immigrants had their toes precariously clinging to the lowest rung of the economic ladder and had to suffer the negative stereotypes of the era, so this was a stellar chance to show their pride in Italian progress. Maria De Grandis Marrelli was eighteen years old at the time and remembers it well:

"There was a group in my neighbourhood that was going so about thirty of us girls got dressed in white blouses, tams, black kerchiefs and skirts. It was so exciting! It was the first time that such a thing happened. Oh my! To be in a huge crowd and to see those young men come out of the planes. We were all waving flags and yelling, *ITALIA, ITALIA, VIVA ITALIA!* We were in heaven, really. It was quite a feat and we were proud to say that they were from Italy."

Balbo and his men were lionized and feted in the United States but his Montreal reception was something less than welcoming. Although fascist leaders in Montreal held two lavish receptions to celebrate the event, also waiting for him was the journalist and anti-fascist Antonino Spada. In 1923 Balbo, as an organizer of fascist gangs that broke strikes and attacked socialists and communists, was suspected of involvement in the brutal murder of the anti-Fascist priest, Father Giuseppe Minzoni. Determined to spoil Balbo's reception in Montreal, Spada printed thousands of photos of the murdered Father Minzoni that were handed out around the Windsor Hotel where the aviators were staying. The mayor of Montreal, Fernand Rinfret, a devout Catholic, went against protocol and decided not to welcome Balbo at City Hall.

It is estimated that during the 1930s support for Fascism and Mussolini among the individuals of Italian origin in Montreal was 90 per cent. (By 1941, there were 112,625 Italians in Canada with the largest number, 28,051 residing in Quebec.) They were, therefore, in perfect sync with the Catholic and anti-communist mindset in Quebec at the time. Mussolini's signing of the Concordat with the Vatican in 1929 was especially welcomed by Catholics in Quebec. Dieni Gentile, Mario Lattoni and others carried the fascist banner to the end while those opposing fascism, like Antonino Spada, while in the minority, were no less determined. For English Canadians, Mussolini, at least in the beginning, was either the man who had done great things for Italy like making the trains run on time (a feat probably more admired by Anglo-Saxons than Italians!) or a buffoonish operatic figure commanding neither respect nor admiration.

In a sometimes unwelcoming city in which many considered them "dirty foreigners", the Italians found support, friendship and help in times of need in their two main churches, Madonna della Difesa and Madonna del Carmine. The churches were the centre of daily life and the women of the parish helped organize the feast day celebrations and other church events. Women also formed a young women's social and volunteer group called Elisabetta di Silvestro which was part of the Order Sons of Italy. These women learned organizational skills that would serve them well all their lives. Maria De Grandis Marrelli was one of these women. It might be said of her that she never met a worthwhile cause that she didn't love. While still a teenager, she was elected president of the Elizabeta de Silvestro. A lifelong Liberal, she served as a Canadian citizenship judge for five years in the 1970s and was made a *Cavaliere della Republica Italiana* in 1986.

The parish priests wholeheartedly supported Mussolini and church parades such as the feast of St. Anthony would usually include lines of marching Blackshirts. The fraternal Order Sons of Italy (Ordine Figli d'Italia) was founded in 1919 by Sam D'Onofrio and thirty-three of his compatriots. In 1936 the community had its dreams realized when the Casa d'Italia opened its doors and became the heart of the community. The beautiful Art Deco building on the corner of Berri and Jean Talon had been constructed on land donated by Mayor Houde, who was a treasured friend of the community. Now the Italians had a place to hold social events, meetings and commercial exhibitions. The Order Sons of Italy, the Casa d'Italia and the local newspapers, *L'Italia* and *L'Araldo del Canada* were under the close supervision of Consul Giuseppe Brigidi who tried to bring the community closer to the Fascist ideals of Mussolini. The consulate organized Italian language classes and many successful students were sent to summer camps in Italy as a reward and to further their ties to the regime. (The Italian consulate in Toronto came to the attention of the authorities when it was discovered that they had a *Squadra d'azione* (Action Squad) which planned to sabotage Canadian industry.) Antonino Spada organized the Ordine Indipendente Italo-Canadese which met in their headquarters in the Sala Mazzini in Ville Emard. Like-minded anti-fascist friends helped him found his own newspaper *Il Risveglio Italiano* which gave voice to an opposing opinion.

Mussolini's invasion of Ethiopia in 1935-36 left some in the community lukewarm while others—as well as many French Canadians—saw it as a way to bring civilization to a poor country. (In one famous story, the parish priests asked all the women to donate their wedding rings to help with the war. This they did with much enthusiasm.) A further lessening of support occurred as Italy signed the Pact of Steel with Germany and finally reached its nadir when Italy entered the war on the side of the Axis in June of 1940. This fateful day left many Italian Canadians worried and insecure. What now? For the vast majority, their total allegiance was to Canada and many proved it by enlisting and buying Victory Bonds, even while their relatives had to register as enemy aliens. Some families had more than one family member in uniform. The Capozzi family had three sons, Billy, Sam and Peter, in the service. The Dilios of Griffintown were another case in point and one of their sons, Jimmy, was killed in Italy while fighting with the Three Rivers Regiment in 1943.

The minute Italy entered the war, the RCMP, assisted by the Quebec provincial police, swooped down on the Casa d'Italia and detained many of its leaders. Their documents were confiscated and the lists of members gave the police a shopping list of future detainees. Allen Calderwood had a ringside seat on this occasion, too: "Some of the Italians, I guess they were spies because the same day war was declared the police were going door to door. I can remember them taking my friend's father away. We got along pretty good with the Italians and a lot of those guys went into the army too." The hard-working Italian community then had to face, in some cases, vandalism of their property, loss of jobs, being declared enemy aliens, confiscation of property with little recompense and internment. The shame felt by families who now had to rely on neighbourhood and family charity and the distortion of family life when wives were thrown into new and unfamiliar leadership roles can only be imagined by those who did not live through this experience. Maria De Grandis's husband Joe Marrelli—a naturalized Canadian and anti-Fascist—was sent home from his job at the Steel Company of Canada, as were all the other Italians. He was reinstated a short while later with an apology but, as an enemy alien, had to report to the RCMP for the next two years.

Of a total of 800 reputed Fascists in the city, 236 were interned. Hundreds were initially arrested but released on condition that they report each month to the RCMP. Those interned represented an eclectic cross-section of the Italian population: professionals, businessmen, workers, a sprinkling of *mafiosi,* a few undercover agents, fascist sympathizers of varying degrees, at least one priest and Guido Nincheri, the frescoe artist known as Canada's Michelangelo, whose works adorn many churches in Eastern Canada and the New England States. His painting of Mussolini astride a horse in the Madonna della Difesa Church (which was commissioned to commemorate the Lateran Treaty of 1929) brought him to the attention of the authorities and he languished in Petawawa for three months until his furious and determined wife arranged his release. (His depiction of Mussolini was "tarped" during the war but may now be seen in its full glory.) Many completely innocent inmates had their lives altered by informers acting on motives of jealousy or vengeance. It was a wonderful occasion to settle scores or gain an advantage over a business competitor. Antonio Capobianco served time at Petawawa while his brother served in the Canadian army. Some prominent fascists like A.D. Sebastiani, the wealthy shoe magnate, and A.S. Biffi were not interned. Being powerful and having the right connections could guarantee being overlooked. It must be noted, however, that many leading Fascists in the city had not the slightest wish to harm their adopted country. It must also be noted that many Italians in Montreal enjoyed a greater degree of prosperity than they ever had before by working in war industries.

Unlike most Italians, Liliana Ferroni Mulligan did not leave her comfortable life in Florence in 1931 for the usual financial reasons. At the age of sixteen she was invited by a prominent Canadian family who vacationed in Italy near the Ferronis to become a governess/companion for their two young daughters. The family wanted a young girl close in age to their daughters with whom they could practice Italian and French. Originally here for six months, the family arranged for an order-in-council in Ottawa so she could

Liliana Ferroni shortly after she arrived in Canada in 1934. At sixteen she became the governess/companion for the two young daughters of a prominent Canadian family while they vacationed in Italy. *Courtesy of Liliana Ferroni Mulligan.*

stay permanently. When the girls left to attend finishing school in England, Liliana moved to Montreal in 1934 and was hired by Eaton's. She was put in charge of the Gift Gallery because of her extensive knowledge of art. In the years before her marriage, she lived with her friend Kay in Westmount. Kay's grandfather, the owner of the house, was an influential person who supported Liliana in the coming stormy events after Italy entered the war.

"The RCMP sent me a notice saying I had to report regularly to them. I must say they were very nice to me but I was the only woman there and all the men were looking at me, 'What has she done?' I was fingerprinted and so on. They showed me pictures of men to identify but I told them that I only knew a few Italians in Montreal through my business and social contacts. When I got home, I told Kay's grandpa that I was worried and didn't know what was going on. He told me not to worry, that he had a good lawyer and would get me any help I needed. I was very comforted by that. They were marvelous to me. I was told that I had to bring any firearms I owned the next time I reported. I didn't even know the word 'firearm' until it was explained to me that it was something one used to defend oneself. I thought: What would I use to defend myself if someone broke into the house? There was a little sitting room in the house with a small fireplace and so, on my next visit, I wrapped up a small brass fireplace poker and took it down. They opened the door and asked me to come into the office. I thought I was going to be arrested although I knew I was protected in every way. When the officer heard my story, he said, 'My name is Gagnon. I'm in charge here and you don't have to come back.'"

Michael Lanese came to Canada at the age of ten in 1917 from the town of Guglionesi in Campobasso. The youngest of thirteen children, he went to work at a very young age, first working at Pastene and eventually going into business for himself. The family moved from St. Henri to the Italian neighbourhood near Madonna della Difesa Church in the early 1920s. In 2009, Michael returned to visit his hometown in Italy for the first time in ninety-two years where he and his family were given a heroes' welcome.

"I was thirty-two when the war started. In the beginning I thought Mussolini was a hero for Italy because he did a lot of good for the country. I remember that my sisters gave their wedding rings which were sent to Italy to help fight the war in Ethiopia. My feelings changed when he went with the Germans. It wasn't the same anymore. I wasn't mixed up too much with the Italian groups like the Sons of Italy because I was too involved with my hat-cleaning business at that time. The Casa d'Italia was a rendezvous place to pass the time and play cards but that wasn't my way of life. I used to go there for weddings and parties.

"I was a Canadian citizen but had to report downtown somewhere to the RCMP as an enemy alien. My mother, who was already an old lady and also a citizen, had to go too. I went for about a year and then they told me not to bother anymore. I was married in 1943 and then they sent me a letter to report to Longueuil for military service. It didn't make sense. I was supposed to be an enemy alien and then I was called for military service. What could I do? I didn't tell my wife. I was afraid that by going into the military my wife and mother-in-law would be left alone. The day I went, I got up and got dressed better than usual. I passed all the examinations step-by-step but, at the end I got a discharge paper probably because of my age.

"Many of the big shots, business people like the shoe manufacturers, contractors, the importers and the statue makers were interned at Petawawa. They took everything away from them. I knew a lot of them personally. They went with the flow and were Fascists but they were not people who were going to hurt Canada. When the war was over, they were let go but they had lost everything and had to start over.

"How did I feel about being declared an enemy alien? I was hurt because I felt I was more a Canadian than a Canadian. I was ten when I came here and was brought up here. We had nobody left in Italy. I never was in any trouble anywhere. I kept myself busy all the time with work. That experience gave me a bad feeling. But time heals everything. They shouldn't have feared the Italians. We came from a poor country to work and build this country and that's what we did. All the railroad tracks and tramway tracks were built by Italians. They worked all day in the heat with a pail of water beside them to drink. They worked very hard and then got into construction—St. Michel, St. Leonard—all built by Italians."

Lucy Fiore Madigan was the youngest of eleven children all born in Canada to Italian immigrants from Campobasso. Having three members of the family in military service did not prevent her mother from falling into the enemy alien category.

“My parents were not political at all. You know, when you have eleven kids...my mother was pregnant just about every year or every second year She was just preoccupied with raising a family. We belonged to Madonna della Difessa parish and my mother went to church almost every day. My father did construction and factory work. I was only two months old when he died in 1931 at the age of fifty-two.

“When the war started, we were worried about the few relatives we had in Italy but, other than that, there was no talk of politics. We were well established in Montreal but, at the beginning of the war, my mother didn’t have her citizenship papers and had to register and report to the RCMP every month. I often wondered why my mother with eleven children would even think of becoming a terrorist. (laughs) My brother Frank was called up. He could have refused because he was the provider of the family but, you know, my brother loved Canada so much. To the day he died, when they played the national anthem, he had tears in his eyes. He didn’t want to go and fight in Italy so he fought and was wounded in the Normandy Campaign with the Royal Canadian Regiment. My mother used to say the rosary every night and try to get us to join her. Maybe that’s what saved him because so many of his friends were killed. I remember the day we got the telegram that Frank was wounded. Oh, my God! My mother was so upset. We didn’t know where it happened because when he sent letters there were always parts that were taken out. My mother stopped crying when she learned that he was being taken care of in England. He was hit with shrapnel in his head and neck. In the end, they couldn’t operate to remove the shrapnel so he had head and neck pain all his life after that. I had cousins who also went overseas but they didn’t want to fight in Italy in case they were involved with relatives. My brother Nick was also called up and served in Canada. He was supposed to go over but the war ended the week before. My sister Lillian joined the Wrens—nice uniform (laughs)—and was stationed in Halifax. There were some positive things that happened to us because of the war. My brother Romeo was a welder and got a terrific-paying job working on ships that were being built in Montreal.

"I had friends who lived on Clark Street. One day I got invited to a concert in their shed. They were going to sing and dance, that kind of thing. I went over there to see this concert and my friend was called in by her mother. She came out and told me that I had to go home. When I asked why, she said, 'You're Italian and you're my enemy.' They never played with me after that. I was just a kid and terribly hurt. I didn't understand...*I'm an enemy?* I went home and told my mother who said to forget it, that I had nothing to be ashamed of. Another time in the country at Orford my sister and I went to a restaurant and someone asked me what nationality I was. I said Italian and they said something to the effect that we were enemies. My sister told them that we had family fighting in the war and they need not be abusive to us."

La Ville Sans Femmes/The City Without Women by Mario Duliani (published in 1945 in French and translated into English by Antonino Mazza in 1994); *Il Duce Canadeses: Le Mussolini Canadien* (a 2004 Radio Canada miniseries); *Barbed Wire and Mandolins* (a 1997 National Film Board production); *Paradise by the River* (a play by Vittorio Rossi, 1998 and 2010) all portray the

Lucy Fiori (left holding her niece) standing beside her brother Frank and her mother Birgida with the backs of houses on Clark Street behind them. *Courtesy of Lucy Fiori Madigan.*

very real financial suffering and emotional torment felt by those interned or by their relatives at home. There was a small minority of fascists who were interned until the end of the war. Photographs of them in camp in Fredericton show them proudly wearing military caps with the fascist motto *Me ne frego* (I don't care). In another photo the men are holding a banner with the same motto. These men were denied release because they said that they did not intend to abide by Canada's laws.

Prime Minister Brian Mulroney's 1990 apology to Italian Canadians for their internment during the war was followed by the adoption of Bill C-302 in the House of Commons. The Italian-Canadian Recognition and Restitution Act of April 28, 2010. Massimo Pacetti, the Liberal Member of Parliament for Saint-Léonard/Saint-Michel introduced the bill to "recognize the injustices carried out against Italian Canadians during the war." Was Canada's internment of Italians a "war on ethnicity" or a justifiable decision—albeit vastly exaggerated—to protect its citizens during wartime? The only certainty is that the innocent Italians who were only trying to carve out a life in a new country and who suffered greatly during this period will never forget the shame and hardships that were imposed on them.

[CHAPTER NINE]

1944

Zoot Suits to Zombies

By 1944, the European war was winding down. The Soviets were on the march west while Hitler, in his desperation, ordered the mobilization of children over the age of ten. The Americans and Australians were making slow but steady progress in the Far East. Allied planes were mercilessly bombing German cities but the Luftwaffe had not yet run out of bombs to drop on London. The monastery of Monte Cassino in Italy was in ruins after the successful Allied attack. The Japanese were being beaten back in India. On June 4 Rome was liberated and the Allies would soon be fighting their way through northwest Europe. Ominously, the first VI flying bombs were launched against England from France. Canadian commander, Harry Crerar was made a full general and, in 1945, during the Rhineland Campaign, he led an army of 350,000 men, the largest force to serve under a Canadian general. In July both Field Marshall Rommel and Hitler were injured; Rommel in an air attack and Hitler in yet another attempt to assassinate him. In August Paris was liberated. The British had a new fear with the first V2 flying rocket landing in London taking only five minutes to make the journey of 192 miles from occupied Holland. Canadian soldiers, including members of the Black Watch and the Régiment de Maisonneuve, both fighting understrength, were involved in the punishing battle of the Scheldt Estuary. This victory opened the Belgian port of Antwerp, a crucial element in the supply line for the Allies. The year ended with the Battle of the Bulge in the Ardennes Forest which was the last German offensive on the Western Front. In Montreal, the population was carrying on as usual but the news that was on the top of the list was the never-ending conscription crisis which was finally dealt with at the end of the year.

On April 25, 1944 residents of Griffintown witnessed a plane crash that made their district resemble the shattered ruins of British cities seen in newsreels of the day. It was not a shot-down German plane or a buzz bomb which caused the damage but a B-24 Liberator flying out of Dorval to England. Observers watched in horror as the plane began losing altitude over downtown Montreal and, barely missing the St. Antoine Street Post Office, scraped the top of the Dow Brewery Building on Notre Dame Street before crashing into six houses at the corner of Shannon and Ottawa Streets, shaking windows all over the neighbourhood. It was a Tuesday, the traditional day of the Devotion to Our Lady of Perpetual Help when people all over the city gathered to pray for peace. The 9:30 a.m. service at St. Ann's Church had just finished and many of the faithful were just arriving at McDonnell's store on the corner of McCord (Mountain) and Wellington for a snack or to buy cigarettes. One of the customers was a Miss Keegan of the Victorian Order of Nurses. She was one of the first to rush to the site but all she saw was fire and smoke. Ten residents of Griffintown were killed as were the mostly Polish RAF crew of five. One of the victims was Constable Louis Lemieux of the traffic police who had left his post at Colborne and Notre Dame Streets a few minutes before the crash to visit his brother-in-law, Wilfred Viens. Thirst saved cab driver William Ferland who had just stepped out to buy a beer. Three young children were also saved by disobeying their mother's order to stay indoors while she went on an errand. Don Pidgeon was a schoolboy at the time: "I remember that day very well. I was seven years old and in school. We weren't allowed to leave school but later on I walked around the site and saw the devastation. You couldn't get that close because the whole area was cordoned off. There were a lot of people milling about—the military, police and firemen—who tried to keep people as far away as possible from the situation. We knew that a plane had come down but we didn't know if it was a military or a commercial plane. The news came out later in the newspapers. I remember a young family named Wells. That day was their fifth wedding anniversary and when the husband came home, he found out that his wife and three-year-old son were both dead. That brought the war really close to us."

The plane crash in Griffintown gave Montrealers a small taste of the reality of war but the Canadian population was mercifully spared the devastation visited upon many areas around the world where carpet bombing of cities and the massacre of civilians was a common occurrence. We were not, however, immune to enemy attacks.

Nazi U-boats were immensely effective in wreaking havoc in the Gulf of St. Lawrence and the St. Lawrence River. Starting in May 1942, twenty-three merchant ships and five warships were sunk or damaged in Canadian territorial waters by U-boats resulting in the loss of 500 lives. Wartime news blackouts after the sinking of the *Nicoya,* the first casualty in the Battle of the St. Lawrence, meant that most Canadians were unaware of these attacks. Those living along the east coast, however, had a hard time ignoring the explosions that rocked their houses and the sight of dead bodies and survivors being dragged ashore. The people of St. Yvon, Quebec were shocked when an attack on a merchant ship failed but broke windows in the community and landed at least three torpedoes on their beach. The sinking of the passenger ferry *Caribou* in October 1942 when it was headed from Sydney to Port Aux Basques was one exception to the secrecy rule. The ship, designated a passenger ferry, on this voyage was carrying 118 military personnel as well as seventy-three civilians and a Newfoundland crew of forty-six. A total of 137 people perished, including ten children, which enraged public opinion. One nursing sister, Agnes Wilkie, the assistant matron of the RCNH (Royal Canadian Nursing Hospital) *Avalon,* drowned in the attack and was the only nurse to die as a result of enemy action during the war.

Thirteen-year-old Allen Calderwood was enjoying a pleasant, warm evening standing around with his friends on Addington Street on

June 3 when a strange thing happened. "Six or seven of us were just hanging around the Lions Club when a taxi pulls up and this guy we knew got out and ran up to the third storey where he lived. He didn't have a stitch on and we were all laughing. He was just a kid, maybe sixteen or seventeen. I guess maybe his sister came down with money for the taxi driver." Allen had some sympathy for the young men defying wartime regulations regarding the quantity of cloth allowed for suits. "Zoot suits. It was the style, you know what I mean. They wore big, baggy pants with a jacket down to their knees. The suits had big chains and many of them wore Fedoras. Everyone wanted to have a zoot suit. My mother would let us wear ordinary pants and go as low as sixteen inches at the cuff but some of those suits had a zipper at the cuff. It was just a cool look."

The lad in question had perhaps been sitting in a downtown restaurant with a couple of pals, walking on St. Catherine Street or dancing at Chez Maurice Danceland. Maybe he and his buddies decided to go to the dance at the Verdun Pavilion but they were in the wrong place to be wearing zoot suits. Tensions between military men and zoot suiters, which had been simmering for a long time, now came to a head. Zoot suiter gangs were often made up of French, Italian and English youths that sometimes clashed with each other, but tensions between French youths and military men had the added spark of the conscription question. There had been brawls in St. Lambert at the end of May between servicemen and civilians resulting in more than fifty arrests but the final straw occurred on June 2 when a sailor and his wife were beaten up in downtown Montreal. The navy was now ready for revenge. On June 3, from mid-evening until early morning, a crowd of about 400, mostly sailors, went on an alcohol- and testosterone-fuelled rampage in downtown Montreal bursting into restaurants and zooter hangouts. The sailors were from HMCS Donnacona, HMCS Hochelaga and HMCS Hyacinthe as well as other sailors in port at the time. Their ranks were bulked up by the addition of some soldiers and airmen. The battles raged with broken bottles, clubs, knives and other weapons much in evidence. The biggest riot was at the Verdun Pavilion, a popular dance hall. Beverly Overall Marsh was a young girl of sixteen who recalls: "A group of us girls used to go for a walk at night to the Verdun Pavilion to watch the people dancing. It was right on the boardwalk with all the screened windows facing the water. It was a very pretty place. One night while we were watching, the navy arrived in a big truck because the zoot suiters were there. When the noise and yelling began, we left and I remember running up Woodland. We knew there was something going on and we didn't want any part of it." What Beverly and her friends missed was a riot that not even the police and the navy's Shore Patrol could control, although one wonders how objective members of the Shore Patrol could be in this case. Allowing some women to leave, the sailors battered their way in with benches from the boardwalk. They beat and stripped the zoot suiters and tore their clothing to shreds. Those hiding in the rafters were pulled down and got the same treatment. Nude zooters were then chased onto Wellington Street and the wrecked Pavilion was not such a pretty place anymore. The final tally was three sailors, two civilians and one police officer taken to hospital and more than forty (mostly sailors) arrested. There was no way of calculating the embarrassment of having to make your way home in the buff. Clashes continued throughout the rest of the week, which resulted in more injuries. Public sympathy seemed to be with the sailors but this event would soon be overshadowed by the invasion of Normandy on June 6.

The zoot suit style of dressing originated in Harlem in the 1930s and was considered a cool but rebellious look. The Wartime Prices and Trade Board didn't care how "hep" it was. It was illegal and tailors were not allowed to create "the drape shape with the reet pleat and the stuff cuff". In the aftermath of the rioting, many zoot suiters visited barbers to modify their "duck tail" hairstyles and kept a lower profile. It is easy to understand the mutual antipathy of the two groups. Many of the sailors had already seen action and, with the invasion of France around the corner, they knew there would be many more casualties. They were subjected to military

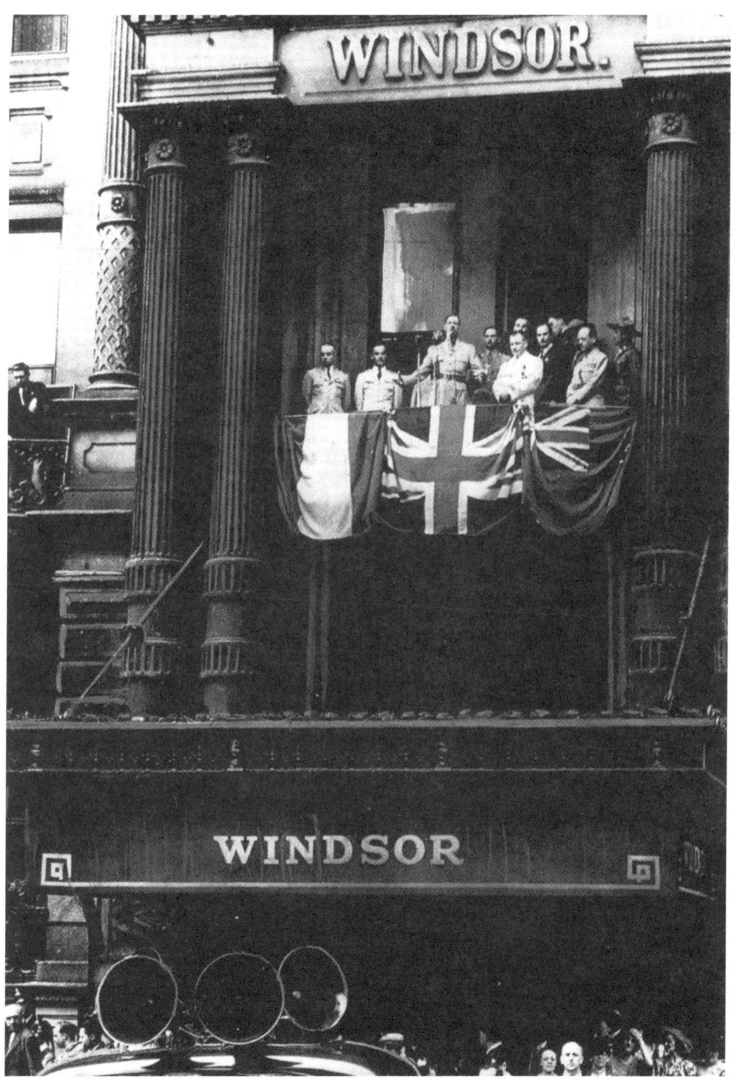

General Charles de Gaulle, leader of the Free French government-in-exile, addressing Montrealers July 12, 1944.
Montreal Gazette.

discipline while the zooters (although many were too young for enlistment) taunted them, called them "suckers" and, worst of all, competed with them for the pretty girls. Allan Marsh, a sailor based at Donnacona recalls: "These guys were against conscription and looked like clowns. That style went on until maybe 1946 when the novelty wore off. I was on the streetcar going back to Donnacona. This young kid, who was about ten years old, I guess, said to me, 'Hey, mister. There's a zoot suiter at the back. Go get him!' I looked at this guy and he probably wasn't too sure what was going to happen because he heard this kid tell me to go fix his clock. I told the kid, 'Why? He didn't do anything to me.'"

The major event of 1944 was the brilliantly-executed Allied invasion of Normandy. In the early morning of June 6, the largest seaborne invasion fleet ever assembled in the history of the world began the final phase of the war. Years of painstaking planning led to the successful attack on beaches codenamed Sword, Juno, Gold, Omaha and Utah. An armada of over 5,000 ships squeezed into the stormy waters of the English Channel and 8,000 zebra-striped airplanes filled the air, providing air cover for nearly 150,000 well-trained soldiers. The German defences were formidable and the weather was unusually bad for early June but, in spite of this, by mid-morning, Canadian soldiers had liberated the town of Bernières-sur-Mer. By nightfall, more than 15,000 troops had come ashore and advanced farther inland than any of the other Allies but with a cost of approximately 1,000 casualties.

Howie Dearlove was a student at Guy Drummond School on D-Day. "We went to school and Mr. McPhee, the principal, came down as soon as the bell rang at 10 to 9 and said it was the most important day in our lives. 'Go home. No school for you today. Go home and come back tomorrow.' I went home. My father was working the night shift at Canadian Propellers and when I got home he was sitting in a chair by the radio. We could hear the planes going over the Channel. I couldn't get my father away from the radio. It was a sad day in many ways but we were getting back at them at last.

We had beaten them in Italy and then they started the invasion. The next day it was back to routine." Those who had loved ones involved could only pray, hope, worry and pray some more that all would go well. The noteworthy achievements of our soldiers fighting in Italy which led to the liberation of Rome just two days before D-Day was pushed aside by the heroic dimensions of the battle to the north, much to the dismay of those troops who had just gone through a difficult slog in the challenging terrain of Italy.

Thousands of Montrealers waited in the rain on July 12, a month after D-Day, to welcome General Charles de Gaulle, leader of the Free French government-in-exile who had kept the flame of resistance alive in his country. By this time, much of the support for Pétain's government had waned and the crowds were anxious to hear what the great man had to say. He did not disappoint. Standing on the balcony of the Windsor Hotel which was decorated with the tricolour of France, the Union Jack and the Canadian Red Ensign, he was effusive in his praise for the Canadian troops who had recently landed in Normandy to begin the liberation of France. "Your soldiers were among the first to land in my—I should say our—dear Normandy," he said. "There was a fine symbol of the great brotherhood of civilized people. Frenchmen, no matter where they may be today, are grateful for what you Canadians have been doing...Love live Canada! Long live France!" After wild applause, the crowd responded with "*Vive de Gaulle!*" "*Vive le Canada!*"and "*Vive la France*!" Then he and his entourage crossed the street to Dominion Square where he laid a wreath at the Cenotaph. Quick visits to the Outremont and Montreal city halls were made and another wreath was laid at the monument to Dollard des Ormeaux in Lafontaine Park. Then he returned to the Windsor for two separate receptions that were attended by thousands of supporters. The stirring *Marseillaise* was sung and again, de Gaulle promised that "France would never forget Canada's friendship." What the public probably did not know was that de Gaulle's niece, Geneviève de Gaulle, a Resistance fighter, had been captured by the Gestapo and was languishing in the Ravensbruck concentration camp for women and children. On another balcony in 1967, Canada's Centennial year, the now seventy-six-year-old de Gaulle struck a far different note when, he ended a speech by shouting "*Vive le Québec libre!*" from Montreal's city hall.

Quebec City hosted the Second Quebec Conference September 12-16, 1944. During the first conference in August 1943, Winston Churchill, Franklin Roosevelt and Mackenzie King met to take steps to unify the Allied command and discuss the Allied invasion of France and other war strategies. In the second conference with the end of the war in sight, the same leaders again met to discuss the future of Germany, American economic aid to Britain and the war with Japan. While the end of the conflict was anticipated by political planners, it was certainly not over for the Canadian infantry fighting their way through northwest Europe in 1944. With their ranks seriously depleted by injuries, deaths and illness, it became necessary to send untrained cooks and clerks to the front lines thus increasing the casualty rate. French regiments were particularly hard hit by this dearth of reinforcements. Canadians, many of whom had suffered family losses, wondered why we still had 70,000 conscripts sitting in Canada and began demanding that the home defence troops be sent overseas to hasten the end of the war. Many couldn't understand why Mackenzie King would put his political survival above the country's obvious needs but King was very concerned with a possible civil rift that might endanger the country's very survival. Serving officers abroad were also desperate for reinforcements. It did not escape notice that Canada, alone among the Allies, did not implement overseas conscription.

Defence Minister, Col. J.L. Ralston was sent on a trip to Europe in September and confirmed the dire facts by seeing first hand the desperation of the troops and their officers. The Mackenzie cabinet's refusal to change the conditions of the NRMA led to his forced resignation. His replacement, the popular Gen. A.G. McNaughton, also confirmed the reality of the situation and stated that 16,000 more men should be sent to Europe to keep the army up to strength.

A public relations attempt by both McNaughton and King failed to increase recruitment. After much dissension and discussion in cabinet in which the argument was put forth that if this solution was not accepted, an election with a possible total-conscriptionist Conservative government win would certainly alienate Quebec and further divide the country. By Machiavellian manoeuvring, King was able to dodge the bullet and save his government. It was agreed that 12,000 NRMA soldiers would be sent to operational theatres. As soon as this decision was made, many NRMA men decided to go active, preferring to go as volunteers, which helped the situation somewhat.

This decision led inevitably, of course, to more rioting in Montreal when mobs tried to attack the offices of English newspapers. A huge police presence prevented that and they had to be happy with smashing the windows of *Le Canada*. Windows were also broken in the National Selection Service office and in several banks. When news reached the troops in British Columbia (these men, unlike rioters in Montreal, were well armed), the reaction was predictable. The men in camps in Vernon and Terrace were having none of it and they mutinied. In Vernon, a crowd of 200 men paraded through the streets holding placards reading: "Down with conscription," "Zombies strike back," and "Conscript money as well". In Terrace, loaded rifles and even anti-aircraft guns were aimed at the troop trains assembled to transport them east. The message was clear: If that train moves, we'll blow it up.

Louis St. Laurent, the avuncular and distinguished Quebec lawyer, had reluctantly agreed to be appointed minister of justice in 1941 to replace Ernest Lapointe who had died in office. The new spokesman for French Canada had made no anti-conscription promises to Quebec. He therefore had a clean slate and was able to go along with King's decision. In spite of this, the turmoil led St. Laurent to remark, "It's happened. I told the prime minister to invite me to celebrate the (Christmas) season here because my people won't have me at home."

The situation in the camps in British Columbia diffused and

the men were sent home for a two-week embarkation leave from which thousands never returned. By early January 1945, out of a total of 10,000 due to sail first, 7,800 did not show up. More than half were still missing by sailing date. There was an ugly incident in Drummondville on February 24, 1945 when members of the Canadian Provost Corps and the RCMP were sent to find deserters. They were attacked by a mob with the riot lasting for several hours and resulting in many injuries. By April 1945, 4,500 were still missing of the original 14,500 destined for overseas service. The departure for overseas in early 1945 was a rather sad scene as dock workers and witnesses reported that some conscripts cried, lay down on the ramp and tried to jump into the water as they were forced onto ships in Halifax Harbour by military police.

In the end, nearly 13,000 Zombies were sent overseas with close to 10,000 making it to the continent. Only about 2,500 of them were involved in action on the front lines. One of the battles in which they fought was the Hochwald Forest in which they acquitted themselves well. When they arrived to join units already fighting, there was some resentment and many felt that they were not well trained. Others said that they were obedient and cooperative and many had no idea that these were not regular recruits. In the end, sixty-nine Zombies died in action.

René Héroux (FMR) was a seasoned soldier and remembers when one of these men joined his platoon: "I had a guy in my platoon who was a Zombie. He used to say, 'I don't want this war but I'm going to kill as many Germans as I can, to hell with you guys.' Sometimes when we were waiting for action he would say, '*Eh, que'ce que on fait!* Let's go! *Awiy! Awiy!*' He was so brave he scared some of us."

[CHAPTER TEN]

The War is Over!

La Guerre est finie!

DURING THE LAST FEW MONTHS of the war in Europe, Canadian newspaper headlines reported hard-won victories that would culminate in total German capitulation. News of grand-scale offences, the crossing of the Rhine by Americans, the unchecked advances by the Allies, the death of Hitler and the liberation of Holland led, finally, to the news that the Allies had been waiting for; the war in Europe was really and truly over. The week of May 8, 1945 had the *Gazette* blazoning the headline: GERMANY SURRENDERS. The *Montreal Daily Star* went for a two-line heading: LAST HUN ARMIES QUIT—WAR ENDS 12:01 A.M. MAY 9. The *Herald* filled its entire front page with three words: HUNS QUIT WAR. *La Presse* was short and to the point: *FIN DE LA GUERRE* while *Le Devoir* on May 7 reported: *L'ALLEMAGNE s'est rendue sans conditions aux Alliés d'Occident et à la Russie dans une école de France.* (*Le Devoir*, of course, could not get totally into the spirit of relief and celebration. Its anti-war stance surfaced in a sobering article by Pierre Vigeant in which he wrote that Poland, the country for which the Allies had gone to war, was now, along with many other countries, "*d'états vassaux*" (vassal states) of the Soviet Union. He claimed that the world was no better off than it was in 1939 with another totalitarian regime again threatening peace.)

After five years, eight months and six days, the war, at least in Europe, was over. In the Hotel De Wereld in Wageningen, the Netherlands, Lieutenant-General Charles Foulkes, commander of the First Canadian Corps, accepted the surrender of Colonel-General Johannes von Blaskowitz on May 6. Prince Bernhard, commander-in-chief of the Dutch Interior Forces, witnessed the reading of the surrender terms. In the early morning of Monday, May 7, at General Eisenhower's headquarters in a technical school in Rheims, representatives of Britain, France, Russia and the United States watched as General Alfred Jodl signed surrender documents. The next day, General-Admiral Hans von Friedeburg signed a separate surrender of German forces to the Soviets in Karlshorst, near Berlin.

Finally, the time for celebration had come. At 9:35 a.m. on Monday, May 7, 1945, Radio Station CKAC was the first to announce the joyful news of the surrender of the German forces. Soon after that, the news went up on the bulletin board outside the offices of the *Montreal Star* on St. James Street causing stockbrokers, secretaries and passersby to begin celebrating. The acting prime minister, J.L. Isley declared the following day, May 8, to be VE-Day and a public holiday and Sunday, May 13, a "day of prayer and solemn thanksgiving." Part of his statement read as follows: "Yet the hearts of Canadians will be filled not so much with the pride of conquest

May 7, 1945. The war in Europe is over. Flags and pure celebration on St. Catherine Street after almost six years of sacrifice and worry. *Montreal Star/Library and Archives Canada.*

as with relief and thankfulness and firm resolution to carry on the war until our enemy in the Far East meets the fate that surely awaits him." Works Minister Fournier followed with a French translation. Mackenzie King and Louis St. Laurent were in San Francisco at the time representing Canada at the founding conference of the United Nations.

Montrealers couldn't wait and throughout the island, streamed out of homes, offices and stores into the streets to celebrate the long-awaited victory in an explosion of joy. Thousands thronged Victoria Square, Dominion Square, Place d'Armes, Champs de Mars and the business district along St. James Street. From the windows in the tall buildings fluttered a blizzard of paper streamers, ticker tape, business statements, blank cheques and even toilet paper that danced in the wind and got tangled in the middle of the street. Chicken feathers emptied from a sack near St. Alexander Street swirled around overhead. Many stores, including Eaton's were boarded up. The corner of Peel and St. Catherine was the heart of the downtown centre of festivities which created a gridlock of trams, cars and flag-bedecked taxis . By noon you could not move through the crowds. Some youths got a kick out of bouncing stalled cars up and down. Jubilant citizens—some borne aloft on friends' shoulders—cheered, sang, hugged, whistled, kissed and danced to music thoughtfully provided by portable radios in a mad frenzy of excitement. Conga lines snaked their way through the happy crowds. Background noise was provided by the roar of a plane flying overhead, blaring car horns, blasting ships' whistles in the harbour, sonorous church bells and celebrants making a racket with firecrackers, sticks, tin cans and whatever they had on hand. "Hail, Hail, The Gang's All Here" was heard and one woman sang "For He's a Jolly Good Fellow" while patting a soldier on the back. One intrepid reveller on a motorcycle, perhaps on a dare, rode down St. Catherine Street wearing a Hitler mask. He barely escaped injury as the crowd threw objects and attempted to clobber him with canes and umbrellas. Two sailors were seen trying to coax a policeman to share their crock of rum. In Point St. Charles effigies of Hitler were hung from trees inviting public ridicule.

Schoolchildren were seen among the festive horde. Although many schools remained officially open, others closed, probably realizing that not many students or teachers were in the mood for penmanship or math that day. The Montreal Catholic School Commission remained officially open and planned to close on the official holiday only. Final exams at McGill were postponed for two days. Students at Loyola College gathered at noon in the chapel for a service of Benediction and the chanting of a Te Deum and were told to return to classes on Wednesday morning.

Union Jacks and Canadian Red Ensigns, as well as flags from many other countries, fluttered from buildings or were carried through the streets. Montreal City Hall hung three flags—a Union Jack with two Red Ensign flags flanking it. Farmers at Bonsecours Market decorated their carts and trucks with everything from carrot tops to ribbons. When red, white and blue bunting ran out, citizens dragged out all the ribbons and decorations they had at home so that Easter, Christmas and St. Patrick's Day colours were also seen draping windows, cars, bicycles, baby carriages and decorating necks and hats. Cars driven by excited young men zigzagged through the streets with celebrants hitching a lift on the running boards and hanging on to door handles, windows and whatever else would provide a grip. Office girls walked in small groups either avoiding or encouraging attention from young men eager to get their share of kisses.

So many customers burned up the phone lines sharing the good news of the day that the Bell Telephone had to issue a warning that calls should be restricted to those that were absolutely essential. Normally sedate members of religious orders allowed themselves a little flutter of excitement. At Collège Mont Saint-Louis, brothers and young boys in their charge stood outside and cheered loudly. On Mount Royal Avenue, nuns marching their teen-age convent girls along the street allowed them to stop and buy newspapers. Stores put "Closed for Victory" signs in their windows. There was little work being done that day and few customers wanted to shop.

Most of the soldiers, sailors and airmen seen in the crowd joined in the celebration but two recently returned soldiers of the Royal Montreal Regiment stood silently by and announced that they would rather be in Piccadilly Circus enjoying a "few pints of Burton".

Chief Inspector Alfred Bélanger assigned every available patrolman and detective in the city to handle the crowds and traffic. Inspector Tom Leggett was put in charge but the good-natured crowd generally responded well to issued directives and, at the beginning, there were only a few incidents reported. Besides a few lost children, some traffic snarls and a few arguments with pedestrians and drivers, there was a bit of mischief when paper in trash cans was set afire, paper bags filled with water were dropped from buildings, a false alarm sent fire wagons screaming downtown, a liquor store on Stanley Street was looted and at least one bonfire was started. Thirty streetcars and buses also had their doors and windows broken but the city was spared the massive looting and rioting that happened in Halifax when drunken mobs took over the city, causing three deaths and damages to the city amounting to $5 million.

Since alcohol is often the engine of mayhem, squads of Quebec Liquor Police members patrolled the city after a provincial government edict forced all bars and taverns to close for the two days of celebration. Of course, not all obeyed and the miscreants had to be warned to stay closed until the morning of May 9. Some early-morning deliveries of beer to licensed groceries had already been made before the news of victory was announced and, fearful of parched mobs hijacking the trucks, brewery officials hurriedly ordered drivers back to the breweries. Most of the larger blind pigs had closed but others remained open to their regular customers. In spite of all these measures, many paper cups were seen in the crowd filled with amber-coloured liquid that certianly wasn't ginger ale. With many downtown restaurants closed, celebrants slowly headed home with some attending evening church services. Others, perhaps, invited in a neighbour or two to share a precious bottle and maybe even get "tight" to round out the historic day.

It was particularly exciting for young people to be let out of school to celebrate. Children had lost part of their childhood with the war and its restrictions and were eager to share in their parents' joy. Howard Dearlove was one on them. "I was ten years old when the war ended. The principal, Mr. McPhee, came down and told us that the war was over and we could go home. McPhee was about seventy years old, an old man, but they kept them on during the war. We got to go home (all the Outremont School Board) for two days this time. We went downtown the next day. My mother took us on a streetcar ride along St. Catherine Street. The street was dead and everything was closed. They hadn't cleaned up yet and the store fronts were full of paper streamers and confetti." Lucy Fiore Madigan: "Oh my Lord! I was at school and the teachers told us that the war had ended and we could go home. I was about thirteen or fourteen. Everybody was dancing in the streets and kissing each other. It was a happy occasion and we knew that our two brothers and sister would soon be coming home."

Beverly Overall Marsh recalls: "Oh Gosh! I remember cars with honking horns and dances on every street in Verdun. It was really exciting and the celebrating seemed to go on forever. Many houses were decorated with flags and banners with WELCOME HOME JOHN and things like that." Don Pidgeon left his home in Griffintown to celebrate. "My mother brought us all up to St. Catherine Street and I remember that on the corner of University there was a newspaper kiosk and some rowdies had overturned it and set it on fire. When they started rocking the streetcars, my mother said that it was too dangerous to stay and we left. People were celebrating but some of them went wild over the fact that the war was over. The war started for us Canadians in 1939 and we had been involved for a long, long period." Phyllis Eperson: "Oh, I remember that day well! We all went down to St. Catherine Street where the crowds were all excited and it was Hip! Hip! and all that. We were so thrilled that the war was over and no one else was going to be killed. My brother was overseas and you always wondered who was going to be next."

Carol Lodge had to live with the disappointment of missing the Montreal celebrations. "I was practice teaching in the Eastern Townships when the war ended. Some other student teachers and I were fit to be tied that we weren't in downtown Montreal but we had the day off and went to a Victory barn dance near Brome Lake. We also listened to all the festivities on the radio."

Not everyone was smiling on V-E Day. Many were seen sobbing or looking reflective. Whether they were crying in relief at the good news or reliving a private loss was not always apparent. Three young women received an answer they did not anticipate when they asked a serious-looking man why he wasn't smiling. He answered, "I can't smile. My boy is not coming back." One can only imagine that many bereaved women lay sobbing across their beds while clutching a silver-framed photograph of a forever-young son or husband. Others might have fingered rosaries as they re-read for the hundredth time the fateful telegram that told them their lives would never be the same. Most were relieved that other families would now be spared the pain of loss but had no idea how they would carry on with the void of their own.

Ruth Swinton Stevenson did not take part in the festivities downtown. "My mother said that we shouldn't go. It was not something to rejoice about." Many were of the same opinion and headed to churches and synagogues to give prayerful thanks that it was all finally over. They lit candles in Catholic churches, made the Stations of the Cross and knelt at the shrines of saints. A service of Benediction was held at St. Patrick's. The bells of St. James Cathedral on Dominion Square and Notre Dame in Old Montreal rang out a call to worship. The regular 12:30 service at Christ Church Cathedral was turned into a VE-Day service. People filed into Temple Emanu-El all day in spite of the fact that no services were scheduled. At the Church of the Advent in Westmount, a little boy's voice was heard asking his mother, "Will Daddy be coming home now?"

Even though the war was officially over, casualty reports were still trickling in. On May 8, the *Gazette* reported the sinking of the *Esquimalt* by a Nazi submarine off the coast of Nova Scotia in mid-

April with a loss of forty-four lives. It was the last Canadian ship to be sunk during the war. While all deaths are lamentable, those occurring at the very end of hostilities seem, somehow to be more needless. That there might be many more casualties was brought home by a sign in a downtown army recruiting office that read: "Open for Business—With Japan".

Stores, businesses and schools were closed for the day and, again, churches and synagogues were open with official services scheduled. The newspapers were full of large and prayerful notices. A typical one read: We Thank Thee, our Heavenly Father, for the Victory Thou hast brought our Cause. We thank Thee that Thou in Thy Wisdom hast permitted Right and Freedom to prevail." None of the ads gloated about the demise of the Thousand Year Reich but rather emphasized the return to peace and the hope for a better future. There was also encouragement to continue the task until the "remaining enemy is crushed and War forever banished from the face of the earth".

Regular radio programming for the day was set aside to allow for special broadcasts and speeches from King George VI, US Secretary of State Edward Stettinius and other military and government officials. Mackenzie King's solemn speech was broadcast from California and was followed by Louis St. Laurent's speech in French. The lights were back on again in England and London was a sea of red, white and blue as Prime Minister Winston Churchill, the voice of dogged resistance, delivered a speech at the Ministry of Health Building to millions of jubilant Britons who had bravely suffered and sacrificed for almost six years. "This is your victory; victory of the cause of freedom in every land! In all our long history we have never seen a greater day than this.....God bless you all." At the end of his speech, the crowd broke into a rousing and heartfelt, "Land of Hope and Glory".

During the hoopla of VE-Day, it was easy to forget for a few hours that the war in the Pacific still raged and hundreds of Canadian POWs were still languishing in Japanese camps under unspeakable conditions. The Americans had been firebombing Japanese cities for the last five months of the war but the worst was yet to come. On July 16, 1945, the first nuclear bomb was detonated in New Mexico. Knowing that an invasion of Japan would be extremely costly for the Allies, a horrible alternative was decided upon. On August 6 and 9, two atomic bombs, code named "Little Boy" and "Fat Man", were dropped on Hiroshima and Nagasaki with a horrendous loss of life. Japanese dithering before the final surrender led to many premature celebrations of the end of the Pacific war in all Allied countries. VJ-Day was officially declared to be August 15 when crowds again tumbled out into the streets of downtown Montreal to celebrate the end of a war that, in its scope, cruelty and depravity was unprecedented in the blood-soaked annals of the world.

Carol Lodge: "This was almost an anticlimax after all the reports of the atomic explosion launched on Japan a few days before. I was at a concert at McGill Stadium on the night of one of the bombings and it was hailed as a marvellous event. We didn't know the true ghastly effects until quite some time later but, being told that it hastened the end of fighting, it was accepted as wonderful. There was dancing in the streets in the afternoon and evening and, in fact, I could pick myself out in a photograph of a small section of revellers on Peel Street."

Although reluctant to commit Canadian forces to fight in the Pacific theatre of war, on May 19, 1945, Mackenzie King announced that 43,500 volunteers would be assigned to fight the final stages of the war. Many veterans of the European war were willing to go and were given a month's leave in Canada in the event, but the dropping of the atomic bombs on Japan ended the war and their services were not needed. One who had volunteered to fight Japan was René Héroux. Still in Valcartier in October, 1945, he was to experience the hostility that was still shown to men in uniform by anti-conscriptionists. "I was a corporal stuck with fifty guys for five weeks and, as the only instructor, I was running the show. I wanted to get out because, as I told the major, 'There's no war here. The only war is with *les canadiens français*'. We had just come back from the front lines and they knew we had wanted to go to Japan. They called us *'les bombes atomiques'*. I didn't go to bars much because, as an instructor, I felt responsible but some guys went to a bar one night and two, three guys came in and said, *'Eh, c'est les criss de bombes atomiques'*. So one guy got up and that was all you needed. The fight was on. Was it difficult fighting with my 'own people'? They were not 'our own people'. They were Zombies and we were the guys that went to war and wanted to go to another war. There was a big difference between us and them. We were not friendly but it was only like that in Quebec City."

Finally, the time had arrived! The boys were returning home! Parties had been planned; food prepared and banners hung. Families dressed in their "Sunday go-to-meeting clothes" and, full of apprehension and joy, went to greet their loved ones, some of whom they hadn't seen in years. Many had to brace themselves to welcome an injured family member and hoped that the shock would not be too great. If the arrival point was Bonaventure Station,

René Héroux as a young recruit, 1943.
"I'm going there to defend the French. The French need us."
Courtesy of René Héroux.

they would find the station awash in Union Jack flags and neatly sectioned alphabetically with sentries posted to keep order. And so they waited—grandparents, parents, siblings, wives and children. As soon as the train arrived, pandemonium would break out and there was no controlling the avalanche of love that greeted the men. "There he is!" "*C'est Jacques!*" "I see him!" Heavily-censored letters from overseas had been the only contact as the long years elapsed but now, everybody hoped, normal life would return. Philip Aspler was winding up his military duties in Montreal and was assigned to welcome soldiers home but his was a difficult task. "We had lists of boys returning home and when they came in at Bonaventure Station, I was sent down to check them off the list as they arrived. It was sad for me because all these fellows were coming back and their families were there to welcome them and I knew that my brother would not be coming home."

Dave McCrindle remembers the day he returned in more splendour than he left. "Going away we were in old colonial cars—worst goddamned railway transportation I ever saw in my life and the food was garbage. A lot of cheese sandwiches, things like that. Coming back we were in newer cars with sleepers. We were treated like royalty; white tablecloths, roast beef, bacon and eggs. It was a very joyful reunion at Bonaventure Station. My parents, my sister, a couple of aunts and two Canadian girls I knew who had joined the CWACS in England were all there to welcome me. We had a big party at home and it was great tasting my mother's cooking again. Canadian beer was a change for me, too. It was a pretty good party with old friends and neighbours coming in until about 1 a.m. Montreal hadn't changed much but I had. I weighed about 145 pounds and had a moustache. I didn't bring any souvenirs home with me because we were warned not to and I didn't want to get nailed. I threw a German Luger in a canal in Holland. The canals in Holland are filled with Lugers."

Arthur Fraser arrived back in Canada an emaciated shell after being held for two-and-a-half years as a POW after the raid on Dieppe in 1942, spending about fourteen months in shackles and enduring the forced march prisoners had to take as the Allies advanced into German-occupied zones. He describes his return and the entrepreneurial spirit that served him well during captivity when wheeling and dealing with guards meant the difference between eating well in the circumstances and just surviving. "I came back in May 1945. Before I left England I bought a dice game called Crown and Anchor. I told myself that I was going to make money with this—and I did! I played this game for five days on the ship. I didn't sleep and I had someone go and get me food. I tipped him half a pound. When we arrived in Bonaventure, the officer said that we were allowed to change English money to the value of $200. I changed my money and passed through. I gave the rest of my money to some friends and told them that I would give them ten bucks if they changed my money. I came out with $700! My mother was waving to me and couldn't understand why I was taking so long but I had to wait for these guys to give me my money. Then I went home to Sanguinet Street and we had a small party—just the close family. I was really glad to see my mother and two sisters again. The next day I opened a bank account and deposited my money."

Stuart Vallières lost a leg when he was shot down over France after completing thirty-two bombing raids and returned to Canada on a hospital ship. Like many airmen based in England, he developed friendships with the local population that were deep and meaningful. "My initial homecoming was in England. Our crew had been very close to two families; one owned a pub and the other owned a café. They had become like parents to all of us. I came back to Canada on the hospital ship, the *Lady Nelson.* My cousin was the chief steward on the ship which made it very nice when they were serving ice cream, and we certainly enjoyed our share of it. The fact that we had two kit bags loaded with cognac and champagne didn't hurt either! I got back to Rockliffe in Ottawa where a reception was held for us. The families who were there to greet the boys coming back were stunned at the quantity of the food and thought we would be impressed, but all most of the guys were interested in was Canadian beer." (laughs)

René Héroux: "On the way back home, I was seasick every day but I still managed to win four or five hundred dollars playing five card stud. I got off the train at Bonaventure on July 23, 1945 and all the gang was there—my family, my cousins, my aunts, my uncles—about fifty people. Some of the neighbours were at the train too, *les Gagnés, les Poiriers*...it was 'Welcome Home' and all that stuff. At home, there was a huge banner over the door, WELCOME HOME RENÉ in English! The party lasted all day and all night. My sister and some of the neighbours looked after the food. I brought back so many souvenirs that I wanted to keep but it was, "*Eh, René, est-ce-que je peux prendre ça?* You can't say no so I came out of there with nothing. I had a pearl necklace which I wanted to keep for my girlfriend. (I didn't have a girlfriend but I was hoping to get one.) My sister got it. I had a revolver in my kit bag and, when they were all looking through my things, my brother-in-law found the gun and fired a shot. It was still loaded and he could have killed someone. I had a 30-day leave and didn't tell my mother that I had volunteered to go to Japan but, as it turned out, the war ended and I didn't have to tell her."

Jacques Boucher: "I remember when my father came home in 1946. In those days there were milk deliveries to the house and my kid sister, Ghislaine, had just picked up two milk bottles at the door. She happened to look across the street when she saw a man in a navy uniform with a kit bag get off the streetcar. She was saying to herself, 'I wish this was my daddy. I wish this was my daddy.' All of a sudden, she recognized our dad. She dropped the two bottles of milk and ran across the street. She could have been killed. There wasn't much traffic in those days but, still. I had seen my father a few times during the war but, for my kid brother who was born in 1938, he was just a man in a uniform. Two more children were born after the war; my sister, Françoise, in 1947 and my brother, Pierre, in 1953 so only the four oldest of us remember the war years."

Beverly Overall Marsh also remembers her father's return before the end of the war. "It was very exciting. Dad came back in

February of 1944. There were just buses, no cars. Not many people had cars. My mom, her sisters and sisters-in-law and my brother and I went to the station. Mom wouldn't let me wear lipstick because she thought it would be too much of a shock for Dad. I was a little girl when he left and a young lady when he came back. I can still see my dad coming up the escalator in Central Station. I hollered, 'HERE HE COMES!' I was leaning over the railing of the escalator and was the first one Dad saw. It was very noisy and there were tears. Many people in the station were holding signs and some of the men arriving were wounded."

In spite of the shadow under which Lucy Fiore Madigan's Italian-Canadian family lived during the war, three family members enlisted. She recalls the day her brother, Frank, returned. "I went with my mother and an elder sister to Bonaventure Station. They only allowed two family members to go in so my mother told me to wait outside in a certain place and not to move. She was afraid that she wouldn't find me when she came out. There were so many people that I didn't dare move. When my brother came out I was a bit scared because he was wearing his uniform and had a handlebar moustache. He hugged me and then we went home and the whole street came to our party on St. Urbain. We just had a small house but *everybody* stopped in to say hello. My mother was so thrilled to see her son. She served wine and I remember that there was food, too. The party lasted all day and then I remember my brother saying that he was tired and wanted to go to bed."

Montrealers, out of a sense of patriotic duty, would go to the harbour to welcome returning veterans. One of them was Phyllis Eperson. "A great mass of people would go down to the harbour to see the soldiers arriving home. The big ships had to stop in Quebec City but the 'Duchess' boats would come to Montreal. You'd see the troops walking off the ship. Some were being carried on stretchers and some were being helped to walk. Family members of returning soldiers were shouting their names. Those who didn't have family members returning would sometimes go down to welcome the boats because you were so grateful that they had arrived home. I was shocked to see a young man arriving with no legs—wouldn't that shock you?"

Don Pidgeon's mother wished to impress upon her children the great toll war takes on young soldiers. "After the war, my mother brought my two sisters, my brother and me up to Bonaventure Station to see the injured and maimed soldiers coming home because she wanted us to always remember the devastation that war brings to people. We stayed and watched until the last one got off the train and was put into an ambulance. Some of them had lost an eye but were bandaged up so you really couldn't see their injuries but when you saw the young soldiers who had lost limbs it was evident and was so strange to us. We saw young men who had to continue life without an arm, without a leg, without both legs sometimes. They seemed to have a look of acceptance at what their fate was. They had done something glorious for their country. They had fought and given their health to save people from the reality of what was happening in Europe. The worst to me was seeing the loss of limbs, especially legs."

Many newly-arrived veterans were anxious to see their old friends but were rebuffed when they tried to get in touch. "Why are you still alive when my son is dead?" That is what happened to Hubert "Dodd" Gray. "I came home and I talked to my mom and told her that I was going to see if I could find some of my friends. I thought I should call first so I started phoning and I got my friend Jimmy's mother and she started to cry and she said, 'Doddy, how come you're back and Jimmy isn't?' What could I say so I stopped phoning for a while."

After the parties were over, the food eaten and the banners put away, veterans had to face the challenges of returning to civilian life, which demanded many adjustments. The first thing they noticed was that, unlike the flattened cities of Europe and the stringent rationing in Britain, Montreal was lit up and and the stores were full of goods only dreamed of overseas while well-dressed people filled the busy streets and restaurants offered amazing choices. Veterans' war experiences had been as varied as the men who enlisted. Some quietly manned desks or sorted letters while others had spent varying amounts of time in hard combat or as powerless POWs. Some had given orders while more of them had, for years, been told what to do. Those on active service had seen and done things that no one should ever have to see or do and remnants of their war service would remain with them forever. Soldiers were broken physically and mentally from the war experience and spent their remaining years in hospital or became alcoholics. In the immediate post-war period, Legion Halls and bars were full of veterans comparing war stories and drinking to excess. Many got a grip on their drinking after a period of adjustment and settled back into normal life. Some felt alienated when there seemed to be little curiosity about what they had gone through while they had to listen as family members complained about the hardships of doing without sugar and tea. While post-traumatic stress disorder (PTSD) was not yet a household word, countless veterans had lasting symptoms—hair-trigger tempers, violent outbursts, insomnia, nightmares, an inability to concentrate, a fear of loud noises, physical pain and other symptoms. Since these men had no physical disabilities, they could expect no assistance, which compounded their frustration. While many were proud to sport their medals and service ribbons, thousands never even applied to Ottawa for theirs. Those who were injured spent time in military hospitals and many had to be fitted with artificial limbs or learn how to cope with blindness, deafness or disfigurement.

Merely getting out of uniform was a big step. They were no longer part of a family and could expect no special treatment. Many Canadian servicemen and women who had spent time in the United States were astonished at the generosity and welcome shown to them by Americans simply because they were in uniform. They were told everywhere they went, "Your money is no good here, son." "Ladies, your lunch bill has been paid." This was treatment they did not always receive in Canada. Hitchhiking was now going to be more difficult if not impossible. The boys who could impress girls just by wearing a uniform now had to try harder to get attention.

On the emotional side, veterans came home older and wiser and had to fit into their families again. Most were still young men in their early twenties but with experiences that aged them beyond their years. For many, cleaning up their language was the first thing they had to do and the "f" word was mothballed forever. Sons were no longer the young boys who went away but seasoned and battle-hardened men. Those who were married had to bridge a gap of years that might have been filled with affairs on both sides, and many veterans returned home to find an extra child or two that couldn't possibly be theirs. Divorce was the answer for many while others buried the past and moved on. Many men returned home to loving wives and found that the spark was still there and they continued where they had left off. Wives had had a taste of freedom, perhaps holding a well-paying job and learning to cope on their own, which meant another adjustment as men tried to reclaim their traditional places as head of the household in the days when "a woman's place is in the home". Magazine advertisements exhorted women to get rid of the coveralls and head scarves and don lacy and floral feminine garb and, of course, the slightly submissive attitude that would guarantee male attention. Children who perhaps were born after their fathers left or were very young at the time were faced with having to acknowledge a stranger as "Dad" and some of these father/child connections simply never "took". Many children had to get used to their father's military discipline which often rankled after Mother's soft touch.

Beverly Overall Marsh certainly remembered the father who went overseas and was delighted with his return but there were many adjustments she had to make. "It was very hard and it was hard for my father too. Dad was three years behind the times and things had changed. We were never allowed to go out and play on a Sunday. Oh my goodness! That was the worst thing in the world. We just used to sit on the steps. Everything like that changed while he was away. I used to wear my Helen Harper cardigans buttoned down the back and my father would say that I couldn't go out like that with my sweater on backwards. You know, it was things like that."

The almost 48,000 war brides Canadian men married overseas had an enormous impact on Canadian life. With thousands of Canadian servicemen stationed in England for years, it was natural that the majority of these marriages (44,886) were to British women but servicemen also married women from Holland, Belgium, France, Italy and there were even six from Germany. (There were also a few "war husbands".) It was a big decision for these women to make and by and large the marriages worked and they adapted to their new country. Nevertheless there were heartbreaking stories of wives abandoned at railway stations and other disastrous unions. Some were shocked at the conditions under which they were expected to live. A young soldier telling his bride that he came from a small village might have made her imagine that it was a friendly and cozy place with a local pub, a fish and chips shop and pretty flower-bedecked stores, which was a far cry from the puritanical and muddy rural reality that she found. Not all marriages survived but the majority did and were very happy and these brave and resourceful women made a huge contribution to Canada. The downside of this migration and the loss of so many young men was that many Canadian women were destined for a life of, in the terminology of the time, "spinsterhood".

Returning soldiers looked around and saw buddies who did not serve or who used influence to obtain a deferment, had made money in war industries, found girls to marry or simply had successful careers and lives. Some were very bitter at these "malingerers" and would harbour resentment all their lives. In Montreal, many English-speaking lads who answered the call, did the job and won the war had nothing but scorn for the French-Canadians who did not enlist. Others had great respect for the unselfish contribution made by so many of them who either fought alongside their English-speaking comrades or served in French-speaking regiments, and did so knowing they did not have the full support of their community.

The majority of returning soldiers had a seamless and happy re-entry to normal life. Even the family dog ran to greet them when they came up the walk to their house as if they had only been gone for the weekend, and their families were happy to see them and eager to make them forget the bad years. They secured jobs or returned to school and prepared for a profession, perhaps joined the Legion—where often they were not welcomed whole-heartedly by the First War veterans who ran the show and were reluctant to pass the torch—and carried on with life feeling empowered by the part they played in a victory against a formidable enemy. Sadness would surface at different times such as Remembrance Day as they recalled lost buddies and they, like many veterans, were often heard to say, "I'm not a hero. The heroes are buried overseas".

While many missed their brothers-in-arms and wondered if they could adjust to independent thinking after years of following orders, most servicemen wanted to get a job, buy a house, find a wife and start a family—a normal life after years of upheaval. Since veterans arrived home on a point system, many worried that the best jobs would be gone by the time they returned. Some stayed in the military and built careers in what was a familiar life to them. Many men had left jobs to enlist and although, by law, these jobs were waiting for them when they returned, they often found them boring and unsatisfying and quit to find something else. Very young men who signed up and Depression boys who had had no job experience at all needed training to fit into a newly industrialized country that needed their talents and labour.

Arthur Fraser describes his difficult re-integration into civilian life. "Life in Montreal had changed. People had money and went to night clubs. I wasn't used to that kind of life. I knew I would be discharged from the army and become a civilian. I was tired of the army. I was so fed up with the army that it was unbelievable. I saw so many people dead on the beach at Dieppe. Later on, I saw dead Germans in a field that were all black. I saw bloated horses and the smell…I felt my back was against the wall. I wanted to get away from the wall and earn my living as a civilian. I had no trade. I worked for a year at Dow Brewery loading trains with beer to be sent outside the province. It was hard work. I only weighed ninety pounds when I got back. We were loading fifteen to twenty boxcars a day. I took the tramway and started work at seven o'clock. Then I bought myself a Veterans' taxi and drove it for eight years. I made money the first five years working seventeen hours a day but then, when they changed to radio taxis I didn't make no money. One of my war souvenirs was that I couldn't hear the fellow who used to broadcast the addresses so I sold my taxi and worked as a private chauffeur for thirty-seven years."

While waiting for the supply of houses to catch up to the demand, finding a place to live was difficult. Landlords demanded "key money" as well as high rents. Some forced their tenants to pay high prices for cheap, second-hand furniture or demanded janitorial services. In 1947, sixteen families were evicted from army barracks on St. Helen's Island. Many, if not all of them were headed by veterans. One ex-serviceman who was then with the RCMP was told to go down and talk to them, thinking that he would be better-positioned to convince them to leave. It was an awful moment for him and he kept quiet about the story for the rest of his life because he was afraid that his RCMP pension would be cut off.

The women who joined the forces often remember those years as having given them a chance to contribute in a very real way to victory. Many also had a glorious good time and missed their friends when the war was over. Although offered the same discharge benefits as men, women were often steered into traditional female jobs if they wanted a career although many did go to university and chose unconventional employment. Women in uniform had challenged society's view of subordinate, feminine womanhood and Canada would never again be the same. The majority of servicewomen, many not the same docile girls who had enlisted, married within a few years and concentrated on making babies and brownies. Things turned out well for Norma Duckworth who served as a Wren. After writing to her navy sweetheart for three years, she married John Dillon in 1947 and they contributed to the baby boom by raising seven children.

Both men and women dreamed of a house with a backyard,

three bedrooms and perhaps a garage and they wanted those houses to be filled with children. One bathroom would do just fine and the powder room would be added later. Wartime housing featuring the typical Cape Cod style of architecture would soon be available and reasonably priced in areas like N.D.G. and Verdun to join those already built for wartime workers.

Madeleine Cloutier Méthot reflects on the end of the war. "We found the time long but the days and years passed and the war was over. We mourned the ones we had lost and picked up our lives where we had left off. I remember the parades on Sherbrooke Street when the troops came back. The soldiers all looked so proud. I will always remember the bad parts of the war but the good side was that my boyfriend returned from serving in the RCAF and we could go to dances at places like Victoria Hall."

Many young veterans arrived home with money in their pockets and an urge to reconnect with the "old gang" to celebrate. Philip Aspler: "I remember in 1946 when the boys were coming home, you could go into the old Bellevue Tavern and order a glass of draft beer for ten cents. (If you went to a night club beer was sixty-five cents a quart.) You'd order nine beers and give the guy a dollar. He kept the last dime. Then a few more boys would come in and order more beer. We'd put four or five tables together and there would be a lot of beer. Unbelievable! This was a gang from our district and anybody coming home, we'd celebrate in the tavern. Those who went overseas got gratuities of $15 for every month they served. It piled up and some of them had $1,500. When they went overseas in 1939, they had never seen that much money in their lives so, of course, some of them went through it like nothing and these were the ones who turned out to be bums, unfortunately. If a guy was smart, he could start a small business or something."

Getting the veterans home proved to be a mammoth problem for Ottawa. Servicemen and women simply had to wait their turn due to the scarcity of available suitable ships. As soon as they arrived home, reintegration began. Although Canada was totally unprepared for war in 1939, it was determined to prepare the way for returning veterans by not repeating the mistakes made after World War I when veterans were badly served by the government, which had left many of them embittered and ready to embrace radical causes. Only one month after the war started and even before the 1st Division left for England in December, plans were underway to ease the return and adaptation of veterans to civilian life. Veterans had given Canada their best years and expected a better life than the Depression Era one they had left. There was no guarantee, however, that their lives would be better and, with the Liberals nervous about the popularity of the CCF and the Conservatives, King's cabinet had to act. Ottawa's aim to help veterans consisted of four elements. They had the right to reclaim their former jobs; find new employment; get retraining or finish their education. In March 1944, the Department of Veterans Affairs was created and The Veterans' Charter was passed by Parliament the same year. It gave generous financial support to both men and women based on years of service. They also received free medical treatment for a year while those suffering war wounds were assured of lifetime care. Life insurance policies worth up to $10,000 could be bought without a medical examination and unemployment benefits could be claimed for up to a year during the first eighteen months after discharge.

Self-employed veterans could collect, for a period of up to one year, a generous living allowance while awaiting the stabilization of their businesses. Spouses of those who had died in the service received war service gratuities amounting to 75 per cent of what a disabled veteran would get. Their children also received additional benefits including financial help with higher education. Disabled veterans had pensions, free medical care or hospitalization and help in finding jobs. Government aid also helped those who wanted to settle on farms. The Veterans' Land Act offered generous loans at very low rates for land and equipment. Government funds also helped thousands of servicemen and women go to university or receive vocational training. Their length of service would determine their time allowed to complete their training. This program produced doctors, engineers and other professionals who helped build post-war Canada. Crammed into overcrowded classrooms and following accelerated programs, they were serious students who knew what they wanted. For many of them, they were the first in their families to go to university. Others did not take advantage of these programs but chose to claim a tax-exempt "rehab grant" to be used to buy, maintain or furnish a home or start up a business. The Zombies who had donned uniforms but stayed in Canada were left out in the cold when these grants were distributed. In all, nearly one million men and women received gratuities amounting to an average of $488 (approximately $5,000 in today's dollars). Although these generous benefits were very costly for the country, Canadians were more than happy to see veterans getting a better deal than had the veterans of the Great War.

The Canada that emerged from the war was barely recognizable from the one that had entered the conflict totally unprepared. Canada became a respected world power, ending the war with the third largest navy and the fourth largest air force in the world. We also had an army of five divisions and two armoured brigades. A total of 1,081,865 Canadians (including 49,963 women) served out of a total population of 11,507,000. The price was high. The dead numbered 44,927 (including 73 women); the wounded 53,145 (including 19 women); POWs 8,271. In terms of the Canadian Merchant Navy 14,000 served on registered ships and 1,146 died. Pre-1949 figures for Newfoundland are: 19,460 served, 704 died, number of wounded and POWs unknown. (the Royal Canadian Legion figures). Although one is repulsed by the term "good war", it is recognized that World War II had to be fought and that Canada played a major part in many ways. From a shaky start in the doomed battle of Hong Kong in 1941 to the fiasco of Dieppe in 1942, we had a lot to learn and we learned quickly.

One of the proudest achievements of Canada's war effort was the British Commonwealth Air Training Plan (BCATP). Canada, far away from active war zones, was well-placed to train airmen for a conflict in which air dominance was crucial. There were 151 training schools and every province had BCATP installations. Thousands of Allied air and ground crew tradesmen received training with the BCATP which was a decisive contribution to the war effort. The war production of tanks, ships, motor vehicles, aircraft and weapons not only provided jobs for Canadians but was also an essential element of victory. Canada took its place on the world stage and was listened to with respect. The country that welcomed back its veterans was wealthy beyond belief compared to devastated Britain, and to what it had been at the end of the Depression, and this was reflected in a new attitude. While English Canadians were still loyal to Britain, they had also developed a stronger nationalistic feeling for Canada. The post-war years would see massive immigration to what many saw as a land of security, plenty and opportunity.

Montreal was still the largest city in Canada and its economic motor. Montreal's clothing industry could now return to peacetime manufacturing instead of making uniforms. Factories quickly switched from war production to manufacturing consumer goods. Years of War Bond savings as well as veterans' benefits could now be spent on clothes, furniture and home appliances. Cars were a sought-after item and allowed Montrealers to leave crowded city areas and move to airy and leafy suburbs like Châteauguay or Lachine. Many were tempted to buy a summer cottage, something that was normally a dream only the rich could afford. With full employment and hopes for the future, the consumer society was launched.

Maurice Duplessis was back at the helm of government in Quebec City and Camillien Houde was again the mayor of Montreal but it was a changed country. Canadians now had unemployment insurance and family allowance benefits. These social safety nets gave a feeling of security to families and led to the baby boom that lasted until the mid-sixties. Women in Quebec—the last group in Canada—had been granted the vote in 1940 and compulsory education was in effect. Changes were on the horizon for Montreal from the advent of television in the early 1950s to the astonishing growth of the city during the 1960s. Montreal had been sanitized

[Top]Guy Bieler with his sister Madeleine, her daughter Elizabeth (Babs) and family friend Dick Ashworth, England 1942. *Courtesy of Guy Bieler's children.* [Bottom] Irene Jones (third from left) was sixteen years old in 1948. Her tap dancing group would visit veteran's hospitals. *Courtesy of Irene Jones Meikle.*

by Jean Drapeau, the prim lawyer who became the mayor in 1954, and the crime-fighting lawyer Pacifique (Pax) Plante. Although no longer Sin City, Montreal would always remain Fun City for locals and tourists. From the crowning glory of Expo 67 to the disruption of political bickering, after thirty years of post-war growth, Montreal finally had to accept second place when Toronto became Canada's largest metropolis.

The loss of a loved one during wartime changes the entire future for the ones left behind. A young bereaved wife who thinks she will never get over the loss of her beloved husband is shocked to find that, many years later, she has trouble even imagining his face, especially if the marriage was a short one. Some war widows were able to find new loves and remarry while others would live in perpetual mourning for the man who, in their eyes, couldn't possibly be replaced. Mothers of "children of the war dead" had an extra responsibility to try to keep their fathers' memory alive. Many women were pregnant when their husbands left so these children and their very young siblings would only know their fathers from photographs and family stories. As the years passed, these children would be forced to realize that they had aged beyond their father's generation and become, in fact, parents to the child. Parents who lost one or more sons coped in different ways. There was the solace of religion; the stiff upper lip that protected others from their grief; the support of friends and family and, in some cases, changed rituals like never again putting up a Christmas tree. Many would never have grandchildren while others would have to take a more active role in their grandchildren's lives. The lost brothers would become a permanent hole in the fabric of the family.

Death came in so many different ways. Soldiers died of illnesses that had nothing to do with battle. Others lost their lives in active combat or were brutally treated as POWs. For the children of Major Guy Bieler, Jacqueline and John, (who now live in Ontario) their case is unusual and haunting. Their father underwent terrible torture before being executed in Flossenbürg Concentration Camp.

His refusal to give away any information meant that he came face to face with pure evil personified in the sadists and sociopaths who ran these camps. For Jacqueline Bieler who had constant nightmares about Nazis, trips to France and Germany filled in some of the missing pieces. In Normandy, she met her father's fellow Resistance fighters who had nothing but praise for "Major Guy". While most of us know that, for example, we get our musical talent from one parent and other qualities from the other, orphans do not have the opportunity to make these observations on their own. While in France, one man noted that Jacqueline had one of the same gestures as her father, which cemented her connections to her father's colleagues. In April 2005, on the 60th anniversary of the liberation of Flossenbürg, she visited the camp with her son and cousin and met with young German hosts who were tactful, frank and helpful and who were working to, if not erase, at least to assuage the pain caused by their parents and grandparents. Faced with visiting the place where her father had undergone unspeakable suffering, she was powerfully affected when placing flowers on the remains of his prison cell. In her book, *Out of Night and Fog: The Story of Major Guy Bieler, Special Operations Executive,* which was published in 2008, she describes that day: "The next morning we return to the remains of cell #23. As I place the tribute on the ground I am overwhelmed. Grief floods through me. What my father must have suffered here, broken, racked with pain and yet able to sustain others in their common purpose. He was the best of what a human spirit can be. And I grieve for myself that I did not grow up knowing the love of this wonderful man."

Her brother, John, whose childish voice was the one heard in Windsor Station telling his father, "Good-bye, Daddy, have a good time", recalls a memory that had a profound effect on him. "I was in the dentist's office when I was eight years old. I climbed up on the big chair and waited for the dentist to arrive. He came in and sat beside me and said, 'Son, I can't look at your teeth today because your mother has not paid me for your last visit six months ago so please ask your mother to pay the bill and then make another appointment.' I didn't know what was going on, but I went home and told my mother and she cried and I didn't know why." More than sixty years later, he had his answer: "Because my father was selected by the British Military to join a clandestine Special Operations Executive group, his records were transferred to the British Paymasters Group and hence…..my mother's income was interrupted by a period of approximately six months so she did not have the funds to pay the dentist. This story has impacted my business life. Personally, bills that come into our house are paid the next day, no exceptions. Ditto when I was managing our manufacturing/sales business. Billed today—paid tomorrow. No exceptions."

For men who were horribly injured, the war would never be over. Irene Jones Meikle was sixteen years old in 1948 and a talented tap dancer. Her teacher, Kathleen Ponting, taught dance at the N.D.G. Community Hall while Ponting's mother, "Pom Pom" took charge of playing the piano for the lessons and making costumes for the shows. After the war, these dancers were much in demand to entertain the veterans at the Ste. Anne's Veterans' Hospital and the Queen Mary Veterans' Hospital. Irene took part in these shows from 1947 to 1949. "We would go out to Ste. Anne's around four in the afternoon to be ready for the show and sometimes we would go and speak with some of the fellows. Some of them were in baskets with just one arm or leg, many of them just a head and a body. They covered them with a sheet but you knew there was nothing there because the baskets were just the length of the body. The first time you see that it takes your breath away. You sometimes saw men in uniform downtown on crutches or walking with canes but seeing the young fellows propped up in baskets was the most crushing experience I had after the war. A lot of them were very young and they were from all over Canada. There were also fellows who were not as badly wounded as that and also old veterans from the First War who perhaps had no families and had come to Ste. Anne's to finish their days.

"We always had an M.C. to open the show. There were singers

and comedians and we usually did three dance numbers. Usually it was a military one to open the show and maybe we'd do a Mexican Hat Dance in the middle and a Spanish one at the end. There were about six or eight of us dancers. On the floor walking around to talk to these boys in baskets was one thing but when the lights came on in the first show I did and I looked down and saw them all in the first row and all the men behind them were able to sit in chairs made me lose my step a few times. It was really heartbreaking. We didn't see then what we now see on TV. We only heard the news. I remember coming home and telling Mother and Father about it and I think they were a little upset that I had to see that."

Naomi Paltiel Lowi, who graduated from McGill Medical School, in 1951, was lucky. Her two brothers came home from the war. "Daniel left the minesweeper HMCS *Guysborough* to take a course just a short time before it was torpedoed. We were all shocked because we got to know a few of his shipmates from the Prairies when he brought them home. My brother Ephrom served on merchant ships because he wanted to do things his own way. I'm very grateful that I was around to experience the war effort. Everything about our life was related to the war. It's hard to describe but it was different then. We were united. There was an *esprit de corps* and an agenda that we were all connected with. There was a friendship that you felt with people in uniform because we were all in it together."

For the veterans who came home seemingly unscathed, many lived a life of remembrance in which the war was never very far from their minds. The Battle of Verrières Ridge in the Normandy Campaign on July 25, 1944 was disastrous for Montreal's famed Black Watch and, like the attack on Dieppe, can rightly be called a massacre. Twenty-six-year old Major Philip Griffin led the attack under orders from his superiors and, many argue, against his better judgement. Of the more than 300 infantrymen who attacked the ridge fewer than twenty made it back; the others were killed, wounded or taken prisoner. John Calderwood was one of the few who survived that day. He died in 2008 at the age of eighty-seven. His daughter, Dale, who was born after the war to John and Hilda, his English war bride, remembers how that experience marked his life. "My dad was a sniper and scout for the Black Watch. He fought through Normandy, Belgium and Holland but recounted to me that Verrières Ridge was the worst experience of all. I've been there. Most people think it is a high ridge but it is really a very gentle slope. The men were promised support that they didn't get. The marched in formation through wheat fields in broad daylight which offered no protection. Essentially, he saw most of the men around him slaughtered and, in a war situation where the men become very close because their lives depend on each other, it must have been totally devastating for him and all these young soldiers. He lived his life, as did others, in absolute fury that Major Griffin was blamed for this massacre. My dad and others I have talked to did not have enough good things to say about Major Griffin. They had the most tremendous respect for him. They said he was tough, fair and a born leader and they considered it a privilege to fight under him. At no time in discussions with my father did I get the impression that they felt less secure because of Major Griffin being a younger officer.

"My father was a staunch Black Watch vet. He never missed a meeting, a reunion or a Remembrance Day ceremony. He was devoted to the men who served with him like Jim Wilkinson, Bruce (Duke) Ducat and others. To truly understand how it affected someone like my dad you would really have to see his face on Remembrance Day. I describe it as a far-away, remembering look. Words cannot describe the depth of feeling and the depth of remembering for lost friends and the love for the men who served with him, which was so apparent in his facial expressions. I've been on a Black Watch military tour of the battle fields and cemeteries in Europe with these veterans and I've seen these elderly gentlemen—who were once so young and handsome—bend down to put a poppy and a small Canadian flag on each Black Watch grave, stand back and salute with tears in their eyes. You *have* to see it. My father was often asked if he could be interviewed about the war but he always refused as he couldn't talk about it. My mother told me that he sometimes had nightmares about Verrières Ridge. When my mom went into a home, I spent a lot of time with Dad and, if a documentary about it was on TV, I would make darn sure I was there to spend the night with him because I knew he should not be alone. It brought back a lot of memories and was very hard on him. Sometimes when he was telling me his war stories his eyes would fill with tears, especially later in life as he became more emotionally vulnerable."

John Calderwood of the Black Watch is welcomed home in 1945 by his parents, Minnie and Jim Calderwood, and his aunt Greta (on the right). *Courtesy of Allen Calderwood.*

Dale Calderwood has her own feelings about history. "War fades into history. When these men came home from war, the streets were full and there were cheers, banners and parades. I'm an artist so I'll describe it in colours. What they were fighting for was in vivid colour and everyone knew they were heroes but, as time goes on, history fades from colours to grey. As young men they were applauded for what they did; as older men they could walk down a street and no one would know or give a damn. My dad lived the war all his life. What he went through became part of his personality. I think when men have an experience like that it becomes part of who they are. There might be negative effects on these men but there could be changes for the better, too—pride, a sense of belonging, a sense of accomplishment and survival. I know what my father and his friends went through and I know their faces. It is a personal history to our direct ancestors but once I'm gone and my son and niece and nephew are gone, then the bright colours will fade to grey and their names will be lost. If children in the future learn anything about the war, it will be a grey thing."

Afterword

World War II forged a special bond between Canadians and the people of the Netherlands that remains strong to this day. Princess Juliana and her daughters, the Princesses Beatrix and Irene, spent the war years in Ottawa. In 1943, the future Queen gave birth to her third child, Princess Margriet at the Ottawa Civic Hospital. For the war-weary people of Holland anxiously awaiting liberation, the first sight of Canadian soldiers was an unforgettable experience and strengthened this bond. It meant that their nightmare years of suffering were over. Although British, Polish and American soldiers also helped liberate this small country, it was Canadian troops who marched into its major cities—Rotterdam, Amsterdam and the Hague— in the western part of Holland. Their arrival meant millions of Dutch citizens were saved from their oppressors and the very real danger of starvation.

The Dutch keep alive the memory of their liberators to an impressive degree, either by tending graves, holding commemorative ceremonies or passing on stories to their children. Every Christmas Eve, approximately three hundred schoolchildren from local schools visit the Commonwealth War Cemetery at Holten where 1,393 young Canadians lie buried. In the presence of local townspeople and dignitaries, the children fan out and place a lighted candle on each grave to remember "the boys who didn't get home for Christmas".

In May 2005, I travelled to Holland for the 60th Anniversary commemoration of liberation. In a large group of 138 fellow pilgrims (including many veterans) headed by the Canadian broadcaster and author, Ted Barris and his wife, Jayne MacAulay, we toured the country and participated in many planned ceremonies, seeing first-hand the gratitude and friendliness of the Dutch. One of the men on our tour, Ronald Charland, a Régiment de Maisonneuve veteran, wanted to visit the grave of his best buddy,

Edouard (Eddy) Paquet of Montreal, who was killed at the age of twenty-one in January 1945. Arriving at Groesbeek Cemetery, Ron Charland found the grave of his friend and in front of it he noticed a rather unusual Canadian flag. Picking it up, he was surprised to see that it was a crayon-coloured flag with a message written by a child on the other side. The message read:

> Dear Canadian Soldier,
>
> I am writing to thank you for sacrificing your life so that others could be free. You gave your life for people you did not know in a land far from home. Canadines (sic) will always be proud.
>
> Sincerely, Patrick, grade 3 student, Oshawa, On.

Ron Charland holds the flag letter from a Canadian Grade 3 student that was placed on his friend Eddy Paquet's grave, May 2005.
Photo by John Tweddell. Courtesy of John Tweddell and Ronald Charland.

This touched Charland profoundly. He reached down and replaced the flag letter with a small Canadian flag and vowed to "cherish this memento for the rest of my life".

Was the sacrifice at home and overseas worth it? The people of the Netherlands; the veterans who survived and shared the euphoria of victory with the ones they liberated; Dutch children and their parents who visit graves and attend liberation ceremonies every year; the Canadians who cherish this gratitude and perhaps even the young men who are buried on Dutch soil would probably say, "Yes, it was".

Contributors

Philip Aspler
Gilberte Belanger
Denise Bernard
Jacqueline Bieler
John Bieler
Jacques Boucher
Allen Calderwood
Dale Calderwood
Rita Melanson Carby
Mike Caron
Howard Dearlove
Kenneth Delamater
Norma Duckworth Dillon
Mary Prendergast Ebel
Phyllis Eperson
Arthur Fraser
Fernande Cloutier Gagnon
Penny Pentland Gélineau
Hubert Gray
Lorne Hamilton
Lois Hashimoto
René Héroux
Betty Kobayashi Issenman
Betty Jennings
Michael Lanese
Eddie Lion
Carol Lodge
Irena Chavchavadze Lomasney
Naomi Paltiel Lowi
Lucy Fiori Madigan

Maria De Grandis Marrelli
Allan Marsh
Beverly Overall Marsh
David McCrindle
Irene Jones Meikle
Madeleine Cloutier Méthot
Liliana Ferroni Mulligan
Joan Byers Mullins
Margaret Neville
Lucille Pacaud
Don Pidgeon
Arthur Stanway
Peggy Ford Stanway
Rosalie Stoss
Ruth Swinton Stevenson
Stuart Vallières
"Frank"
"Fred"
"Jo"
"Roger"

Selected Bibliography

BOOKS

Barris, Ted. *Days of Victory, Canadians Remember, 1939-1945.* Toronto: Thomas Allen Publishers, 2005.

Bieler, Jacqueline. *Out of Night and Fog: The Story of Major Guy Bieler, Special Operations Executive.* Ottawa: CEF Books, 2008.

Bilson, Geoffrey. *The Guest Children.* Saskatoon: Fifth House, 1988.

Black, Conrad. *Duplessis.* Toronto: McClelland & Stewart Limited, 1977.

Bothwell, Robert. *Canada and Quebec, One Country: Two Histories.* Vancouver: UBC Press, University of British Columbia, 1998.

Broadfoot, Barry. *Ten Lost Years 1929-1939: Memories of Canadians who Survived the Depression.* Don Mills, Ontario; General Publishing Co. Ltd., 1973.

_______. *Years of Sorrow, Years of Shame. The Story of the Japanese Canadians in World War II.* Don Mills, Ontario: General Publishing Co. Ltd., 1979.

_______. *The Veterans' Years: Coming Home from the War.* Vancouver/Toronto: Douglas & McIntyre, 1985.

Burton, Pierre. *The Great Depression 1929-1939.* Toronto: McClelland & Stewart, 1990.

Canadian Naval Centennial. Centenaire de la Marine Canadienne. A Souvenir Photo Album History of 100 Years of the Royal Canadian Navy, 1910-2010. The Naval Officers'Association of Canada, 2010.

Crone, G.H. *Holland and the Canadians.* Amsterdam ,Holland: Contact Publishing Company, 1995.

Dear, I.C.B.; M.R.D. Foot. *The Oxford Companion to World War II.* Oxford University Press, 1995.

Ellis, Jean M. *Face Powder and Gunpowder.* Toronto: S. J. Reginald Saunders & Company Limited, 1947.

Feasby, W.R. *Official History of the Canadian Medical Services, 1939-1945.* Vol. 1. Ottawa: Queen's Printer and Controller of Stationery, 1956.

Gouin, Jacques et quelques anciens du Régiment de Maisonneuve. *Bon Coeur et Bon Bras, Histoire du Régiment de Maisonneuve 1880-1980.* Montreal, 1980.

Hurst, Alan M. *The Canadian Y.M.C.A. in World War II.* National Toronto: War Services Committee of the National Council of Young Men's Christian Associations of Canada, 1950.

Iacovetti, Franco; Perin, Roberto; Principe, Angelo. *Enemies Within. Italians and Other Internees in Canada and Abroad.* Toronto: University of Toronto Press Inc., 2000.

Ito, Roy. *We Went to War.* Ottawa: Canada's Wings, Inc., 1984.

Jones, Ted. *Both Sides of the Wire. The Fredericton Internment Camp.* Vol. 1. New Ireland Press, 1988.

Keshen, Jeffrey. *Saints, Sinners and Soldiers: Canada's Second World War.* Vancouver: UBC Press, University of British Columbia, 2004.

King, Joe. *Fabled City. The Jews of Montreal.* Montreal: Price-Patterson Ltd., 2009.

Koch, Eric. *Deemed Suspect; A Wartime Blunder.* Toronto: Methuen Publications, 1980.

Lehmann, Heinz. *The German Canadians, 1750 1937: Immigration, Settlement & Culture.* St. John's, Newfoundland: Jesperson Press, 1986.

Lennon, Mary Jane; Charendoff, Syd. *On The Homefront.* Erin, Ontario: The Boston Mills Press, 1981.

Linteau, Paul-André; Durocher, René; Robert, Jean-Claude; Ricard, François. *Quebec Since 1930.* Toronto: James Lorimer & Company, Publishers, 1991.

MacKay, Donald. *The Square Mile, Merchant Princes of Montreal.* Vancouver: Douglas & McIntyre, 1987.

MacLaren, Roy. *Canadians Behind Enemy Lines, 1939-1945.* Vancouver: UBC Press 1981.

Marrelli, Nancy. *Stepping Out: The Golden Age of Montreal Night Clubs.* Montreal: Véhicule Press, 2004.

McLaughlin, K.M. *The Germans in Canada.* Ottawa: Canadian Historical Association, 1985.

Morton, Desmond; J.L. Granatstein. *Victory 1945: Canadians from War to Peace.* Toronto: Harper Collins Publishers Ltd., 1995.

Nigel Fountain, editor. *WW II: The Peoples Story.* Montreal: Reader's Digest Association Ltd., 2003.

Nish, Cameron. *Québec in the Duplessis Era, 1935-1959: Dictatorship or Democracy?* Toronto: Copp Clark Publishing Company, 1970.

Nord, Max (editor). *Thank you, Canada.* Amsterdam: N.V. De Abeiderspers, 1967.

Peate, Mary. *Girl in a Sloppy Joe Sweater.* Montreal: Optimum,1988.

RCMP Security Bulletins. *The War Series.* Committee on Canadian Labour History, Dept. of History. St. John's, Newfoundland: Memorial University.

Robinson, Jennifer. *Montreal's Century: A Record of the News and People who Shaped the City in the 20th Century.* Outremont, Quebec: Éditions du Trécarré, 1999.

Roy, Gabrielle. *The Tin Flute.* New Canadian Library. Toronto: McClelland & Stewart Ltd., 1964.

Salvatore, Filippo. *Fascism and the Italians of Montreal: An Oral History, 1922-1945.* Toronto: Guernica Editions Inc., 1998.

Shimizu, Yon. *The Exiles.* Wallaceburg, Ontario: Shimizu Consulting & Publishing, 1993.

Stacy, C.P. *Arms, Men and Governments. The War Policies of Canada 1939-1945.* Ottawa: The Queen's Printer, Ottawa 1970.

_______. *Official History of the Canadian Army in the Second World War.* Vol. 1. Ottawa: Queen's Printer and Controller of Stationery, Ottawa, 1955.

The Canadians at War, 1939-1945, Volumes 1 and 2. Montreal: Reader's Digest Association Ltd., 1969.

Weintraub, William. *City Unique: Montreal Days and Nights in the 1940s and '50s.* Toronto: McClelland & Stewart Inc., 1996.

Williams, Dorothy W. *The Road to Now: A History of Blacks in Montreal.* Montreal: Véhicule Press, 1997.

OTHER

Canada Remembers, Le Canada se Souvient. Second World War Fact Sheet Series. Veterans Affairs, Canada.

Livingston, Neal (producer and director). *Both Sides of the Wire.* Documentary film. Mabou, Nova Scotia: Black River Productions Ltd., 1993.

Also many Internet sources and newspaper reports, especially the *Montreal Gazette's* "Canada at War" series, 1989.

Index